The Jar of Severed Hands

The Jar of Severed Hands

Spanish Deportation of Apache Prisoners of War, 1770–1810

MARK SANTIAGO

University of Oklahoma Press : Norman

Also by Mark Santiago

The Red Captain: The Life of Hugo O'Conor, Commandant Inspector of the Interior Provinces of New Spain (Tucson, 1994)

Massacre at the Yuma Crossing: Spanish Relations with the Quechans, 1779–1782 (Tucson, 1998)

Library of Congress Cataloging-in-Publication Data
Santiago, Mark, 1959–
The jar of severed hands : Spanish deportation of Apache prisoners of war, 1770–1810 / Mark Santiago.
p. cm.
Includes bibliographical references and index.
ISBN 978-0-8061-4177-0 (cloth) ISBN 978-0-8061-6456-4 (paper)
1. Apache Indians—Relocation—New Spain—Nueva Vizcaya—History. 2. Apache Indians—Wars—New Spain—Nueva Vizcaya—History. 3. Apache Indians—New Spain—Nueva Vizcaya—History. 4. Indians, Treatment of—New Spain—Nueva Vizcaya—History. 5. Nueva Vizcaya (New Spain)—History. 6. Mexico—History—Spanish colony, 1540–1810. I. Title.
E99.A6S355 2011
972'.02—dc22
2010042826

The paper in this book meets the guidelines for permanence and durability of the Committee on Production Guidelines for Book Longevity of the Council on Library Resources, Inc. ∞

To Dawn

Forever and Always

Contents

Illustrations

FIGURES

MAPS

Preface and Acknowledgments

The genesis of this work was sparked by an examination of a pair of reports in the Archivo General de la Nación of Mexico, under the section called Provincias Internas. Together, they tell the story of two *colleras*, or chain gangs, of Apache prisoners of war captured by the Spanish and deported from their homelands in the years 1791 and 1792. The reports are grouped together for quite logical reasons. One is that they both deal with expeditions that involved the transfer of individuals from one governmental authority to another, in this case from the commandant general of the Interior Provinces to the viceroy of New Spain. That transfer of authority involved many of the mechanisms of government, including the overlapping roles of military officers and civilian bureaucrats. Similar letters and reports, certificates and testimonies, and even receipts for expenses are found in both reports. Transfers of funds for costs incurred in the first expedition are listed as finally repaid in the report of the second.

Yet the similarities that led to the juxtaposition of these two reports are stripped away upon an examination of the actual events they describe. The first expedition, of 1791, details a story that places a large group of Apache prisoners of war in the company of three *Apaches de paz*—"peaceful Apaches." These three were members of a community that had agreed to settle under Spanish supervision in what was essentially a reservation. As part of the terms of that agreement, they had aided the Spanish in attacking their recalcitrant kinsmen. Now these three peaceful Apaches were accompanying this latest chain gang in hopes of redeeming kinsmen already sent into exile. At first glance, the image of one group of Apaches traveling with and tacitly witnessing the deportation of another group of Apaches while hoping to recover still another group of Apaches already deported appears incredible. In addition, the treatment accorded enemy Apaches by their Spanish captors in the expedition of 1791 seems to indicate, at least at times, the recognition of a common humanity that belies the usual callousness engendered between warring peoples.

This touch of pathos stands in marked contrast to the records of the second expedition, of 1792. In this tale, the hopeless desperation of the captives collides with the disciplined ruthlessness of the captors. Death comes, not stealthily like the illnesses that carried off the members of the first expedition, but explosively and suddenly in a full-scale irruption of violence. In this second account, the treatment of the prisoners betrays no hint of compassion and is instead a cold testament of the horrors of war.

Why were the stories contained in these two reports, only a year apart, so glaringly different? This question seemed to demand an answer, given the close association of the documents. Yet on closer examination it became clear that these tales were not as different as they appeared. As more and more reports detailing the colleras came to my attention, the overall nature of the Spanish deportation policy came into focus. The two colleras of 1791 and 1792 became poles, opposite to be sure, but nevertheless still within the sphere of an understandable whole. They represented the totality of a policy that included violence and compassion, confrontation and accommodation, the mailed fist in the velvet glove — all elements within a design to force the Apaches to bend to the will of Spanish officialdom. That will required the Apaches to stop their raiding of Spanish settlements, or at the very least to curtail the raids to an acceptable level. Further, it became clear that the deportation policy played a significant role in developments surrounding the system of reservations the Spaniards had set up, which later came to be called *establecimientos de paz*. That system, it is generally agreed, marked the apparently peaceful culmination of decades, if not centuries, of violence between Spaniards and Apaches.

Although two noted historians, Max Moorhead and Christon I. Archer, have produced excellent overviews of the deportation policy in journal articles, and other historians have included the topic as discussion points, a detailed description of the colleras themselves has not yet been undertaken. In this work I have endeavored to balance the history of the development of the overall deportation policy with narratives of several of the most representative and, in all honesty, most dramatic of the collera journeys. This approach not only allows for a more in-depth examination of the historical antecedents of deportation and its actual implementation in the late eighteenth and early nineteenth centuries, but also offers an opportunity to touch on the humanity of the participants — Spaniard and Apache alike — and provide at least a pale reflection of the circumstances of their lives. In this effort, the most relevant concepts and ideas are those of the participants and their own time, and I have tried to limit as much as possible the preconceptions and judgments of our own day.

Most of the primary sources used in this work are available as microfilm copies from Spanish and Mexican archives and from separate independent collections held at several universities. I would like to thank individuals at these institutions for their assistance: Nancy Brown-Martinez, Reference Specialist at the Center for Southwest Research, University of New Mexico, Albuquerque; the staff of Media and Microforms and the C. L. Sonnichsen Special Collections Department, University Library, University of Texas at El Paso; and Christian Kelleher, Archivist, Nettie Lee Benson Latin American Collection, the University of Texas Libraries, Austin. All translations and interpretations of these primary sources are my own, and I bear responsibility for any errors or omissions.

As I prepared this manuscript for publication, Roger Myers, Archivist, Special Collections, the University of Arizona Libraries, Tucson, helped me gather illustrations. Also, close friends Richard and Barbara Collins of Tucson reviewed early versions of the manuscript and provided keen insights and suggestions, as well as offering stimulating discussions on the Spanish military in the Interior Provinces.

I would also like to thank my sons, Edward, Alexander, and Justin, for their love and support over the years and for the opportunity to watch them all become honorable men. Finally, I could not have accomplished anything without the inestimable support and superb editorial skills of my wife, Dawn.

The Jar of Severed Hands

Introduction

The bodies had been decaying for several days, and the stench must have been overpowering. Despite the smell, the man ignored the discomfort and set about the task he had been ordered to fulfill. Whether he conducted the amputations himself or sought the help of the soldiers of his escort is not recorded, but regardless, the twelve corpses were located, the arms pulled into suitable positions, and the hands—all left—were removed from the bodies. If the hands were hacked from the arms by the stroke of a sword or removed by the measured incisions of a knife, the result was the same. As he had been directed, the man placed the severed hands into a container, most likely a jar, for future inspection. So it was that the last earthly vestiges of twelve Apache men were noted in the annals of history and sifted into the sands of time.[1]

The brief narrative of the men's tale is simple enough. They had been part of a larger group of Apache prisoners captured by Spanish soldiers along the northern frontier of New Spain, what is today the southwestern border between the United States and

Mexico. In late March of 1792, they were among eighty-two Apache men, women, and children ordered transported south from the frontier to Mexico City, guarded by some thirty Spanish soldiers. Several days into their sojourn, at a desert arroyo, the prisoners attempted a desperate break for freedom by rising up and attacking their captors. But the Spanish soldiers were better armed, and using swords, lances, and firearms, they quickly killed twelve of the Apache men and cowed the remaining prisoners, mostly women and children, back into submission. Eventually, the Spanish would offer proof of the attempted breakout by gathering and displaying to their superiors the severed hands of the dead Apaches.

After the escape attempt, the surviving prisoners and their escort journeyed for another forty-five days until they reached Mexico City. There the prisoners were handed over to the military authorities of the capital and most probably subjected to imprisonment and death. The soldiers of the escort turned in the accounts for their expenses and headed back north. Bureaucrats haggled over the cost of the expedition and assiduously determined who should pay for what and why. With the closing of the financial accounts, the story ends. The book of the lives of the players is closed forever.

This tale is one of a series of reports dealing with the fate of Apache captives grouped together in colleras, or chain gangs. During the late eighteenth century, the Spanish began systematically to apply the policy of deporting captured Apache prisoners of war beyond the area of conflict into regions of the empire from which they could never return. For the Spanish, the policy of exile became a powerful weapon in the arsenal they employed against those they regarded as among their most implacable enemies. Yet within this tale there is reflected a more complex story that enmeshed both peoples in a struggle that had begun at least as early as the seventeenth century and that had forced both sides to develop and adapt to what seemed a never-ending cycle of violence. Over time—and to a large extent forced by the tenacity of Apache resistance—the Spaniards finally hit upon a strategy that produced results that were, at the very least, acceptable. This strategy called for the application of an apparent dichotomy: on the one hand, to encourage Apaches to settle on reservations, known as establecimientos de paz, or "peace establishments," where they would be placed on the government dole; and on the other, to wage unrelenting war on those who failed to accept or chose to ignore the deal. Beginning in the last decades of the eighteenth century, the Spanish system of establecimientos de paz attracted thousands of Apaches to come under at least some form of Spanish control, and led to a general arrangement among both peoples that even in its most negative light resembled peace more often than it did war.

Yet side by side with these settlements lay campaigns against recalcitrant Apaches that ended in the policy of deportation, a policy that, at a minimum, saw the forced removal of at least two thousand Apaches at the same time that like numbers were being congregated onto reservations. From the Spanish point of view, the policy of deportation could be seen as a successful counterpoise to the alternative offered by establecimientos de paz. It presented to the Apaches the ultimate choice, either the velvet glove or the mailed fist—to accept accommodation or to risk death and deportation. As the pendulum of Spanish policy swung between humane and savage treatment of the Apaches, it mirrored the quandary of all human conflict. The contrast of humane and rational treatment afforded to the enemy amid the brutal and often irrational exigencies of warfare underlies much of the story of the Apache chain gangs. Yet as far as this story is concerned, this conflict emanated from the highest levels of government and then diffused downward to the regional, local, and individual level.

This contrast may to a great extent be explained by the origins and nature of Spanish power as applied to the people generically labeled "Apache." Despite a worldview that tended to see most "Indians" in a set-piece pattern of existence, over time, the Spanish developed a more complex view of the Apaches than their official policies often cared to admit. This was especially true during the era of the so-called "Bourbon Reforms," roughly from 1760 to 1790, when the Spanish government implemented sweeping changes along the northern frontier of New Spain designed to deal in many respects specifically with the Apaches. The changes in Spanish official policy against the Apaches, even in the context of constant warfare, reflect difficulties that clearly were not originally foreseen. These difficulties in turn caused a confusion of power, or more precisely, of the application of power. That the Spanish believed they had the means to control the Apaches was not at issue. What was at issue was the cheapest, easiest, and quickest way to do it.

Eventually, two designs for the application of Spanish power emerged: either reach some level of accommodation with the Apaches or crush them militarily. Initially, the military option was seen as the policy to employ always and everywhere. When this proved unsatisfactory, accommodation would then be applied. In many instances, elements of both designs would be attempted, with decidedly mixed results. There would even be moments when the military solution was sought along one part of the frontier while accommodation was the policy along another.

Over time, the confusion of power shown by the Spanish became a vehicle that the Apaches came to exploit and use to their own advantage. If hard pressed by the Spaniards, they would offer to make peace, which was often granted. Then, after regaining their strength, the Apaches would return to their habit of raiding, and the cycle of violence would start anew. If the Spaniards in one area refused to treat with local Apache groups, the latter always had the hope of obtaining peace with Spaniards in a different area. Given the overlapping nature of Spanish authority, the Apaches could—and did—repeatedly manipulate this system to their own ends.

At the same time, the Spanish began to focus more and more on something they had known for many years but had never fully exploited—"the Apaches" were a disparate and complex group of people, often with no sense of deep commonality. Apache groups along the frontier were markedly different from one another in their behavior. Sometimes these differences reflected geography, sometimes proximity to other peoples, and sometimes the whims of individual personalities. Whatever the reason, the Spanish came to realize that the official policies regarding "the Apaches" could not be totally uniform. The clear distinctions that the Indians drew among themselves required that the Spanish show flexibility in the means they employed against them, even if the ends remained consistent.

However, the Spanish themselves showed deep division over how flexible they should be in seeking to control the Apaches. In the late 1780s, they adopted an overall policy designed to foster Apache dependency and gradually break down their traditional ways. Nevertheless, several senior Spanish officers insisted on waging campaigns designed to first crush the Apaches militarily. In the western portion of the frontier, the Spanish generally applied a more pragmatic approach, while in the east, the rule was dogmatic aggression. Not surprisingly, these differences influenced the behavior of the many Apache groups throughout the region. The "western Apaches" were characterized as more pliable, if no less violent, while the "eastern Apaches" came to be viewed as more or less inconstant and unable to curb their violent predispositions. That these opinions in many ways became self-fulfilling prophecies did not prevent Spanish officials from embracing them. Differing methods of treatment for Apaches from the western and eastern portions of the frontier eventually became the rule even if the "official" policy remained intact.

From 1786 to 1792, when the Spanish formally separated the governments controlling the frontier into western and eastern halves, the differing attitudes and actions became further entrenched. It was only after 1793, with the reuniting of the frontier under a sole command, that the Spanish policies regarding the Apaches began to resemble something approaching unity of purpose.

Yet throughout this era of ever-changing tactics, one of the most consistent Spanish methods of dealing with the Apaches was that of deportation. Whether the mailed fist was ascendant over the velvet glove or not, the exile of Apaches from the frontier continued unabated. The ready deployment of deportation reflected the realities of the age. In the eighteenth century, deportation of those the state regarded as dangerous or undesirable was fairly common. The nation of Australia, for example, was founded as a location to which sentenced British prisoners were transported, and within a few decades of its founding, the United States would also resort to deporting large numbers of Indian groups beyond the Mississippi River. Thus a government's removal of those deemed as problems was a normal procedure and one regarded as a more humane policy than the practice of times past wherein prisoners were routinely slaughtered by their captors. In the context of the times, the deportation of Apache prisoners was not only predictable, but—to many Spaniards—enlightened.

The sheer length of the conflict between Spaniards and Apaches produced situations of appalling inhumanity perpetrated by both peoples. The ease with which brutality can become routine has been and perhaps always will be one of the darkest truths about war, and this conflict was no different. Both sides resorted to what jurists have labeled *bellum terrorum*—a war of terror. The killing of women, children, and the elderly and the mutilation of the dead were common. In this context, the Spanish policy of exiling captured Apaches could be construed as simply another tactic to use against the enemy. Yet even amid this brutality, decent treatment of the prisoners was required. Through this small opening, the light of a shared humanity sometimes broke through to both sides: clothing given to the ill-clad in winter, doctors sought out to heal sick children, the dead interred decently. A genuine concern for the "saving of souls" was felt for those whose bodies were condemned to a slow death. The policy of deportation itself gradually became a battlefield where both Spaniard and Apache strove to negotiate, or at least mitigate, the enmity that defined their relationship.

In the end, the "peace" policies first adopted in the late 1780s became the dominant method Spaniards employed to deal with the Apaches. It was at best an attempt at accommodation and at worst, forced acculturation. On the other hand, the alternative was unrelenting war and all its concomitant terrors—not the least of which was deportation. Some may argue that the peace policies amounted to a Spanish acknowledgment of defeat or at least weakness in their ability to completely subdue the Apaches. If true, then it seems that the Spaniards, in the midst of their "weakness," nevertheless still devoted the time, energy, and money to pursue, capture, and deport large numbers of Apaches at least until 1810 and the beginning of the Mexican War of Independence. This fact alone speaks to the value that the Spaniards themselves placed on the practice.

While this conflict and the policies it engendered are evident, how they affected the many groups of Apache prisoners remains less so, as the historical documents simply do not give the background or details that would make them clear. None of these reports contains anything approaching a dispassionate account of events, and the point of view is obviously that of the Spanish captors, the men who conceived, wrote, submitted, and approved the documents. The Apaches are, for the most part, relegated to the role of "items" to be transported and delivered, and when they are mentioned, it is always through the lens of Spanish ideas, thoughts, and beliefs. This is, of course, not surprising. The narratives of incidents are recorded in official reports that tend to obscure the humanity of their subject in the midst of facts and figures.

Still, the drama of these expeditions remains a story that deserves to be told. The participants, Apache and Spanish alike, were flesh-and-blood human beings with all the emotions, nuances, and reactions of any of us. The official documents offer a few glimpses into their lives. Some of their names, ages, and sexes are recorded. The clothes they wore, the food they ate, the places they slept or passed through are known or can be discerned. Perhaps most important, the reasons they found themselves in the situations recorded can be placed in the larger context of how and why these two groups of people, Spanish and Apache, had come to be such bitter enemies. For it is within this larger conflict that the story of these individuals is hidden and the strands of their lives preserved, if only in the briefest mention, in the stark image of a jar filled with severed human hands.

CHAPTER 1

A Cruel and Bloody War

Campaigning in wintertime was never easy, but Captain Manuel de Echeagaray was a seasoned veteran. At age thirty, he had been in the army since he was a boy of ten, and he had been an officer along the northern frontier for over seven years. By January of 1788, he had, by his own reckoning, participated in a dozen campaigns and numerous other forays in pursuit of "the enemy," a term that along the northern frontier almost invariably meant the Apaches. Seven days into the new year, Echeagaray gathered a force of 186 officers and men and set out on yet another campaign to harry the enemy in their own lands.

Departing from the Presidio of Santa Cruz in northeastern Sonora, the expedition headed east into the lands of the Mimbreños, as the Spanish designated the Apaches in this area. Moving between the mountain ranges and desert basins of what is today southwestern New Mexico, Echeagaray and his men came across numerous tracks of horses and people. Relentlessly pursuing them, on the night of January 15, the soldiers saw campfires high up on a mountain range. The captain ordered his men to press on, and at four o'clock in the morning, they surprised and attacked a small encampment of Apaches, killing four women and capturing another two, along with an adult man and five children. In addition, they freed an Indian man and a boy who claimed they were prisoners.

Echeagaray interrogated the man, who informed the captain that he knew of another encampment farther to the east. Following up on this intelligence, the soldiers rode for two more days until they located the Apaches. Again they achieved a complete surprise, killing three women and a man and taking five other people captive. An Apache woman told her captors that yet another group of Indians was farther east and that they had stolen many Spanish horses. Despite being forced to stop for half a day due to heavy snowfall, the soldiers' pursuit bore fruit when at dawn on January 20, they located the tracks of many horses driven by six men in the Sierra Florida near present-day Deming, New Mexico.

Pushing his men onward, Captain Echeagaray reported that by midnight of the next day, he reached a mountain called El Potrerito, where he found seventeen horses that the Apaches had abandoned. If the Apaches hoped that their pursuers would be satisfied with the recovery of the animals and turn back with these spoils, they were dreadfully wrong. Without hesitation, the captain ordered his men to ride through the night after the Apaches as they fled toward the Rio Grande. "I continued after them," Echeagaray noted in his field diary, "until ten the next day, and I attacked them on the banks of the said river."

There were six Apache men and nine women with five small children. Despite being overwhelmed by a force of over a hundred soldiers, the Apaches resisted desperately. They managed to kill one of the Spanish officers, Alférez Rafael Tovar, much to the chagrin of Captain Echeagaray, who wrote that Tovar "was carried away to his destruction by his valor." Despite this loss, the fight raged for over six hours, the Spanish continuously firing their guns on the Apaches, "who made a stiff resistance." Perhaps stung by this and the loss of one of their leaders, the Spaniards were not inclined to show mercy, and they killed all the Apaches, even the children, sparing only a single woman. Tersely concluding his report of the action, Captain Echeagaray noted, "This hard fight ended at four in the afternoon, at which hour I ordered the burial of the fallen officer and the cutting off of the ears and heads [of the Apaches]." Although the campaign would continue for another seventeen days, the soldiers would not encounter any more Indians. On February 7, Captain Echeagaray reported to his superiors that the expedition had succeeded in killing twenty-eight Apaches of both sexes and all ages, capturing fourteen more, and recovering forty-one horses. Within a few months, the captain would set out again, this time on his fourteenth campaign.[1]

As a career military officer, Echeagaray's constant campaigning may have inured him to the horrors and violence of combat; the struggle against the Apaches had been going on for so many years that the killing of women and children and the taking of heads and ears to establish "body counts" had become routine. Like so many human conflicts before and after, both sides came to dehumanize the other to the point that such practices were viewed as normal. For example, Spanish officers referred to captured Apache prisoners as *piezas*, or "pieces," a term derived from counting the number of animals bagged during hunting. Expeditions into Apache territory were often termed *mariscadas*, literally, "gathering shellfish." The Apaches also indulged in such hyperbolic wordplay, referring to the Spaniards as "herds" or "crops" from which they harvested their spoils. The bitterness and hatred engendered between Spaniard and Apache would perversely sustain the cycle of violence. In later years, one of Echeagaray's brother officers, Antonio Cordero, would tellingly characterize the conflict as "a cruel and bloody war." But despite his long years of service, even Echeagaray probably did not know the true length and depth of the struggle.

When the Spanish and Apaches first came into conflict is a matter of conjecture. Between 1540 and 1542, the expedition of Francisco Vásquez de Coronado entered the American Southwest in search of the fabled Seven Cities of Gold, and among the many peoples it encountered were the Querechos, an Apache group. Whether they witnessed the warfare that Coronado's men unleashed, and whether they suffered from diseases brought by the conquistadors, is not known, but the Querechos and other Apaches undoubtedly realized that a powerful new force had entered their world.

That force became manifest when in 1598 the expedition of Juan de Oñate returned to establish a permanent Spanish presence in what he termed the Kingdom of New Mexico. By 1610, Oñate and his successors had crushed overt Puebloan resistance and established themselves in permanent settlements that drew on the various native communities for supplies and labor. The Spanish demand for goods and services disrupted production cycles and trade relationships between various indigenous peoples, including the Apaches. In addition, new plants and animals brought by the Spaniards changed forever the lifestyles of the natives and profoundly impacted the environment. As the competition for resources escalated, warfare, long a part of the native peoples' lives, intensified.[2]

During the late sixteenth and early seventeenth centuries, references to the Apaches began to appear regularly in the written records of the Spanish. For example, in the 1630s, the chronicler Fray Alonso de Benavides referred to the "Apaches de Gila" dwelling southwest of the Spanish settlements in New Mexico and to several other Apache groups to the east and north. Despite having identified only a few Apache groups by name, as the seventeenth century progressed, the Spanish gradually became aware that the Apaches occupied a much wider geographic area. Pushing northward from central Mexico into Sonora, Nueva Vizcaya, and Coahuila, by the 1670s they had encountered various groups of Apaches in all of these locations. Beginning with the Pueblo Revolt in New Mexico in 1680, numerous indigenous peoples throughout the region rose up against the Spanish in what historians have called the Great Northern Revolt, and by the time the Spanish had quelled this series of uprisings in 1695, many more Apache groups had been brought into focus. Combined with the Spaniards' efforts to thwart French expansion into Texas during the same period, the limits of the lands inhabited by the Apaches began to take shape.[3]

By the beginning of the eighteenth century, what has been referred to as the "Apacheization" of many Indian groups began to occur. Several peoples such as the Jocomes, Sumas, Mansos, and others who had been identified in earlier times as different peoples began to meld with the Apaches. Whether this process was the result of increased competition for scarce environmental resources, the alliance of hitherto independent bands into larger groups for protection against Spanish encroachment, or a combination of these and other factors, the term "Apache" began to be applied to a growing number of peoples along a swath of territory stretching the entire length of Spanish settlement.

Along the eastern portion of the Spanish frontier, a primary stimulus to the growing Apache presence was the irruption of the Comanches onto the scene about 1709. Developing as a highly aggressive and expansionist people, the Comanches began to vie with other tribes for control over the southern buffalo plains. They gradually overpowered and defeated the eastern Apache groups who were among the major competitors for the same territory. A large factor in the Comanches' success was their ability to procure firearms through indirect trade from the French settlements east of the Mississippi River. Relatively quickly, the Comanches began to exert a marked military

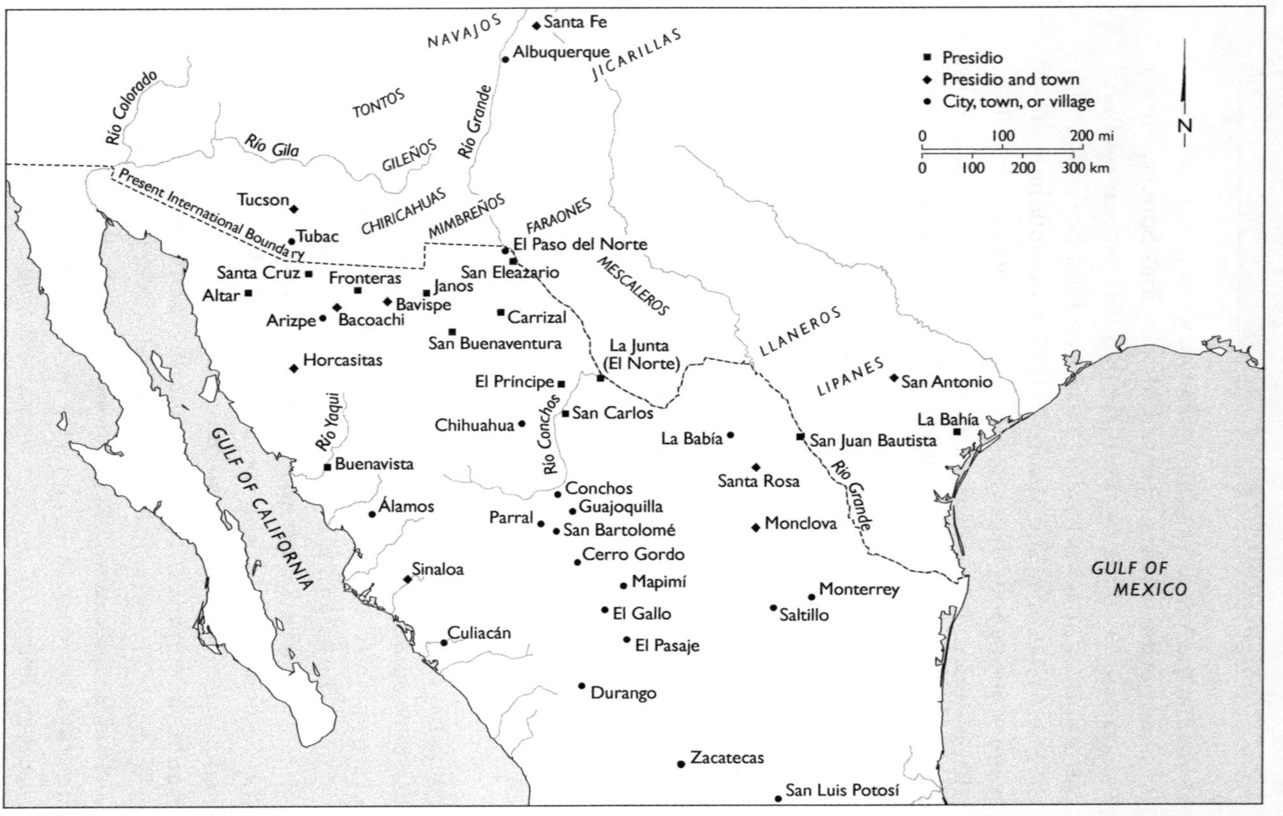

Apache groups and the line of presidios, 1772–1810. Adapted from Max L. Moorhead, *The Presidio: Bastion of the Spanish Borderlands* (Norman: University of Oklahoma Press, 1975).

superiority over the eastern Apaches. Unable to stand against them, the Apaches began to be pushed out of the southern plains and into the zones of Hispanic control.

In 1722, the Spaniards identified many different Apache groups inhabiting the eastern area between the settlements at San Antonio in Texas and Santa Fe in New Mexico. By about 1730, more Apache groups were known to range along both sides of the Rio Grande at least as far as the Big Bend country, while others occupied lands farther west along the drainage of the Gila River in what is now southern New Mexico and Arizona. Eventually the Spaniards would come to call the whole area "*la gran Apachería*."[4]

But it was not merely the extent of the lands the Apaches traversed that drew the attention of the Spanish; it was the actions of the Apaches themselves, who had emerged as among the most effective and sanguinary raiders the Spanish had encountered in the New World. The Apaches lived in relatively small communities that the Spanish labeled *rancherías*. Usually grouped around extended families or local groups, rancherías could contain anywhere from a few individuals up to several dozen, and it was with the ranchería that individual identity was most closely connected. Generally speaking, the Apaches traced descent through both the male and female, but they were a matrilocal society, with married men moving to live with the families of their wives. Groups of kindred might come together at various times of the year for mutual protection, for common hunts, for harvests of wild plants or sown crops, or for religious ceremonies. Specific regions were inevitably considered the "home" of various rancherías.

Over time, the Spanish and other Western peoples would group the Apaches into units based on their geographic location as well as their cultural characteristics. By the eighteenth century, the Spanish identified the Apache peoples living to the east as the Lipans, Lipiyans, Jicarillas, Llaneros, Faraones, Natages, and Mescaleros. To the south were other distinct groups labeled Gileños, Mimbreños, and Chiricahuas. To the west were the Navajos, who had begun to develop a heavily pastoral society and a unique identity that gradually differentiated them from the Apaches. Furthest west were the Tontos and the Coyoteros, also known as White Mountain Apaches.[5]

However, despite these broad characterizations, for many Apaches, the notion of belonging to a tribe or band was often imposed by outsiders in an attempt to understand their society. It is unclear if such identifications existed among the Apaches themselves. While certainly aware of a shared language, same ethnicity, and common customs, the identification of members of one local group or one ranchería with those of another, especially those at some distance, was never certain. Their recognition of belonging to a larger "tribe" and even of being "Apache" did not amount to the overriding sense of identity seen in other peoples.

Their form of self-identification derived ultimately from the nature of leadership among the Apaches. Leadership within each family and ranchería—especially among adult males—came to be based on individual success at all times and in every circumstance. Thus, leadership could be, and often was, fluid and ever changing. If a man scrupulously carried out the obligations demanded by kinship, if he practiced religious or cultural ceremonies properly, if he showed generosity to friends and exacted vengeance from enemies, then others would accept his leadership.

Still, even if an individual Apache was recognized as a leader within the local group, leadership was most often temporary and subject to the whims of individual members. Even forceful personalities and successful leaders held control and garnered respect only up to a point. Those who disagreed with the pronouncements or actions of a leader were free to make their own way. This extreme independence ensured that leadership was atomized to the most basic level within Apache society. This cultural trait was to have an enormous impact on two other linked aspects of Apache society: raiding and warfare.

Before the Spaniards arrived, the Apaches had engaged in raiding and warfare against other native peoples and against other Apaches. The control of natural resources and hunting grounds, the acquisition of food supplies and trade goods, the taking of slaves and captives, and the wreaking of vengeance for real or perceived insults were all reasons for action. By the time the Spanish arrived in the region, Apaches were regarded by some of the Puebloan peoples as aggressive raiders who, although they might engage in trade, were often hostile.

As Spanish settlements began to move north at the end of the seventeenth century, the Apaches found that the newcomers' habit of establishing settled communities provided them with increased raiding opportunities for food, goods, and wonderful new metal implements. But the most tempting prizes were the herds of horses that the Spaniards brought. As with numerous other indigenous peoples, the horse quickly became a major cultural denominator. By the early eighteenth century, the eastern Apache peoples had become "horse cultures" that exploited the mobility the animal gave them to greatly increase their capability to hunt buffalo. Apaches living farther to the south and west also took to the horse but added it as a source of food in lieu of ready access to the buffalo plains. Regardless of such nuances, horses quickly became the favorite target of Apache raids.

Within several generations of contact with the Spanish, horse ownership had become crucial for the Apaches. A man's ability to supply horses to his family and friends, to use them to acquire a bride, or to trade them for other goods became the primary mark of his worth and renown. One of the primary ways to acquire horses was through raiding. As the horse helped coalesce Apache cultural patterns, the extreme individualism of the Apaches accelerated the imperative for raiding. The relative proximity of Spanish settlements spurred countless forays by the Apaches to steal horses and raid for other goods. The atomized nature of Apache leadership meant that raids could be as small as one or two individuals rustling strays, all the way up to organized expeditions with scores of men seeking to drive off whole herds. Inevitably, during such raids, there would be resistance from the animals' owners, and often Apaches would be killed. Such a loss, in turn, triggered another requisite of Apache culture: vengeance.

The Apaches, like many other peoples throughout history, regarded the death of one of their own at another's hand as an act demanding retribution. Whether it was a homicide or accidental killing among the Apaches themselves or a death in a raid or battle against outsiders, Apache cultural mores stipulated that those who had suffered the loss would wreak vengeance. While this pattern was recognized and accepted among the Apaches, when applied to outsiders, it took on added dimensions.

When dealing with different peoples, the Apaches directed vengeance against "the other" and not necessarily against the actual perpetrator or group. Thus, if an Apache was killed while raiding a Spanish horse herd in one region, Spaniards far removed from the event might be attacked in retaliation for something they had no part in. To the Spanish, it was unjust to hold one individual responsible for the actions of another. But to the Apaches, this was irrelevant. "The other" must pay in a collective sense in order to balance or repay the loss. In addition, the Apaches often took the view that there was no *final* payment. Vengeance could be exacted for as long as one felt aggrieved; it could continue for a long time and involve many different attacks.

These two cultural imperatives—raiding and vengeance—became a focal point for Apache relations with outsiders. As Spanish settlements began to push up against the Apaches' homelands from Sonora all the way to Texas, it was inevitable that these settlements would become prime sources for raiding and convenient targets for vengeance. The Spanish would just as inevitably seek to halt these raids by counterattacking the Apaches. However small the amount of blood first spilled between the two peoples, over the course of the late seventeenth century and into the eighteenth, the flow gradually increased. Soon it threatened to become a torrent.[6]

Until the middle of the eighteenth century, the Spanish had not developed a coherent and consistent military policy for dealing with the Apaches or any other native peoples along the northern frontier of New Spain. There were several independent *presidios*, or forts, of professional soldiers in the region, but these were scattered haphazardly across thousands of miles of territory. The presidios had come into existence mainly in response to two outside forces: first, as protective agents for the missionary endeavors of the Catholic Church; and second, to protect lucrative but often ephemeral mining strikes. The missions and mines competed for the souls and labor of the local Indians. When the Indians resisted the missionaries or threatened the mines (which almost always occurred), the response was to establish a presidio to restore and maintain order among the Indians.

Aside from these few presidios, all other military needs along the frontier were supposed to be met by local militias. In a tradition that harks back to the Iberian medieval Reconquista against the Moors, emergency defense fell to an armed citizenry ideally made up of all the able-bodied males, armed and equipped at their own expense. However, along the northern frontier, where there were very few cities and towns, such a system was at best inadequate. The function of the militia was often carried out not by the population of Europeans or mixed-blood *mestizos*, but by Indians, either tribal bands in alliance with the white men, or semi-Christianized levies drawn from the mission communities.

While there had been some attempts to bring uniformity of command and organization to the presidios and militia along the northern frontier—most notably the 1729 Regulations of Brigadier General Pedro de Rivera—Spanish military power remained decentralized despite the increasing conflicts with aboriginal peoples between 1730 and 1750. This laissez-faire attitude came to an abrupt halt in 1763, not because of events along the northern frontier but because of the Seven Years' War.[7]

This war, which became generalized throughout Europe in 1756, saw the building of a confederation that eventually came to include France and Spain allied against Great Britain. Spain initially remained neutral, but when a new king, Charles III, ascended the throne, he watched in awe as Britain marshaled its military and maritime power to decisively defeat the French in North America and India. Hoping to aid his French cousins, Charles brought Spain into the war in 1761. But the British, turning against the Spanish latecomers, quickly overwhelmed and captured the city of Havana, Cuba, Spain's most powerful and strategically crucial American fortress. On the other side of the globe, another British expedition captured Manila in the Philippines. Unnerved by the British ability to employ massive force on such a wide scale, Charles III ignominiously sued for peace.

Although Spain was able to recover both Havana and Manila in 1763 by the terms of the Peace of Paris, Charles III had learned a harsh lesson. The superiority of the British Navy allowed it to rapidly deploy forces against Spain's overseas empire while at the same time preventing reinforcements from being sent from Europe. Spain's only defense was to position sufficient military power in Spanish America to repel a British assault. To accomplish this, the king launched a complete overhaul of the military and financial machinery of his empire. For over a decade, Charles III and his ministers attempted to revamp and revitalize the economic and military underpinnings of Spain's colonies. The impetus of reform and retrenchment would eventually reach the northern frontier of New Spain and bolster the continuing war against the Apaches.

The most crucial aspect of Spain's North American defense was to protect the silver flowing from the mines of central Mexico back to the mother country. To this end, the Spanish devised an elaborate system of defense designed to wear down an attacker while securing the delivery of Mexican silver. The first and outermost layer in this defensive system was the construction and garrisoning of fortifications at strategic locations throughout the islands of the Caribbean, such as Cuba and Puerto Rico. A second ring of powerful coastal defenses was established on the Mexican mainland at Veracruz and Campeche. These would have to be overcome before an enemy could proceed inland. To meet this last threat, the crown began the formation of a standing army designed to confront and overwhelm an invading force between the coast and the Mexican interior.[8]

It was only at this point, around 1764, that the policy makers in Madrid began to consider the military situation along the northern frontier of New Spain. Yet, even then, they addressed the problem from a continental perspective. By the terms of the Peace of Paris, Spain had lost Florida but in turn had gained the Louisiana Territory. The already vast northern frontier of the Viceroyalty of New Spain had grown enormously and now stretched west to California, east to Illinois, and south to Florida. Much of this area bordered on British possessions in Canada and those east of the Mississippi River. Although a British invasion from these regions was unlikely, smaller diversionary attacks were a potential threat.

To assess not only the frontier situation but the entire military and financial capabilities of the viceroyalty, Charles III dispatched several of his ablest advisors to New Spain. The most powerful and influential of these was the *visitador* José de Gálvez. Arriving in Mexico in 1765, Gálvez advocated two complementary programs that dealt directly with the northern borders. The first called for the reorganization and retrenchment of the frontier zone between the Gulf of California and the Gulf of Mexico, to be known as the Interior Provinces of New Spain. This area was to be placed under a unified military command, the better to cope with the incursions of hostile Indians. Second, Gálvez recommended a military drive northward along the Pacific coast into what is now the state of California. He hoped that these two projects would together provide an added buffer against both European and indigenous enemies.

Gálvez understood that Spain's immediate enemies affecting the Interior Provinces were not Europeans, but numerous native groups, such as the Apaches and Comanches. Although these peoples did not actually threaten Spain's hold along the northern frontier, they did drain financial and military resources that were needed elsewhere. Furthermore, the Indians' proximity to the British colonies created the specter of hostile tribes directly assisting the British or at least acting as surrogates. These ideas had largely been shaped by the recommendations of the Marqués de Rubí, one of four field marshals the Spanish had sent in 1764 to reform the military throughout Mexico. Rubí had been assigned the task of assessing the northern frontier. After a two-year, 7,600-mile inspection that took him from Sonora to Louisiana, he compiled a comprehensive plan for dealing with the region.

Realizing that Spain claimed much more territory than it controlled, Rubí recommended that Spanish forces be arranged in a defensive cordon along the edge of settlement. To accomplish this, he advocated repositioning most of the presidios of Spanish soldiers garrisoning the northern frontier into a vast arc following the irregular course of the Rio Grande and a line approximating the thirtieth parallel. The presidios would be spaced close enough together to offer mutual support, and more important, they would be controlled by a single, unified command.

Rubí's idea for a line of presidios was not unique. Similar cordons had been employed successfully in Europe and by the

Spanish themselves in South America. But from the crown's perspective, two points about Rubí's plan *were* unique. One was its confirmation that there was little danger of a European invasion of Mexico via the northern frontier. The second was its argument that the threat posed by the Indians of the region, while irksome, could be overcome by the local forces already available, given proper training and leadership—and avoiding a troop buildup promised to save the treasury a substantial sum. These two conclusions would form the cornerstone of all Spanish military policy regarding the region for the next forty years.[9]

As a result, in 1771, Viceroy the Marqués de Croix, with the backing of Gálvez, provisionally adopted Rubí's plan. Charles III, somewhat tardily, gave formal approval the following year. Thus was born the famous royal Regulations of 1772 for governing the Interior Provinces of New Spain. The Regulations of 1772 recognized that the primary enemies to be dealt with along the frontier were the Apaches. Because the Apaches lived in autonomous bands from Sonora to Texas and habitually raided for plunder and vengeance, the regulations called for unrelenting warfare against them. To that end, the regulations even advocated that other aboriginal groups hostile to the Spaniards, such as the Comanches, be enticed into alliances against the Apaches.

The Regulations of 1772 created a new military position to oversee the war against the Apaches: the commandant inspector of the Interior Provinces, who would be appointed by the viceroy. This officer was assigned three interrelated tasks. He would oversee the formation of the cordon of presidios at the locations the Marqués de Rubí chose. At the same time, he would institute a new program for the disciplining, training, equipping, and financing of the presidial garrisons. Finally, he would coordinate the actions of the garrisons to block Apache raiding parties and simultaneously attack them in their homelands.[10]

Yet, amid the detailed instructions for reforming the conditions of service for his soldiers to reinvigorate them in their war against hostile Indians, Charles III and those writing in his name devoted a considerable portion of the new regulations to ensuring that these same enemies "be treated with humanity." The regulations are replete with the seeming contradiction of calling for a most brutal war while simultaneously arguing that it be waged with a degree of temperance. Indeed, the main goal of the regulations was stated as being the "welfare and conversion of the gentile Indians and the tranquility of the frontier areas." That the first part was not necessarily compatible, or perhaps even possible, with the second may seem obvious in retrospect, but for the king and his ministers there was no contradiction: "The most effective measures for attaining these useful and pious ends are vigor and activity in war and good faith and gentle treatment of those who surrender or are taken prisoner."

The Regulations of 1772 specified that once the soldiers of the frontier had accomplished the prescribed reorganization and reforms, they were to direct all their powers toward "waging an active and incessant war against the Indians who are declared enemies, wherever possible attacking them in their own villages and lands." Yet, in the midst of these activities, the same soldiers were enjoined to treat any prisoners they captured with compassion. "With the prisoners who are taken in war, I [the king] prohibit all bad treatment and impose the penalty of death upon those who kill them in cold blood; they shall be sent to the vicinity of Mexico City where my viceroy may dispose of them as seems convenient. I order that prisoners be assisted with the same daily rations that are given Indian auxiliaries; and the women and children that are apprehended will be treated equally and assisted, in order to procure their conversion and instruction."

Still, while the regulations prohibited "bad treatment" of individuals, there was no such caution when dealing with larger groups; they noted that while "gentleness and good treatment with individual prisoners are useful, with the entire nation they are pernicious. . . . Especially is this true with the Apaches." Obviously referring to the numerous times that ephemeral treaties had been concluded with various Apache groups, the regulations clearly determined to stamp out this practice. "When their forces are inferior, or they are overwhelmed by our victories, they profess a desire for peace; afterwards they abuse our clemency at the first opportunity, interpreting as weakness the kind treatment that they were given." Undoubtedly angered by these tactics, the king was unequivocal in this matter, writing, "I prohibit the commandant-inspector and the captains of presidios from granting them peace." Temporary truces and pauses in hostilities would be granted in order to negotiate the exchange of captives, but any formal peace with the Apaches would have to be approved by the viceroy in Mexico City.[11]

The Apaches were clearly identified by the Regulations of 1772 as "the enemy." The most brutal warfare could be, and undoubtedly was, waged against the group, but mercy was to be extended to the individual to meet the demands of a Christian and civilized society. Thus, it was through the context of individuality that the king and his ministers sought to try and temper the cruel and bloody war against the Apaches. Through the prism of their own history and culture, the Spaniards had come to define and apply what they understood to be the correct "rules of war." The use of terror and brutality and the place of mercy and humanity had all undergone centuries of development that had led to the idea that war, despite all its concomitant evils, could be regulated in certain ways. Just how those ideas should be applied to the Apaches was still an open question.

CHAPTER 2

Prisoners

By late July of 1765, the *cárcel,* or public jail, at the presidio and town of El Paso had become crowded with Apaches. Since the beginning of the year, newly appointed captain Pedro José de la Fuente had seen the soldiers of his command, the citizens in the adjacent *villa,* and the allied Indians in the nearby missions all contribute to the accumulation of captives. The soldiers had seized seventeen women and children in a foray that De la Fuente himself had led into the nearby Sierra de los Órganos. The citizens had helped catch four Apache men attempting to rustle horses. The allied Indians had taken three Apache women they had encountered while scouting the other side of the Rio Grande for signs of enemy activity. The question now before the captain, however, was what to do with them all.

It was a long-standing custom on the northern frontier that Apaches who were captured, especially women and children, were parceled out as "servants" among those Spanish families that promised to raise them as Christians. Captain de la Fuente adhered to this tradition, noting, "I decided to distribute the twenty captured Indian women and children, whom I apportioned among the principal residents of the town, advising and suggesting they give them kind treatment and above all instruct them in the principal mysteries of our Holy Catholic Faith and [in] good manners. Of this number there are eleven who have not yet reached the age of reason and who are ready for baptism."

Still, there remained the four Apache men to be dealt with. They had clearly been trying to steal horses and were from a group that was avowedly at war with the Spaniards. But they had not been taken in battle and had not actually committed any known depredations. Were they to be treated as thieves subject to Spanish criminal justice, or were they prisoners of war seized as combatants from a hostile nation? Could they legally be placed in servitude and their labor used for the benefit of their captors? Captain de la Fuente was in no position to answer these questions and he knew it. As a result, he ordered that the Apaches be held in the cárcel, "awaiting the superior orders of His Excellency the Lord Viceroy of these Kingdoms, whom I have notified so that he may make the final decision as to what is to be done with them." It was a situation that greater minds than the captain's had wrestled with for centuries.[1]

From the earliest times and in almost all societies, "prisoners of war" were enslaved, regarded as the property of their captors to be disposed of as they saw fit. All members of a belligerent group, whether they had performed as combatants or not, were included in this category, regardless of age or sex. As property, prisoners became the responsibility of their captors, and if the captor chose to feed and shelter them, he did so at his own expense. Indeed, this expense was often pointed to as the reason for the usual practice of slaughtering prisoners—the captors simply did not have the resources to care for them. Enslaved prisoners were spared only if they could bring some benefit to their captors, and usually this benefit was their personal labor.

In many societies throughout the world, the number of captives was often a delineator of individual success, increasing the wealth and power of the captor. Among some tribal societies, captives might even be adopted into the group to increase its size and power. In state societies, captives and their labor could be transferred to other individuals or to the state itself in exchange for goods or money. As such, prisoners of war often became a marketable commodity. Prisoners might also be ransomed for large sums or exchanged for captives held by an enemy, although ransoms were usually sought only for wealthy or powerful elites.

In Europe during the Middle Ages, the attitude toward prisoners of war became less severe. Among Western Europeans, spurred by the merciful enjoinders of a unified Christian Church and a shared worldview, the ransom and exchange of nobles and of valued and expensive mercenaries became more common, and the enslavement or slaughter of prisoners diminished. In the heat of battle, however, the killing of prisoners might still be undertaken. Perhaps the most famous example was at the Battle of Agincourt in 1415, when Henry V of England ordered the massacre of several hundred French prisoners of war, including a large number of valuable noblemen.

During the sixteenth and seventeenth centuries, European jurists and clergy began to trace the outlines for the so-called "laws of war," which, among many other precepts, advocated for more humane treatment of prisoners. Still, even the most influential of these thinkers, Hugo Grotius, in his great work *On the Laws of War and Peace*, maintained that captors could lawfully enslave prisoners of war, although he personally advocated that they be ransomed instead. However, at the end of the Thirty Years' War in 1648, the Treaty of Westphalia resulted in the release of prisoners without ransom and established a precedent among the European nations. By the eighteenth century, further developments in international law began to take hold, and thinkers such as the French philosopher the Baron de Montesquieu in his 1748 work, *The Spirit of Laws*, held that captors could hold prisoners only to prevent them from rejoining the fight and that they did not have the right to treat them as chattel. Reflecting on the perceived advancements of his age, Montesquieu noted, "All nations concur in detesting the murder of prisoners in cold blood." Sentiments such as these continued the process of classifying and treating prisoners of war differently from slaves.[2]

Despite these advancements, many of these ideas were considered applicable only among Europeans who shared a similar cultural heritage, and even then there were no guarantees. Treaties and general attitudes were often seen as applying to specific conflicts or participants and might not be uniformly respected. During the American Revolutionary War, for example, the British regarded their prisoners as "rebels" who had broken faith with their natural sovereign and as such were not lawful combatants. The result was that they treated American prisoners of war horrifically, causing many thousands to die of neglect and maltreatment. In a similar vein, the ideas of the "laws of war" were often felt to be different in combat against non-Europeans, such as Turks or the polities of the Indian subcontinent.

For the Spanish, however, long proximity with non-Europeans had produced a more complex view on the laws of war that in some ways anticipated these general European trends. In Spain, many of the attitudes regarding the treatment of prisoners of war had evolved over centuries of conflict with Islamic powers. Ideas regulating the conduct of certain types of warfare as well as rules for the enslavement and release of prisoners were especially relevant in the struggle involving the so-called corsairs.

Throughout the sixteenth and seventeenth centuries, while many governments in the rest of Europe began to advocate for better treatment of prisoners, the populations that lived along the coast of the Iberian Peninsula were being subjected to the depredations of Muslim corsairs, who routinely carried off men, women, and children to be sold into slavery among the Islamic states in North Africa and the Levant. Conversely, many Islamic peoples along the North African coast were exposed to Christian corsairs, who sold their slaves in Spain, Portugal, France, and Italy. In all these instances, slaving raids by corsairs were recognized as a more or less legitimate species of warfare, a "low intensity conflict" directed by cities or nation-states against longstanding enemies of a different culture. Indeed, captives seized by corsairs were regarded as the very sinews of war; the oared galleys that predominated in Mediterranean navies by the sixteenth century were almost always manned by enslaved rowers.

During this period, slave raiding by all the powers of the Mediterranean had developed to such an extent that many aspects had become institutionalized, and a type of "international law" came into existence. Islamic and Christian corsairs, for example, were generally regarded as privateers, not pirates, and as a result were seen as agents of the warring parties. Among Muslim states, such as Algiers and Tunis, the corsair trade in slaves came to be a substantial source of their revenue, and they developed intricate rules and regulations that both sides came to recognize. Several Catholic religious orders, such as the Mercedarians and Trinitarians, were thus viewed as honest brokers that negotiated ransoms and helped expedite exchanges for imprisoned Christians.

By the eighteenth century, technological and economic considerations began to influence the rules of warfare in the Mediterranean. The use of oared galleys for naval operations declined in the face of larger and better armed sailing ships. Prisoners seized by corsairs began to be used less to row galleys and more for other purposes. Many of the Christian powers commenced employing their Muslim slaves in public works. In Spain, for instance, the naval arsenal at Cartagena contained hundreds of Muslim slaves who were deemed essential to the base's operations. Christian slaves similarly provided the labor to upgrade most of the fortifications and to build and maintain the palaces, streets, and harbors of Muslim strongholds like Algiers. Prisoners as labor commodities began to be factored into the equations of the state finances of all the powers. As a result, the costs associated with their acquisition, maintenance, and disposition received greater scrutiny, and general rules regarding their treatment began to take shape, all to protect this important source of labor.

Among the Muslim cities of North Africa, the prisoners represented a valuable commodity in other ways. The extortion of ransom was very lucrative. A "price scale" developed in official circles that set the ransom to be paid for various classes of individuals, ranging from nobles, military officers, and clergy all the way down to fishermen, old people, women, and children. This taxonomy of ransom further influenced the treatment of prisoners, with the value of an individual captive tied to the set cost of purchasing his or her freedom.

A prisoner's liberty could also be obtained through the policy of exchange, wherein captured Muslims were traded for captured Christians. Exchange, in turn, furthered the idea of reciprocity or proportionality, wherein prisoners of equal standing were traded for their like, or a number of low-level slaves were traded for a single higher-level one. Although exchange had existed since the beginning of the corsair trade, by the eighteenth century it had become a highly refined, even ritualized, affair, which promoted improvement in the treatment of captives.

Many of the Christian powers in the Muslim cities of Algiers, Tunis, Tangiers, and other North African enclaves maintained formal embassies to oversee the operations of ransom and exchange. The constant flow of money needed to purchase various types of prisoners or to oversee their transfer resulted in formal treaties that guaranteed particular status to the representatives of the Christian states resident in the Islamic ports, as well as securing their persons and property. All of these developments accumulated to provide a general framework that helped to regulate the nature of conflict and the treatment of prisoners among the warring states of the Mediterranean. For many Spaniards, the policies that had evolved in the long struggle with Muslim corsairs would influence the way they acted against other perceived enemies, especially non-European ones. Nowhere would these actions and the ideas behind them be more pertinent than in the Spanish conflict against the American Indians.[3]

In conquering and controlling its American empire, Spanish notions of waging war had undergone many evolutions. From the first expeditions of Columbus, conflicts between Spaniards and the indigenous peoples had spurred intense debate over how to apply the concept of a "just war" to the peoples of the New World. By the eighteenth century, the laws of war as they pertained to Indians had become increasingly categorized and somewhat regularized. Native peoples who had been brought under some degree of control were usually considered "subjects" of the empire. Therefore, if these groups engaged the authorities in warfare, they were most often deemed "rebels" and, under the Spanish rules of war, were subject to a much harsher and narrower stricture than if they had not been part of the empire. It was therefore "legal" from the Spanish perspective not only to kill rebellious Indians, but to enslave any captives taken, as they had lost most of their legal rights as a result of their insurrection.

However, Spain also laid claim to large swaths of territory that it did not actually control. Natives within and beyond these "zones of conflict" were clearly not yet subjects of the empire. Warfare with these groups presented several problems that troubled the sensibilities of many Spaniards. As *bárbaros*, or barbarians, the Indians were viewed as having either implicitly or explicitly rejected Spanish and Christian ideas, thus proving that they were "irrational" beings. As a result, they could be and were enslaved after being taken captive in battle. But the Spanish government, at least officially, recognized that many of these Indians were, in fact, prisoners of war and consequently subject to a different set of legal constraints than slaves. From the Spanish view of justice according to the "laws of war," this issue presented an ambiguity that defied an easy solution. By the 1700s, perhaps no other indigenous group in Spain's North American possessions was affected more by this ambiguity than the Apaches.

When the Spanish first entered the Southwest in the 1540s, they found slavery a common denominator between themselves and the natives. For example, the Puebloan people routinely acquired slaves both by barter and through warfare, as did the ancestors of the Apaches and the other numerous Indian peoples of the region. Melding European practices with those of the indigenous groups they contacted, the Spanish on the northern frontier had by the seventeenth century tapped into and expanded the existing lucrative trade in slaves. Spanish slave-raiding expeditions secured numerous Indian captives as sources for cheap labor in mines and at haciendas and as domestic servants. Indian retaliation against the Spaniards or their native allies provoked further raids, with more captives seized and enslaved, trapping both sides in a seemingly unbreakable cycle.[4]

Although the Spanish crown outlawed Indian slavery at least as early as 1542, enforcement of the law remained problematic at best. Presidial captains on the northern frontier routinely placed Indian prisoners, especially women and children, in the care of prominent families with the promise to the crown that they would be civilized and Christianized by their new owners. Indian men, on the other hand, were usually set to hard labor at mines, ranches, farms, or public works. Many prisoners were retained in or near the presidios, to be exchanged for Spanish captives. As the frontier moved into lands inhabited by the Apaches, they too became engulfed in the rolling tide of Indian slavery.

By the mid-eighteenth century, warfare escalated to the point that Apache prisoners of war were so common that numerous Hispanic settlements along the northern frontier held captured Apaches. Often these communities contained both enslaved Apaches and some free individuals who had become integrated and acculturated. Although many individual Spaniards benefited from the enslavement of these prisoners, the practice itself often proved disastrous for the government's efforts to pacify the region. In an attempt to regain family members, Apache groups inevitably escalated attacks on Spanish settlements to exact revenge or take prisoners for exchange. Additionally, Apache prisoners held by the Spanish often contrived to escape and rejoin their people, which only fueled more hatred and gave impetus for more revenge attacks.

An attempt to deal with the problem of Indian slavery occurred in 1729 after Brigadier General Pedro de Rivera had finished his inspection of the northern frontier. In the Regulations of 1729 for presidios established after Rivera's inspection, it was decreed that "none of the officers who happen, by plunder, to capture Indians of any sex or age in an expedition of war . . . can claim said prisoners for themselves or divide them under any motive or pretext. Rather they shall send them under guard to the outskirts of Mexico so that what His Majesty orders . . . is enforced." Further, Rivera sought to ease the cycle of revenge by returning noncombatant Indian prisoners to their families. "Whenever the commanders and captains of the presidios take any of the aforementioned as prisoners they will return to their parents and spouses any captured children and women. This action encourages them not to take revenge and curbs their outrage." The Regulations of 1729 reiterated that the Apaches and other Indians were not to be treated as slaves but as "prisoners of war," more akin to criminals. Thus, they were to be sentenced to forced labor for a set period of time, usually ten years. The first recorded application of this policy being employed against the Apaches occurred in 1732 when a group of fourteen prisoners under the leadership of the chief Cabellos Colorados was captured in Texas and shipped off to Mexico City from whence they never returned.[5]

Despite the government's efforts, the long-standing frontier practice of holding captured Apaches as slaves and servants in Spanish communities in the Interior Provinces remained the norm for many more years. When the Marqués de Rubí inspected the area in 1766, he found the keeping of Apache slaves to be widespread and noted that it was "an abuse against all their humanity and right as a people" for prisoners to be distributed among Spanish citizens, "who treat them as slaves, even to the point of selling them." Despite his aggrieved sense of justice over the treatment of prisoners, Rubí believed that harsh measures were needed to defeat the Apaches, and he reiterated that the standard practice called for Apache prisoners of war to be deported to Mexico City, where they would then be dispersed to work on the fortifications at Veracruz and Havana.[6]

Soon after Rubí completed his inspection, Spanish authorities began to regularly concede to the Apaches the status of prisoners of war. Although at the local level the enslavement of prisoners remained the norm, the increasing control of the central government began to alter the equation. The reforms that culminated in the Regulations of 1772 and the formation of the Interior Provinces as a separate military entity were most responsible for this alteration. A more unified command structure resulted in greater consistency in the application of Spanish military force. The Apaches were relatively quickly identified as the "official" enemy, and as such received more scrutiny at higher levels in the military chain of command. Among the numerous designs implemented to defeat the Apaches, there began to be formulated ideas about what to do with prisoners. Increasing efforts were made to retain Apache captives at the frontier presidios to exchange for prisoners taken by the Apaches. Perhaps reflecting Spain's dealings with the Muslim states, the regulations formalized these ideas of reciprocity and exchange. For example, it was stipulated that "the exchange will be man for man, etc., but if this is not possible and it is necessary to give more for my [the king's] troops, it will be two or three Indians for each Spaniard. By no means will this be extended to Indian auxiliaries or scouts, who will be exchanged at an equal ratio." The advantages of exchange were to be made self-evident to the Indians so that "[their] self-interest will destroy [their] cruelty that so many times has led them to murder their captives, and [to] awaken in them sentiments of humanity."[7]

Yet, the most significant development lay in the policy of deporting captured Apaches from the area altogether. As with the recognition of prisoners of war as a distinct class, deportation was not a new phenomenon for the Spanish. The transfer of individuals and even whole populations that a government deemed undesirable or dangerous dated to ancient times and was practiced almost universally. The Assyrians and other peoples of the ancient Near East routinely deported enslaved peoples far from their homelands in order to secure a conquered area, perhaps the most famous example being the Babylonian exile of the Jews circa 586 B.C. The Chinese also practiced the forced relocation of populations over a period of some fifteen hundred years, beginning with the Ch'in Dynasty and reaching up to the Ming Dynasty in the fourteenth century. Deportations continued among many Islamic states in the late medieval period, with the Turkish Ottomans and Persian Safavids both forcibly relocating enormous numbers of ethnic minorities, such as Greeks, Turkomans, Armenians, and Kurds. The indigenous peoples of the Americas also deported their enemies, as when the Incas transplanted conquered groups such as the Chimu to help control the boundaries of their empire or to serve as laborers for the construction of state projects. The Spanish themselves had engaged in large deportations with the expulsion of the Jews in 1492 and the Moriscos in 1609–14, although in these cases the populations were sent to areas outside of Spanish control.

In the seventeenth and eighteenth centuries, all the European powers regularly used deportation. In some countries, it became a favored method of social control. Britain especially favored the policy of transportation of criminals, rebels, and other undesirables to far-flung imperial outposts. Transportation served the dual purpose of ridding the mother country of potential troublemakers while at the same time using these same people as cheap labor. Large numbers were transported in the 1600s to Jamaica and other British Caribbean islands, where they were enslaved and forced to labor in the sugar fields. In the same fashion, more convicts were sent to Britain's thirteen American colonies on the mainland of North America. Often euphemistically referred to as "indentured servants," many of these people were enslaved in fact, if not in name, although technically only for a set period of time such as seven years. Whether they were English convicts sentenced to transportation in lieu of hanging, Irish boys and women kidnapped by British slave dealers, or Jacobite rebels from Scotland, all were treated as a labor commodity, with many sentenced to serve on "plantations" from New England to Georgia. Through the last decades of the eighteenth century, as many as fifty thousand men, women, and children may have been sent to the American colonies. The number was so great that the renowned English author and lexicographer Samuel Johnson, discussing the Americans with a friend, remarked, "Sir, they are a race of convicts and ought to be content with anything we may allow them short of hanging." When the Americans gained their independence, the British quickly found another dumping ground in 1788 with the founding of the colony of Australia, where transporting the prisoners not only served to rid the mother country of undesirables, but also made them the first agents of empire.[8]

In Spain, as well, the deportation of condemned criminals was a widespread means of control. From the early 1600s, prisoners from the homeland were routinely deported to the presidios along the North African coast to labor at the fortifications and even to serve as soldiers in these Spanish enclaves in Muslim lands. Others were sentenced to be sent to the Philippines, where they acted as settlers in Spain's most distant colony. Beginning in the middle of the eighteenth century, the construction of a series of huge coastal fortifications throughout the Spanish-held islands and mainland coastlines of the Caribbean required large numbers of prisoners sent from Spain. Such was the demand for labor to help build and maintain these defenses, that many more prisoners from other parts of the Spanish empire were sentenced to work on them. Most of those deported were condemned criminals, but many were other groups or individuals who caused problems for the authorities. Unfortunately for many Apaches, they fit all too well into the latter category.[9]

During the first half of the eighteenth century, Spanish authorities in the Interior Provinces sporadically deported Indians to work on the fortress of San Juan de Ulúa in the port of Veracruz. These included some Apaches, both individuals and small groups, whom they deemed particularly troublesome. For millennia, the Spanish, like many other peoples worldwide, had used a brutally simple method of restraining groups of captives, whether they were slaves, criminals, or prisoners of war. This was to tie a halter around the neck of each individual and link them together with ropes or chains passing through each halter. Fastened together in small groups of up to ten or twenty at a time, the prisoners would find it nearly impossible to attempt to escape. Further, a small group of guards could control a much larger number of prisoners. The Spanish came to refer to groups of captives secured in this fashion as either a *collera*, from the colloquial term for the halter the prisoners wore, or as a *cuerda*, referring to the "cord" of chain or ropes linking them together.[10]

The use of halters to link large numbers of captives became over time a thing of the past. Manacles for the hands and leg shackles of iron, leather, and rope were far more economical and more readily available. On the northern frontier of New Spain, their use became standard practice. Given the long distances that prisoners were often forced to travel, it became impractical to have them tied together by the neck while marching on foot. Instead, they would usually be mounted on horses or mules, often in pairs, with their legs or wrists bound to each other and sometimes to their mount. The groups of prisoners retained the old name of "collera" or "cuerda" despite the change in the methods of their restraint.

Many of these colleras of Indians had either fought against enslavement or forced labor in Spanish mining camps or had been deemed to be "rebels" who had resisted acculturation by missionaries or governmental entities. Yet only in a very few instances did the Spaniards seek to remove an entire ethnic population—the labor provided by these Indians was too valuable a commodity to be lost. The Seris of Sonora, who inhabited the coastline of the Sea of Cortez, were a notable exception. Despite their small number, the Seris for decades succeeded in defying the Spaniards and had become such violent opponents that by 1764 the Jesuit Father Juan Nentvig could see no alternative but "that they should be deported or made to serve as oarsmen in the Royal galleys." Nentvig maintained that "the expense incurred for their transportation would be more than offset by the benefit to the rich mining settlements, pearl fisheries, haciendas, and estancias which are now abandoned because of their hostilities."[11]

Although the Spanish would never successfully quell Seri resistance, they would continue to deport groups of Indians from the northern frontier throughout the eighteenth century, despite the lack of a specific policy regulating the practice. However, the adoption of the Regulations of 1772 transformed all that. With the change directed primarily against the Apaches, from that point on the disposition of Apache prisoners of war, at least officially, became fairly straightforward. All those taken in war were to be sent from the Interior Provinces to Mexico City, where the viceroy would decide their fate. The regulations specified that the Apaches were not slaves, that they were not to be mistreated or killed arbitrarily, and that the prisoners were to be given the same daily pay allowance for food that Spanish Indian auxiliaries received. Women and children were to be treated with kindness and efforts made to convert them to Christianity. But in the end, they were all to be sent into exile. Unfortunately for the Apaches, the officers chosen to implement the regulations against them were to do so with zeal and efficiency.

CHAPTER 3

Regulations and Instructions

From his desk in the Villa de Chihuahua, Don Hugo O'Conor, commandant inspector of the Interior Provinces, set about to write a report to his superior, Viceroy Antonio María de Bucareli. It was January of 1772, and O'Conor had recently been appointed as the military commander of a region stretching from the Sea of Cortez in the west to the Gulf of Mexico in the east. In preparing his report to the viceroy, O'Conor had consulted numerous records in the archives of the region, detailing the course of the long war against the Apaches. One bundle of papers contained a particularly grisly account of the recent destruction of a small settlement within several leagues of where O'Conor himself now sat.

On Wednesday, February 7, 1770, at seven o'clock in the evening, an exhausted and bedraggled youth had ridden to the house of Don Juan Joseph Barrendegui, *alcalde ordinario* of the Real de Santa Eulalia, some fifteen miles east of Chihuahua. Breathlessly, the boy reported that "Indian enemies" had attacked his home at the Rancho del Potrero, a league and a half away. Alcalde Barrendegui ordered an armed horseman to ride back with the boy to confirm the story, and by Thursday evening, both returned with the terrible news that the entire ranch had been destroyed and all within killed. Barrendegui then sent word to the chief civil authority of the area, Juan Joseph de Lemus, *corregidor* and *justicia mayor* of Santa Eulalia, to spread the word. Both officials organized a group of mule drivers, accompanied by a guard of seven Yaqui Indian bowmen and some armed citizens, to return to Rancho del Potrero and recover the bodies and bring them back for a decent burial. Even for men hardened by the violence of the frontier, the scene they came upon was shocking.

The majordomo of the rancho, a mulatto named Ramón González, was found with four lance thrusts in the chest, his genitals hacked off and stuffed in his mouth, and arrows pushed into his rectum. Nearby lay a widow named Hana Andrea Ortega, "pierced through the breasts with three lance thrusts, the womb destroyed, and within they filled it with beans, and in the privy parts they stuck in a bow, leaving this abused body totally naked." The bodies of fourteen other residents, including three Tarahumara Indian men who worked at the ranch, were scattered about. Among the dead were "nine children, the oldest of which appeared to be about seven years, the rest smaller on down to the youngest, a newborn of three or four months." A short distance outside the buildings they found the body of Joseph Manuel González Zamora, "a youth of about thirteen or fourteen years, his whole body run through with ten lance thrusts, his hair pulled out by the roots from the skull." After scalping the boy, his killers had cut off the thumb and forefinger of his right hand and stuck them on top of the scalped head, "placed in the sign of the cross." The marauders had destroyed everything, killing all the sheep and cattle, the chickens, "and even the cats and dogs."[1]

As he continued to read through the listings of depredations, Commandant Inspector Hugo O'Conor confirmed in his own mind that the Apaches were, as a people, barbarous in the extreme. In characterizing the Apaches in his own report, he stressed their ferocity and described them with vicious hyperbole. "The cruelty of the barbarians," he wrote, spared no one, "regardless of age or sex, even ripping infants from the breasts of their mothers and even from the womb, and executing on their bodies the most detestable excesses." Whether or not O'Conor knew or cared if the Spaniards committed equally "detestable excesses" against the Apaches was a moot point. Decades and decades of violence and warfare had led both peoples to a situation where they were inured to the vagaries of guilt or innocence. Extraordinarily ferocious acts failed to garner much attention anymore, and even "the most detestable excesses" were now seen only as one more reason to crush the enemy. As the man now in charge of the Spanish military on the frontier, O'Conor was determined to use all the resources at his disposal, including the deportation of prisoners, to do just that.[2]

Don Hugo O'Conor was an Irish exile with more than twenty years of military experience by the time he came to serve as commandant inspector of the Interior Provinces. He was a regular officer who had served in Europe and the Caribbean and had been governor of Texas. Now, in his new position, he was given command of all the military forces in the Interior Provinces, subject only to the viceroy, Antonio María de Bucareli. Establishing his headquarters in the Villa de Chihuahua in the central province of Nueva Vizcaya, O'Conor systematically between 1772 and 1775 began the erection of a line of presidios starting from east to west. As called for in the Regulations of 1772, within each of the Interior Provinces, the presidial garrisons were reorganized and refitted and their locations adjusted. Many of the garrisons were moved, some were suppressed, and a few were left in their current position.[3]

As with the other articles of the regulations, the policies regarding deportation of Apaches were also soon put into practice.

During his journeys along the frontier, O'Conor conducted several regional campaigns against various Apache groups that resulted in the capture of a substantial numbers of prisoners. Between July and November of 1774, for example, O'Conor and his soldiers attacked the Apaches "located in the mountains some distance from the presidio of Janos and sixty leagues toward the northwest," most likely indicating the Chiricahua and Gileño Apaches in what is now southeastern Arizona and southwestern New Mexico. "I luckily was able to attack and capture some of the Enemy," he later wrote, "and took them to the presidio of Carrizal for safekeeping." Although the number of prisoners taken is not known, they were held for four months as O'Conor continued his reorganization of the presidial line. When the commandant inspector left Carrizal in the early spring of 1775, he finalized the disposition of the prisoners: "Reaching Chihuahua on the fifth of April, I ordered the captain of dragoons, Don Manuel Pardo, to bring from Carrizal the chained Apache captives who were in prison there." Soon thereafter, as required by the Regulations of 1772, O'Conor had a total of ninety-three Apaches sent to Mexico City in a collera commanded by Pardo, to be disposed of as the viceroy saw fit.[4]

By late summer of 1775, Commandant Inspector O'Conor had finished selecting the sites for the presidial line, and with many of the garrisons in place, he began organizing a massive offensive designed to attack the enemy along the entire length of the *gran Apachería* that fronted the Interior Provinces. In September, eight Spanish columns totaling two thousand men moved against the Apaches in a series of three consecutive envelopments moving from east to west from Texas and Coahuila, from New Mexico, and from Nueva Vizcaya and Sonora. Spanish regulars, presidial soldiers, citizen militiamen, and Indian allies all took part in the assault. By the time the campaign ended in November, the Spanish had killed 132 Apache warriors; captured 104 men, women, and children; and seized almost two thousand horses and mules.

Although most of his officers hailed these results, O'Conor himself was dissatisfied. The Spanish offensive had failed to eliminate Apache raiding and indeed had escalated the conflict throughout the frontier. O'Conor nevertheless had his soldiers continue small-scale offensive operations, and by April of 1776, another substantial number of Apache prisoners were reported as being held captive in Chihuahua. Many of these probably included the 104 Apaches "of both sexes and all ages" that had been seized in the recent general campaign. A report from the following month indicates that all of these Apache prisoners were also deported to Mexico City.

Despite suffering from deteriorating health, O'Conor determined to press on with his aggressive strategy against the Apaches. He therefore organized a second general campaign designed for the fall of 1776. Once again, three converging Spanish columns sought to envelop and destroy the Apaches in the area between the headwaters of the Gila River and the Big Bend of the Rio Grande. By December, Spanish forces had killed sixty-seven and captured sixty-four Apaches of all ages and both sexes. But the greatest loss of life for the Apaches came at the hands of other Indians. Large numbers of Mescalero and Mimbreño Apaches fled northeast before the Spanish columns. Somewhere near the upper reaches of the Pecos River, they came across a general war parley of the Comanches. Exulting in this unexpected prey, the Comanches fell upon the Apaches with a vengeance, reportedly slaughtering three hundred families, numbering perhaps one thousand individuals. Even the Spaniards were appalled by the carnage.[5]

The fate of the Apache prisoners taken in O'Conor's second general campaign was now clear. Manuel de Escorza, the official in charge of the military treasury along the frontier, reported in

May of 1777 that one of O'Conor's officers, Lieutenant Ygnacio de la Cadena of the Dragoons of Mexico, had been entrusted with the sum of 1,134 pesos for the expenses needed to conduct a collera of 150 Apache prisoners to exile and imprisonment in Mexico City. The captives had been held for two months in the cárcel of Chihuahua City as well as at the town of El Paso and at the presidios of Junta de los Ríos and Carrizal, which may indicate that they were from a variety of Apache groups along the northern frontier. This collera included the sixty-four prisoners that O'Conor had reported taken by campaign's end in December of 1776, along with a substantial number of others seized since then. The pattern of deporting Apache prisoners southward into exile appeared to be firmly established.[6]

Despite these campaigns, the Spanish still had not solved the problem of Apache raiding along the frontier, and indeed, in many areas, the war continued unabated. Further large-scale offensives might have brought results, but they were not to be. Two events combined to stall the war against the Apaches. First, Commandant Inspector O'Conor's health was broken by his years on the frontier, and he was granted a promotion and transfer to less-stressful duties. At the same time, the Interior Provinces experienced a monumental change in governance, revolving around the ambitions of José de Gálvez, who had emerged as one of King Charles III's most powerful advisors. In 1776, Gálvez was named first minister of the Council of the Indies and concluded that the viceroyalty of New Spain was too vast for effective military control. He advocated forming a separate government, independent of viceregal authority, for the Interior Provinces. That same year, the king agreed to create a new position, the commandant general of the Interior Provinces. This new official, possessing full civil and military powers along the northern frontier, was ordered to cooperate with the viceroy on most matters but remained independent in many areas.

The first commandant general was Teodoro de Croix, known as the Caballero de Croix, who arrived in Mexico City in December of 1776 to assume his duties. No stranger to Mexico, the caballero had been employed in several governmental posts when his uncle, the Marqués de Croix, was serving as viceroy of New Spain between 1765 and 1771. Yet his command experience was limited and his knowledge of the northern frontier nonexistent. Still, the caballero possessed an arrogant and imperious assurance of his own abilities and importance. Soon after his arrival, tensions developed between the Caballero de Croix and Viceroy Bucareli. Despite assurances from Madrid to the contrary, Bucareli naturally felt that the establishment of a new, separate government for the Interior Provinces reflected on his abilities. Croix did not help matters by publicly and repeatedly condemning the state of affairs on the northern frontier. The caballero was especially critical of the tenure and achievements of Commandant Inspector O'Conor, a loyal supporter of Bucareli.

Aggravating the animosity, the Spanish crown had deliberately left the precise jurisdictions of both men vague, and consequently their responsibilities often overlapped. The inevitable result was a bureaucratic reshuffling that stalled military operations throughout the Interior Provinces. The Caballero de Croix delayed matters further by first gathering detailed reports from a variety of sources on the state of his new command. As a result, it was not until October of 1777, almost a year after his arrival in Mexico, that Croix finally arrived in the Interior Provinces.[7]

Establishing his headquarters in the Villa de Chihuahua, Croix found himself beset by a complex series of military problems. His orders stated that "the defense and extension of the great territories included in your command" were his primary duty. Yet these same orders bid Croix to undertake "the conversion of the numerous heathen Indians who live in the north of western America." The caballero quickly realized the impossibility of converting the nations hostile to Spain, especially the Apaches, without first subduing them militarily, and he concluded that he would have to reorganize and retrench his forces. Although the Regulations of 1772 were still in force, Croix, in his position as commandant general, possessed extensive flexibility in how they were to be applied. He decided to postpone O'Conor's policy of massive campaigns against the Apaches until the presidial line was readjusted a second time and the presidial garrisons restructured. Only then, the caballero felt, would large-scale offensive operations be effective.[8]

Throughout 1778, from his headquarters in Chihuahua, Croix concentrated on the internal arrangement of his forces. While reforming and reinforcing his command, the caballero also concentrated on adjusting the presidial line, which in many cases had proven quite porous. He shortened the line by pulling back several of the exposed posts to more defensible locations. More significantly, Croix established a defense in depth by deploying provincial militiamen in strategic towns behind the cordon of presidios.

By 1779, Croix's reorganization and reform policies throughout the central and eastern Interior Provinces had progressed to the point where he felt he could move further to the west, where the Apache problem appeared more dangerous. He planned to establish himself in a new capital, Arispe, Sonora, from which he would begin operations for a massive offensive he planned against the Apaches. But before he could depart, he received orders from Madrid to suspend his plans indefinitely. War with Great Britain was about to begin, with Spain on the side of the American colonies, and in order to save funds and materiel, the king ordered Croix to keep his troops on the defensive throughout the Interior Provinces. Indeed, with Spain's entry into the War of the American Revolution, the entire Spanish policy regarding the frontier was now to be reviewed. Croix was ordered to try and induce the Apaches and other hostile tribes to make peace by offering them alliance and distributing gifts. This would lead the Indians into increasing dependency on the Spaniards for guns, alcohol, and other items they desired. Force was to be used only as a last resort.

These changes caused a dramatic shift all along the frontier. Unlike his predecessor O'Conor, Croix had not initiated any large-scale campaigns during the first two years of his administration, although many smaller offensive operations did take place. And now, with the defensive orders, the number of punitive operations against the Apaches slowed considerably; consequently, deportations seem to have practically ceased. Small numbers of Apaches were captured from time to time, but they were mostly detained along the frontier and not shipped south to Mexico City. Just three Apaches, for example, were reported as incarcerated at the jail in Chihuahua City in January of 1779, and between January and April of 1781, Croix noted the delivery of seven Apache prisoners sent from New Mexico to Chihuahua, from whence he had them transferred to the public workhouse at nearby Encinillas.[9]

However, by 1782, the war against Britain began to draw to a close, and Croix was allowed once again to conduct offensive operations against the Apaches. In subsequent small-scale attacks, the Spanish began to take more Apache prisoners, and the deportation policy was quickly renewed. In February of 1782, Croix petitioned to dispatch to Mexico City a collera of 95 Mescalero Apaches, requesting that the viceroy ensure that they be disposed of in such a way that they could never return to cause trouble on the frontier. By January of the following year, Croix's men had gathered together another 145 Apache prisoners in Chihuahua City slated for exile to the capital. Among the group was the Mescalero chief Patule, who had for a brief time in 1779 led his followers to settle outside the Presidio del Norte, located in the modern Mexican town of Ojinaga, across from present-day Presidio, Texas. They had lived in a specially constructed village that the Spaniards hoped would serve as a model for other Apaches. However, by late 1781, Patule and his people had abandoned the reservation and headed southeast into the Bolsón de Mapimí and begun raiding. The Spanish counterattacked and eventually captured Patule along with many of his people.

The Mescalero prisoners were dispatched south on January 20, 1783. Eleven days into their journey, however, the Apaches staged a successful uprising, and Patule and fifty-five of his compatriots succeeded in breaking free. The soldiers of the escort pursued the prisoners vigorously and hunted down and killed nine of them including Patule. Still, forty-seven Apaches, including thirty-one men, fourteen women, and two small children, managed to elude their pursuers and presumably were able to make their way back to their homeland.

Undoubtedly reacting to this outbreak, in May of 1783, one of Croix's officers, Commandant Inspector Felipe de Neve, requested that the caballero allow him to bring extra security for twenty-eight Apaches who had been captured in the eastern portion of the Interior Provinces. Neve had brought the prisoners to the town of Monclova in Coahuila, from which they were destined for deportation to the capital, but in light of the recent escape, Neve was worried that the Apaches might succeed in another breakout, "as those taken in the past have continually done." Whether the extra precautions were successful is not known.[10]

Security measures were also in the forefront for yet another collera of Apache prisoners sent from Monclova later that same year. It was made up of thirty-three captive Mescalero Apaches (six men, twenty-four women, and three boys) but also contained four Comanche men and one woman, as well as "two mulatto youths" who were captives of the Mescaleros and had apparently been acculturated and adopted into their society. Governor Pedro Tueros of Coahuila was particularly concerned with the actions of the latter pair and wrote to Viceroy Matías de Gálvez that "there were two mulattos that were captive among them, that caused some damage more or less." The governor observed that while the two youths were among the Mescaleros, they had been exposed to the "liberty and barbarity introduced by the Enemy, to the desolation of the lives and lands of the vassals of His Majesty." Tueros stated that as a result, he would employ the strictest measures to guard these prisoners, "in particular the *Indios Gandules* [adult men] and the mulattos, that are the most perverse and inhuman, and owing many lives that they have taken from the *vecinos* [citizens] of this Province."[11]

The deportation of this group of Mescaleros heralded a return to the Spanish design for large-scale offensives. Indeed, Croix had continuously made plans for launching a massive operation against them as had not been seen since the days of O'Conor. But just as his plans were solidifying, Croix's tenure as commandant general drew to a close in 1783, when he was appointed viceroy of Peru. Despite all his preparations, it would fall to others to conduct the campaigns for which the Caballero de Croix had laid the groundwork.

Croix was succeeded as commandant general by Brigadier Felipe de Neve, promoted from commandant inspector. A career soldier who had served with distinction as governor of California, he assumed office in October of 1783 and continued Croix's planning for a series of coordinated campaigns against the Apaches across the entire Interior Provinces. In April of 1784, Neve launched a force of over eight hundred men from Sonora and Nueva Vizcaya in five columns, striking first against the Gileño Apaches. In two months, the Spaniards killed sixty-eight Apaches and captured seventeen others, and although Neve was disappointed with the results, he was determined to keep up the pressure.[12]

Neve's aggressive policies against the Apaches included the continued deportation of prisoners, and he showed particular concern for ensuring the secure delivery of the captives to their final places of exile. In January of 1784, Neve even went so far as to take a direct role in the deportation of a Chiricahua leader named Pacheteju, who had proven an ardent opponent of the Spaniards for many years. After Pacheteju and his wife were captured by Spanish soldiers the previous year, they, along with a number of other Apache prisoners, were scheduled for a four-part journey from the Presidio of Fronteras in Sonora to the Presidio of Janos; from there to the *obraje*, or workhouse, at the Hacienda de Encinillas outside of Chihuahua; and from Encinillas south to Mexico City.

Neve was concerned that the followers of Pacheteju might try and rescue their leader, but the commandant general was determined not to let that happen. He ordered that a strong escort commanded by "a trustworthy officer" be assembled and that it was to guard against any attack in transit and to make sure the prisoners did not flee. If the captives attempted to escape or if other Apaches tried to rescue them, Neve bluntly ordered that they should be killed, "especially Pacheteju, as it would be very prejudicial if he were to be freed." Once they arrived at Encinillas, the administrator of the workhouse would secure the Apaches and inform Neve when they were dispatched to Mexico City.[13]

But less than seven months after overseeing the deportation of these prisoners, Commandant General Felipe de Neve died suddenly outside the Villa de Chihuahua on August 21, 1784. With his death, large-scale Spanish offensives again faltered, and the number of colleras sent to exile in Mexico City appears to have slowed yet again. There was no shortage of Apaches seized by Spanish forces, but they were now congregated along the frontier. Many were sent to the obraje of Encinillas, where they were held while their ultimate fate was still being decided. Others were kept in the frontier presidios, undoubtedly to be used as barter for potential exchange, to provide domestic labor for the

Spanish, or to be acculturated. This last may have been the fate of a group of Apache children noted by Lieutenant Manuel Delgado, the commander of the Presidio of San Buenaventura in Nueva Vizcaya, who wrote in the monthly post return of January of 1785: "On the 20th of this month there entered here the Alférez of Janos, Don Francisco de Yesco, with seven infants, Apaches, who were made prisoner in this presidio, and these were also joined by the corporal of Janos, Balthasar Acosta, who took them, along with the cattle from the Enemy in the Paraje del Alamo on the first of December this past year; and all were brought in [for] the Señor Commandant General."[14]

After Neve's sudden demise, Commandant Inspector José Antonio Rengel was named as interim commandant general, but he had barely assumed office when the entire structure of the Interior Provinces was radically altered. Exercising a talent for nepotism, in 1785, José de Gálvez managed to have his nephew, Bernardo, the captain-general of Cuba and conqueror of English Florida, named viceroy of New Spain. Wishing to invest his nephew with as much power as possible, Gálvez then persuaded the king to place the Interior Provinces once again under the direct control of the viceroy.

Bernardo de Gálvez, soon given the title of Conde de Gálvez, actually brought impeccable qualifications to the viceroyalty and had extensive experience in dealing with the Interior Provinces. As a young officer, he had served as military commandant of Nueva Vizcaya, where he had personally fought against the Apaches, albeit with varying success. He had been wounded in combat and had even captured two Apache warriors, who later served him for several years as a sort of personal bodyguard. Later, during his service as governor of Louisiana, he had seen firsthand the French and English policies of dealing with Indian tribes through trade, bribes, and shifting alliances, a radical change from the traditional Spanish policies of forced acculturation. The result was that Gálvez came to view the Indian problems

Bernardo de Gálvez, Viceroy of New Spain, 1785–86. From Manuel Rivera Cambas, *Los gobernantes de México*, 1 (Mexico, 1872–73). Courtesy Special Collections, The University of Arizona Libraries, Tucson.

of the Interior Provinces with a pragmatism that sought to fuse the traditional Spanish patterns with those he had seen employed successfully by other European powers in Louisiana.

In 1786, Gálvez codified his policies in a lengthy document entitled *Instructions for the Governing of the Interior Provinces of New Spain*. Although later seen as an important turning point, the instructions were in reality nothing new. Most of the policies called for had in fact been employed on the northern frontier since 1779, when the king had ordered the Caballero de Croix to cease offensive operations. What was unique about the instructions was that they synthesized the most effective programs of past administrations into a coherent and calculated strategy.

Gálvez's plan was simple. The Indians were to be given a stark choice between peace and war. If they chose peace, they were to be plied with food, weapons, and supplies that would foster dependence and help break down their cultural and social traditions. As the price of their sustenance, they would be enlisted to attack those groups that remained hostile. On the other hand, if they chose war, they were to be attacked until they were either destroyed or forcibly settled near Spanish presidios. Either way, the results would be the same. Gálvez succinctly summarized the instructions' aims: "They [were to] employ the ancient hatred, factional interest and inconsistency and perfidy of the heathen tribes to their mutual destruction." He reserved a special ire toward the Apaches, writing, "I am very much in favor of the special ruination of the Apaches, and in endeavoring to interest other tribes and even other Apache bands in it, because these Indians are our real enemies in the Interior Provinces."

After almost two decades of continuous but erratic warfare, it appeared that the Spanish had finally determined a strategy to deal with the Apaches once and for all. This called for individual Apache rancherías to be settled near Spanish presidios on what later historians would call establecimientos de paz—peace establishments. Here the Apaches would be given food, clothing, and other supplies in exchange for stopping their raids against Spanish settlements. Apache men would be enlisted to serve as scouts and auxiliaries against those rancherías that refused to accept the offer, and they would be rewarded for their service with horses, weapons, and other gifts. Apache women and children would be encouraged to coexist with their new Hispanic neighbors and to adopt their habits—and their vices—including learning agricultural techniques, attending school, and gambling at cards. For those Apaches who refused the Spanish offer, the alternative was stark: they would be hunted down and killed and those captured would be transported from their homelands forever. The Spanish policy offered the Apaches a clear choice between two alternatives: to be crushed by the mailed fist or to be restrained by the velvet glove. However, the question remained as to just how much death and violence both peoples would have to suffer before the Apaches were persuaded to accept the Spanish offer.[15]

CHAPTER 4

The Confusion of Power

Alférez Domingo Vergara was a bit of an anomaly among the frontier officer corps. Unlike almost all of his brother officers, Vergara was not a career military man, but started as a businessman serving as the *armero principal*, or chief gunsmith, of the Province of Sonora. However, he had become so frustrated with the mounting losses from the continuing conflict with the Apaches that he had had enough. In April of 1783, he had taken matters into his own hands and organized, at his own expense, a party of militia made up of citizens and Ópata Indians from the pueblo of Bacoachi. Launching two pursuits against the Apache raiders, Vergara "maintained and paid the citizens and Indians of the Pueblo and provided supplies and other aid to the people, totaling 3,500 pesos." Building on these successes, he continued to supply money, matériel, and leadership for other operations. His actions eventually attracted the attention of the military authorities, and by 1786, Vergara had been named *alférez graduado*, or brevet ensign, for the Presidio of Bacoachi. There he operated with the recently raised infantry company drawn from the warlike Ópatas, inveterate enemies of the Apaches. Now leading these Indian warriors, Vergara continued to use all his efforts to hunt down the Apaches in the area. Thanks in part to his endeavors, Spanish expeditions soon began to take a toll on the Apaches of northeastern Sonora, especially the Chiricahuas.

Just how successful the Spanish attacks were soon became evident. In September of 1786, a chieftain named Isosé, joined by twenty-three other warriors, cautiously approached Vergara, requesting peace for himself and his people. Realizing his opportunity, Vergara opened negotiations with the Chiricahuas with the goal of having them agree to establish themselves under the watchful eyes of the Spanish garrisons, as called for in the recently implemented 1786 Instructions issued by Viceroy Gálvez. Somewhat surprisingly, Isosé and his followers seemed disposed to comply. Although neither Isosé nor Vergara realized it at the time, they had just laid the foundation for an agreement that would last for over forty years and transform Spanish-Apache relations throughout the frontier.[1]

Yet, while progress was being made on the local level, at the upper end of Spanish officialdom, unforeseen problems soon emerged. At the same time that Viceroy Gálvez was drawing up his Indian policy, he also implemented a change in the governance of the Interior Provinces that was to trigger a great deal of confusion and overlapping authority. In August of 1786, he ordered that the northern frontier be divided into three semi-independent administrative commands, ostensibly to better coordinate military operations. Brigadier General Jacobo Ugarte y Loyola, who had replaced Neve as commandant general, was nominally in charge of the entire frontier, but he was to be personally responsible only for the western provinces of Sonora and Upper and Lower California. Colonel José de Rengel retained the title of commandant inspector and was assigned to oversee the military operations of the two central provinces of New Mexico and Nueva Vizcaya. Colonel Juan de Ugalde was named *cabo segundo*, or secondary commander, under Ugarte and was to oversee the four eastern provinces of Coahuila, Texas, Nuevo León, and Nuevo Santander. Determined to increase operational efficiency, Viceroy Gálvez believed that this division would allow for more rapid military responses by each of the three frontier commanders in their own districts. All three officers were enjoined to cooperate closely with one another, and to ensure that they did so, Gálvez himself would closely monitor their actions. It was a system that promised tactical flexibility at the local level, balanced with a strategic unity supplied by the viceroy. However, these changes had hardly been implemented when word reached the frontier that Viceroy Bernardo de Gálvez had died suddenly on November 30, 1786.

The death of Viceroy Gálvez threatened to leave his *Instructions for the Governing of the Interior Provinces* stillborn. Although the ideas in the 1786 Instructions were now viewed as official Spanish policy, in the interregnum after Gálvez's death, there was no authority to guarantee that either the intent or the spirit of the policy was carried out. Indeed, the choice whether to seek out the Apaches and destroy them or seek accommodation with them by placing them on reservations now depended on the predispositions of individual Spanish military officers. The clearest indication of this was the differing actions and attitudes of Jacobo Ugarte y Loyola and Juan de Ugalde.

Both Ugarte and Ugalde were regular officers with long years of service on the northern frontier. Prior to being named comandant general, Ugarte had served as governor of both Coahuila, where he had confronted eastern Apaches such as the Lipans and Mescaleros, and Sonora, where he contended with southern and western Apaches such as the Chiricahuas and Gileños. Ugalde, on his part, had also served as governor of Coahuila, where he seems to have developed a particular animus toward the Mescaleros. Perhaps because of his greater exposure to the Apaches, Ugarte came to view the policies of the 1786 Instructions as the most pragmatic means of dealing with them. As a result, he came to favor the inducements offered by the establecimientos de paz as the surest method of controlling the Apaches. Conversely, Ugalde came to favor the policy of crushing the Apaches militarily; he apparently regarded the peace establishments as merely temporary and local expedients. The death of Bernardo de Gálvez left the situation unsettled, and inevitably a power struggle soon developed between the two officers.[2]

Nevertheless, for almost nine months, Ugarte, due to his higher rank, was left as the de facto commander of the Interior Provinces. Under the assumption that he was still bound by the Instructions of 1786, Ugarte pursued the policy of offering the Apaches peace if they agreed to settle near presidios subject to Spanish control. The Chiricahuas who had negotiated with Alférez Vergara had set themselves up outside the Presidio of Bacoachi in Sonora, and by March of 1787, some 251 Apaches were living on the reservation. Also in March, a large group of Mimbreño Apaches, estimated to number approximately eight hundred men, women, and children, had agreed to congregate outside the Presidio of San Buenaventura in the central province of Nueva Vizcaya. Then, on March 29, 1787, several hundred Mescaleros had requested and been granted a truce outside the Presidio del Norte at the junction of the Conchos River and the Rio Grande. Although these Mescaleros did not set up permanent establishments, they accepted other terms demanded by the Spanish and agreed to remain within clear boundaries in the surrounding mountains. Ugarte felt that a corner had finally been turned in the long war against the Apaches. But no sooner had the Commandant General begun to make plans to expand the peace programs than the whole system seemed to collapse. The key to much of this unraveling was Colonel Juan de Ugalde.

Ugalde had arrived to take up his command of the Eastern Interior Provinces on October 11, 1786, when he reached the Hacienda de Patos in the province of Coahuila. Having served as governor of the province between 1779 and 1783, Ugalde felt he had more than enough background to assess the current situation, and he determined to pick things up from where he had left them three years earlier—namely to attack any eastern Apache groups that continued to plague his command, especially the Mescaleros. For the next two months he assiduously planned a massive campaign to strike into the Bolsón de Mapimí, a desolate depression separating Coahuila and Nueva Vizcaya that served as the prime pathway for the Mescaleros to raid both provinces. In January of 1787 he set out on a general campaign with over four hundred soldiers and militiamen, hundreds of horses and mules, and enough supplies to last for seven months.

Disappearing into the Bolsón de Mapimí, Ugalde scoured the region for Mescalero raiders. He engaged in mostly fruitless search for almost three months before deciding to head north toward the mountains bordering the Big Bend country of the Rio Grande. By April he found and attacked several large gatherings of Mescaleros. Unfortunately, these were the same groups that had made peace with Commandant General Ugarte a few months earlier. When Captain Juan Bautista de Elguezabal, who was at the nearby Presidio del Norte, intervened and attempted to stop Ugalde, the latter took umbrage and maintained that he was acting within his authority. Further, he added, with much justification, that the Mescaleros constantly raided into Coahuila and when pressed would retreat to Nueva Vizcaya to seek shelter, in what he labeled a sham peace. The infuriated Ugalde informed Captain Elguezabal that he would continue to attack the Mescaleros wherever and whenever he found them. As quickly as he had appeared, the colonel left, crossing the Rio Grande and heading north, still searching for Apaches. Elguezabal immediately sent word to Commandant General Ugarte about the confrontation. Ugarte understood that Ugalde might not have known about the truce that had been arranged with the Mescaleros; he was willing to concede that Ugalde's attacks were the result of poor communication. Nevertheless, from that point on, he issued a specific order directing Ugalde not to hinder the peace negotiations. Unfortunately, these clarifications came too late.

Clearly antagonized by the attacks they had suffered at Ugalde's hands, four of the eight Mescalero bands around the Presidio del Norte broke off peace negotiations and went back into the hinterland, and those that remained complained bitterly and were filled with mistrust. Then, on May 21, 1787, almost all of the eight hundred Mimbreños gathered outside the Presidio of San Buenaventura in Nueva Vizcaya rose up and fled, killing several Spaniards and three Chiricahua Apache auxiliaries who attempted to stop them. The timing of the Mimbreño uprising, although most likely coincidental, occurred so close to the partial breakdown of the Mescalero truce that it confirmed the opinions of many Spaniards that the Apaches simply could not be trusted to live in peace. As if to prove this suspicion, on July 20, 1787, over half the Chiricahuas settled near the Bacoachi establishment in Sonora fled the reservation, although there was no violence. Stung by the flight of so many "peaceful" Apaches, Commandant General Ugarte organized a large-scale operation directed primarily against the Mimbreños in Sonora and Nueva Vizcaya. In June, a Spanish expedition guided by the remaining Chiricahuas from the Bacoachi reservation attacked several Mimbreño encampments and killed or captured 102 men, women, and children. Throughout the summer and into the fall of 1787, the Spanish launched more attacks, inflicting further Apache casualties.[3]

Ironically, Ugarte, the Spanish leader who so much favored the peace policy, was now engaged in large-scale warfare, while the hawkish Colonel Ugalde was trying his hand at peace. During his campaign north of the Rio Grande, Ugalde parleyed with a powerful chief named Picax-ande, whom the colonel identified as a member of the Lipiyan group of the Llanero Apaches. As a mark of how little the Spanish understood the complexity of the Apaches, this same chieftain was known as El Calvo, or "the Bald One," by the soldiers of Nueva Vizcaya and had been identified as one of the Mescalero leaders seeking peace at the Presidio del Norte. Whether Ugalde recognized this fact or not, in July of 1787 he negotiated a treaty with Picax-ande that the colonel hailed as the first step in bringing a lasting peace to the frontier. Capitalizing on this agreement, Ugalde continued to push for peace, but strictly on his own terms. He demanded that all the Mescaleros establish themselves outside the Presidio of Santa Rosa in northwestern Coahuila. Any that refused to relocate, including those seeking peace outside the Presidio del Norte in Nueva Vizcaya, would be considered hostile and would be attacked. By October of 1787, a group of approximately 150 Mescaleros, led by eight chiefs who Ugalde claimed "spoke for the entire nation," had settled in a reservation along the Río Sabinas outside Santa Rosa.

When Commandant General Ugarte heard of Ugalde's actions, he was incredulous. The Apaches settled at the Río Sabinas represented only a small number of all the Mescaleros and did not include most of the primary leaders. To require those who had already agreed to terms for peace to be bound by conditions they had no part in negotiating seemed duplicitous. Finally, the idea of forcing them to move several hundred miles away was simply not feasible, and Ugarte knew the Spaniards did not have the power to force them. Ugarte once again issued a series of orders to Ugalde requiring the colonel to follow the peace policies as called for in the Instructions of 1786. But even as he composed these orders, Ugarte's authority had already been swept away.[4]

Manuel Antonio Flores, Viceroy of New Spain, 1787–89. From Manuel Rivera Cambas, *Los gobernantes de México*, 1 (Mexico, 1872–73). Courtesy Special Collections, The University of Arizona Libraries, Tucson.

In March of 1787 the king appointed Manuel Antonio Flores to replace Bernardo de Gálvez as viceroy of New Spain. A career military officer, Flores had served in a high position in the Viceroyalty of Río de la Plata and from 1776 to 1782 had been the viceroy of New Granada. In the latter post, he had shown great energy in revitalizing the economy and in upgrading the military capability of the viceroyalty in expectation of war with Britain. However, when war did come, his inflexible policies in raising revenues had given fuel to the fire that became known as the Comunero Revolt, which erupted in 1780–81. Although Flores was instrumental in crushing the uprising, his ruthlessness caused great resentment, and he was eventually forced to resign his office. But his abilities were clear, and after several years, he was again brought into royal service.

Flores arrived in Mexico City in August of 1787 and assumed office as viceroy of New Spain. After several months of review, he concluded that many of the more aggressive policies of the Regulations of 1772 were better suited to the situation than those encompassed in the Instructions of 1786 as drawn up by Bernardo de Gálvez. While conceding that the policy of settling the Apaches into establecimientos de paz was his ultimate goal, Flores nevertheless believed that they should be compelled to surrender by force of arms; those who refused should be annihilated. And, while he disagreed with Gálvez's maxim that a bad peace was better than a good war, nevertheless, Flores felt that the policy of dividing the military responsibility for the northern frontier was sound. Like Gálvez, the new viceroy believed that the region was simply too vast for a single individual to manage effectively and that a division of authority would allow for a more efficient and effective use of military power. To this end, he recommended to the king that the Interior Provinces be divided, not into three sections, but into two halves. The Western Interior Provinces would include the Californias, Sonora, New Mexico, and Nueva Vizcaya. The Eastern would include Coahuila, Texas,

Nuevo León, and Nuevo Santander. Each half would be under the control of a commandant general with equal rank but with the more senior man in the west. Both officers would report directly to the viceroy, who would ensure that they worked in tandem.

Assured of royal support for his plans, in the fall of 1787, Flores informed both Ugarte and Ugalde that the new administration would become effective in January of 1788. Commandant General Ugarte felt that this decision reflected poorly on his abilities and his honor and immediately offered his resignation. Flores quickly assured him that this change was designed solely to improve military operations and was not meant to slight him in any way. However, in other, more confidential reports, Flores admitted that he felt Ugarte was too old to handle the rigors of the northern frontier and that age had dulled his once aggressive spirit. Such was not the case with Juan de Ugalde, who demonstrated an indefatigable and bellicose nature more in line with Flores's own style. It soon became obvious to all that the new viceroy favored Ugalde and his policies over those of Ugarte.[5]

A clear indication of this preference came on November 21, 1787, when the viceroy ordered Ugarte to have all the Mescaleros who were congregated around the Presidio del Norte transferred to the Río Sabinas and settled at that reservation under the terms Ugalde had set up. Should those Mescaleros refuse, they were to be regarded as having broken their word and immediately attacked. In addition, the viceroy made clear that from this point onward, no Mescaleros were to be admitted to peace in Nueva Vizcaya, only in Coahuila. Convinced that this policy was dangerously counterproductive, Ugarte managed for several months in early 1788 to stall the removal of the Mescaleros while he tried in vain to persuade Viceroy Flores to change his mind. Ugarte even wrote directly to the king to plead his case, but to no avail.

Nevertheless, Ugarte dutifully continued to manage his command, and on October 1, 1787, he sent Viceroy Flores a detailed overview of frontier operations. Ugarte noted that in Sonora, between May of 1786 and October of 1787, the Spanish had killed 294 Apaches and captured 305 more, causing "much consternation among them so that rather than conspire to attack, they have retired to Nueva Vizcaya, where as yet they live in the eastern part without the rumor of eruptions." These blows had forced many Chiricahuas to sue for peace and settle near the Presidio of Bacoachi. When these Apaches had submitted, Ugarte's men turned "afterward against the Gileños of the West and . . . the Mimbreños or Gileños of the East in the Frontier of Nueva Vizcaya . . . and against the Mescaleros before the peace with that nation. The successes in that Province consisted of 117 Indians killed and prisoners." As Gálvez's Instructions had not dealt with the treatment of Apache prisoners of war, Ugarte concluded that the policies laid out in the Regulations of 1772 were still in effect, namely that all captured Apaches were to be sent from the frontier to Mexico City for disposition by the viceroy. As a result, the commandant general decided that exile was to be the fate of many of the three hundred Apache prisoners his men had taken.[6]

Beginning in the summer of 1787, Ugarte dispatched 154 of the captives from Arispe, Sonora, to Guadalajara and from there eventually to Mexico City. He had the prisoners broken up into three groups and sent south at intervals of approximately six weeks. As a mark of the importance Ugarte placed on this operation, he had the prisoners escorted by contingents from the only two units of regular troops he had under his command. The first group, under Lieutenant Ygnacio Ullate of the Regiment of the Dragoons of Spain, left Arispe on August 1 and consisted of two men, twelve women, and twenty-seven children. The second *remesa*, or remittance, as Ugarte termed it, set out on September 24 with twelve adult men, twenty-three *mujeres grandes* (adult women), and forty-four children, under Sergeant Manuel Terminel of the Voluntarios de Cataluña. The final batch, escorted by Alférez Joseph Loredo of the Dragoons of Spain, left on November 9 with seven men, twelve women, and fifteen children.

That same day, Ugarte wrote to Viceroy Flores reporting on the status of the expedition. Regarding the first group, the commandant general had ordered the escort commander, Lieutenant Ullate, to leave "in Los Alamos and populations between there and Guadalajara the prisoners less than 12 years old . . . to the citizens who can accommodate them and who can assure their Christian education." As for the adults and older children, Ugarte required that they be turned over to the authorities of the Royal Audiencia in Guadalajara, "to the end that they be placed in secure Workhouses or Jails."

The second group of prisoners, commanded by Sergeant Terminel, had a much more eventful journey, for after leaving the Real de los Álamos on October 16, it suffered losses of over a third of its seventy-nine prisoners. Two adult Indian women managed to break free and escape. But their flight was overshadowed by an unknown sickness that had quickly spread among the rest of the prisoners, killing another adult woman, an adult man, and eight children. Sergeant Terminel concluded that another eighteen children were too ill to move, "and he distributed the remaining small piezas that were sick among the citizens who could care for them." By the time they reached Guadalajara, only forty-nine Apache captives remained.

Commandant General Ugarte approved allowing many of the Apache children to be given over to the subjects of the crown who requested them, who would undoubtedly use them as domestic servants. But he cautioned that only the youngest Apaches should be thus placed, who would not remember the country of their birth, thus "extinguishing in them the inclinations and knowledge of which the older *Indios* and *Indias* conserve, anchoring them to return and reunite with their relatives." Even the Bishop of Sonora, Fray Antonio Barbastro, requested that Ugarte turn over the very young Apache children to repopulate the missions along the frontier. If Ugarte complied, Barbastro offered "to educate and sustain them along with the native Indians." The bishop felt that the Apache children would over time become acculturated, and "forgetting their language, would speak Pima or Ópata according to the Mission where they were found and would be ignorant of their origin." Still, Ugarte had declined the bishop's request, believing that the Chiricahua Apaches who were settled near the presidios might try and reclaim the children "since the kinship ties that these Indians have stretch from themselves to the Mimbreños."

The bonds of country and kin were even stronger among older Apache prisoners, and Ugarte was fearful of allowing any adults and older children to be distributed among Spanish households, even those far removed from the frontier. He requested that the viceroy ensure that these captives be sent "overseas or . . . placed in the Castillo of San Juan de Ulúa where they cannot flee." Ugarte knew all too well that in the past, many Apaches had managed to escape from captivity and had returned to the frontier, "breathing vengeance," and that even those held as far away as Guadalajara and Mexico City had been "restored to these territories despite the enormous distance between them."

Ugarte's concerns were validated when it was reported that the Apache prisoners of the third group, commanded by Alférez Loredo, were apparently overheard plotting "to attain their liberty if they were left in that capital." One Apache man was said to have remarked that some Apache women who had been given to private citizens along the way would "guide him in his return," and the man concluded by saying that it appeared "very easy to be freed," especially if the women "fled the houses where they were distributed." Ugarte said he had misgivings about the

Apaches' ability to lull the Spaniards who held them into a false sense of security, stemming from "the confidence that they inspire by their apparent meekness among those ignorant of their bloody character."

While the practice of distributing some Apache prisoners as domestic laborers among Spanish households never seemed to be an issue, *where* the distribution occurred clearly was. The ability of Apache captives, even the very young, to escape and return to the frontier argued for moving all the prisoners as far from their homelands as possible. Ugarte knew too well that Apache prisoners, once deported, should "never return to these Lands, for if they returned they would swell up the ranks of our Enemies and, having attained their liberty, multiply their barbarous hostilities."

Viceroy Flores addressed Ugarte's concerns in a letter of December 18, 1787, wherein he assured the commandant general that he would deal with the Apaches. "To prevent the flight of the Apache Gandules," Flores wrote, "I am dispatching them to destinations overseas and placing the bigger Indias in the prisons or in secure depositories." As for the smaller children, Flores felt it would be better to "distribute the *Piezas chicas* in this city [Mexico City] and in Guadalajara rather than in territories near the frontier." To this end, he would give the children over to "decent subjects" of the capital who would "receive them with the precise obligation to maintain them and educate them Christianly." The viceroy noted, in conclusion, "It seems to me that this is the best destiny that can be given to these gentile children."[7]

While Ugarte was occupied with maintaining the official policies of deportation in the west, to the east, Ugalde, now promoted to brigadier general, was busily pursuing his own agenda. In late February, he ratified a peace treaty with the Lipiyan leader Picax-ande, which he hailed as a great achievement. However, no sooner had Ugalde left the area to inspect the Province of Texas than on April 8, 1788, the Mescaleros who were gathered at the Río Sabinas reservation rose up, killed seven soldiers, and raided several settlements in Coahuila before fleeing into the mountains. Within weeks of this outbreak, Ugarte finally issued orders for the Mescaleros gathered at the Presidio del Norte to leave and relocate to the Río Sabinas. But, as he had warned, they headed back into their homelands upon leaving and soon began to raid into Nueva Vizcaya.

By July, warfare had intensified all along the northern frontier. Incensed by what he labeled the "treachery" of the Mescaleros, Viceroy Flores ordered both Ugarte and Ugalde to escalate offensive operations against all Apaches. Throughout the remainder of 1788, both commandant generals complied and launched large-scale attacks in their jurisdictions. In addition, the Spanish continued to cultivate the alliances they had formed in the past few years with several Comanche groups, as well as the Navajos and Utes, and persuaded these tribes to join them in these new offensives. Pressed on numerous fronts, large numbers of Apaches soon began to sue for peace.[8]

The surge in violence throughout 1788 was reflected in the deportation of two more groups of Apache prisoners of war, one from the eastern portion of the frontier and the other from the west. Commandant General Ugalde reported in April that he was sending out a collera of twelve Apaches into exile from San Antonio, Texas, bound for Mexico City via San Luis Potosí. This group included "two youths, one of eleven and the other of fifteen, three women each of twenty years, five of the same of twenty-four years, two of the same of forty [years]." The prisoners, most likely Lipans, had originally numbered seventeen, but five had died before they even left Texas, and the remainder did not reach Mexico City until early June. Ugarte dispatched a much larger group of seventy-seven Apaches from the Western Interior Provinces in August under the command of Don José María Rivero, cadet of the Presidio of El Pitic in Sonora. Gathering his prisoners in Chihuahua, Rivero saw two small children die and a woman become too ill to travel even before he set out. Nevertheless, over the next two months, he was able to move the remainder of the prisoners south, where they were delivered to Mexico City for Viceroy Flores's disposition.[9]

The greater number of prisoners dispatched from the western portion of the frontier echoed the generally successful operations Commandant General Ugarte had undertaken in 1788, and he was convinced that things were improving once again after the disasters of the previous year. Not only had his troopers been successful in numerous expeditions, but more and more Apaches were again soliciting peace and asking to relocate near presidios. Ugarte felt that allowing these Apaches to settle down, if only for brief periods, was the key to achieving long-term progress. He instructed his officers to permit those Apaches who requested peace, and who agreed to strict regulations, to stay at the reservations. While these actions skirted the commands of Viceroy Flores, Ugarte saw clearly that it was more pragmatic to enlist these Apaches as allies and try to control them at the peace establishments than to hunt them down in the hinterland.

However, Ugarte saw additional value in the prisoners of war. He realized that some of them could be used as barter or exchange for Spanish subjects held prisoner by the Indians. Better yet, they could be used as hostages to induce or reward good behavior among those living at the establecimientos de paz. Then, the following September, Ugarte was handed another opportunity to emphasize this reward system. His troops had recently captured the wife of a prominent Chiricahua chief named El Compá. When El Compá approached the Spanish about redeeming her, Ugarte had his officers tell him that the only way he could get his spouse back was to settle in peace outside the Presidio of Bacoachi. El Compá agreed and joined the other Chiricahuas already resident at the post.[10]

Thus the tactic of controlling the residents of the establecimientos de paz by selectively granting the release of prisoners of war gradually became another successful weapon in the Spanish arsenal. But the effectiveness of this tactic lay in the Apaches' awareness and dread of the fate of the prisoners taken by the Spaniards. At the end of 1788, the recent capture of over one hundred prisoners doomed to be sent into exile during the next few months underscored this threat. Their tale served as a template of how the Spanish could, on one hand, reward those Apaches deemed loyal and under control, and on the other, deliver a clear warning of what would befall them should they continue to resist.

After extensive campaigns into the Apachería during late 1788, Spanish forces under the command of Captain Manuel de Echeagaray had captured a substantial number of prisoners. He had his men escort most of the captives to the Presidio of Janos, the gathering point before they were sent into exile. Echeagaray dispatched, along with the prisoners, a note to the commander of the presidio, Lieutenant Colonel Antonio Cordero, requesting that one of the women prisoners not be included in the collera. The captain reported that "an Apache from the newly pacified who was here with the troops . . . presented to me and to those with me that in examining them [the prisoners] he recognized the garb of a loved one on one of the women prisoners and he manifested to give me his security [for her]." The Apache man, later identified as Tujlainla, was "generally known as having courage and agility and is destined for spying." As Echeagaray hoped to use him in the future, he requested that the captive woman, whom the Spaniards named María, be released to Tujlainla. Cordero concurred with this assessment and had María given over on his own authority. On December 4, the commander reported to Ugarte about this turn of events, writing, "I hope that the circumstances that I have undertaken will meet with the superior approval of Your Lordship." Nine days later, at what may have seemed like the last moment, Ugarte allowed a glimmer of hope to shine through when he approved having

María turned over to Tujlainla. Whether an act of compassion or calculation, the release clearly demonstrated that the Spaniards would reward the Apaches who aided them, while those who resisted would be exiled forever. The subsequent fate of the captured compatriots of María made the lesson all too clear.[11]

Cordero had arranged for one of his officers, Lieutenant Don Manuel Carrasco, to take "the collera of enemy prisoners consisting of the number that set out from here of 103 piezas of all ages and [both] sexes" to the Villa de Chihuahua. Ninety-nine Apaches had originally been brought into the post on December 2, but, as Cordero explained to Ugarte, several casualties had occurred. During their short stay at Janos, "there died immediately three infants who were baptized and some Indian women who did not wish to be baptized; and to the remaining number of ninety-five were added nine that were found here."

Carrasco arrived in Chihuahua with his prisoners on December 22. Records show that they were apparently to have been held temporarily in the obraje of the villa. But the journey from Janos south appears to have taken its toll. The day after the prisoners arrived, three children died, followed by one more on December 24. All four children, recorded as "párvulos de Nación Apache," or infants of the Apache nation, were laid to rest in the cemetery of the parish church of Chihuahua by a resident cleric, an indication that they had been baptized before they died.

In the meantime, preparations for the Apaches' journey to Mexico City were underway. Upon arriving in Chihuahua from Janos with the Apaches, Lieutenant Carrasco turned his charges over to the officer selected to oversee their deportation, Lieutenant Juan Sartorio of the Voluntarios de Cataluña. Although he had served as a field officer, Sartorio possessed very good organizational and financial skills that drew the attention of his superiors, so much so that he would eventually be seconded as secretary for the commandant general. These skills undoubtedly contributed to his selection for this latest assignment, and when the Apache prisoners began to be congregated in the Villa de Chihuahua, it was Sartorio who held their fate in his hands.

On December 30, 1788, Sartorio took delivery of more prisoners, noting that "another seven piezas were brought from New Mexico by Lieutenant Don José Maldonado." On New Year's Day, however, more deaths occurred. Another little boy died and was buried in the cemetery of the parish church with his compatriots, but an Apache woman at the point of dying could not or would not be baptized. For her, Antonio Mendes, "the administrator of the obraje of this Villa," delivered a written note, stating: "I certify that today on this date there passed away an Apache Indian woman of thirty years old and as she was a Gentile, I had her interred *en el campo*," indicating a burial outside the cemetery. Despite these deaths, during their confinement in Chihuahua, the Apache prisoners seem to have been treated humanely. Lieutenant Sartorio purchased ninety-two blankets to cover the captives of the collera soon after their arrival. During the course of the fourteen days in the villa between December 22 and January 4, they were supplied with over fifty *quintales*—about 5,000 pounds—of *carne fresca* (fresh meat) as well as ten *fanegas*, or twenty bushels, of maize for their rations.

As part of his preparations, on January 2, Sartorio had the prisoners reviewed by Domingo Bergaña of the royal treasury. Bergaña's count showed forty-six children between one and five years old, seventeen children between six and fourteen years old, and thirty-three adults over fourteen years old. For the captives' transport, maintenance, and rations, the royal treasury had overseen the contracting of thirty-nine mules and had supplied Sartorio with 1,200 pesos in cash and drafts for a total estimated expense for the seventy-day trip to Mexico City amounting to 2,043 pesos.[12]

On January 5, 1789, Lieutenant Sartorio was ready to depart with the prisoners, but on that very day he found that two of his charges, both children, were too sick to move. Turning once again to Antonio Mendes, Sartorio had him fill out a receipt reading, "I certify that today on this date there was left in the said obraje and remain with me two párvulos of the Apache nation." With the two children accounted for, Sartorio had the remaining ninety-four Apache prisoners mount their mules, and surrounded by their guard of soldiers, head south, bound for exile.

After one week of steady travel, on January 13 the collera and its escort reached the Presidio of Conchos, the headquarters of the Tercera Compañía Volante, or Third Flying Company. Here one of the women fell deathly ill. The chaplain of the company, Father Sebastián Florez, a Franciscan, ministered to the Apache woman. When her condition deteriorated completely, the priest recorded that he had "baptized and buried on the same day an India of the said nation." Perhaps due to the required ceremonies, the expedition remained in Conchos for two days before pressing on.[13]

By January 19, Lieutenant Sartorio had pushed his command farther south until it reached the settlements in the Valle de San Bartolomé. Here, another Apache woman became too sick to continue the journey. As he had done previously, Sartorio sought out a suitable public official to confirm the delivery of the prisoner. He located one Mariano Oviedo, who listed himself as "the commissioner of the Subdelegate of the Royal Hacienda for the Valle de San Bartolomé." Oviedo wrote out a certificate that he had "received in this royal cárcel a sick India."

Moving on, three days later, on January 21, Sartorio reached the Río Florido, where he turned the Apaches over to Sergeant Nicolás Tarín of the Third Flying Company. Tarín would be responsible for the collera for the remainder of its journey to Mexico City. Ninety-two prisoners remained of the original ninety-six who had set out from Chihuahua. But on the same day that he reached the Río Florido, Sartorio found more prisoners waiting for his arrival.

After the large group under Sartorio had left the Villa de Chihuahua at the beginning of the month, six more Apache captives had been brought in. Carabinero José Manuel Carrasco had been charged with delivering these latecomers to Río Florido in time to join the main collera. To sustain his charges, Carrasco had purchased four blankets, beef, bread, and sweets. Departing on January 14 with only six prisoners, Carrasco was able to travel at a faster pace than the large group and arrived at Río Florido the same day as Sartorio. Having fulfilled their mission, both Sartorio and Carrasco filled out their paperwork required to complete the transfer of the prisoners to Sergeant Tarín. Carrasco, being illiterate, had to turn to a young officer cadet, Don Mariano Varela, for help. Varela took time out from assisting Sergeant Tarín with the collera to certify the costs Carrasco had incurred on his journey.[14]

The newly enlarged collera departed from Río Florido soon afterward, but unforeseen problems soon began to arise. After only four days of travel, Sergeant Tarín became gravely ill and could not continue. After reaching the town and one-time presidio of Cerro Gordo, Tarín concluded that Cadet Varela was the only soldier of the escort fit to take over, most likely because he was literate. Dispatches were quickly sent to Commandant General Ugarte informing him of the events, and he hastily approved what was a fait accompli. On February 1, Varela officially took control of the prisoners and the seventeen soldiers of the escort. The group once again headed south, bound for Mexico City.[15]

Six days later, Varela and the collera reached the settlement of El Pasaje, where for unknown reasons he left a number of Apache girls "for the disposition of Captain Don Joseph Yrndiola." Whatever the reason, for the remaining thirty-eight days of the journey, the losses among the prisoners continued to mount. By the time Varela turned over his charges to the military authorities in the capital, only seventy-three Apaches were left of the original ninety-eight he had started out with. The records of the expedition do not contain information on what happened to the twenty-five missing captives. Judging by the fate of prisoners in the earlier part of the journey, it seems most likely that the losses were attributable to those who died of sickness or were left behind to become servants or slaves. Whatever the cause, the loss of more than a quarter of the collera during the journey was startlingly high.[16]

Whether they were aware of the mortality rate of these prisoners or not, the continuous exile of their kin was a clear indication for those Apaches who had settled at the establecimientos de paz that they had chosen the wiser path. As the months wore on, the soldiers sent out more and more raiding parties to attack any Apaches who did not agree to congregate near the peace establishments. In addition, any of those who had settled but returned to raiding were also targeted. By the early part of 1789, Commandant General Ugarte continued the relentlessly aggressive cycle that guaranteed more dead and captured, and thus more deportations. For the Apaches de paz, the inevitable fate of those captives sent into exile drove home, yet again, a lesson that they were learning all too well: those not with the Spaniards risked a most terrible doom.[17]

CHAPTER 5

Severed Heads and Chained Necks

The number of reports to be reviewed was voluminous. Still, he would have to read as many as he could, or at least the summaries prepared by his secretary. Depending on the content of each report, he would have to respond in writing and provide answers, comments, or at the bare minimum, his signature. Yet some items stood out among the stack of papers—namely a report that had originally been accompanied by twelve cut-off heads and a string of desiccated ears.

For Commandant General Jacobo Ugarte y Loyola, the grisly body parts were tangible proof of the continuing warfare waged by the soldiers he commanded. For twenty years he had been serving in the region, and for twenty years he had been fighting almost exclusively against the same enemy—the Apaches. The ebb and flow of the conflict had seen thousands killed on both sides, and for many Spaniards, the war seemed never ending. But in the spring of 1789, Ugarte may have felt things were finally looking up.

For the past year, his men had been engaged in the relentless pursuit of any and all Apaches within reach of Spanish power. Monthly patrols scoured the areas between Spanish forts and settlements, looking for any signs of Apache raiders. Larger military expeditions were sent out at least twice a year to attack the Apaches in their own homelands beyond the edge of Spanish control. Harassed at all turns, the Apaches were gradually being worn down in a savage war of attrition. Clear evidence of the pressure was the growing number of Apaches who were voluntarily relocating near Spanish presidios in the establecimientos de paz. There, they were given food and supplies and, tellingly, required to join Spanish military expeditions to hunt down those Apaches still at war.

Determined to gauge the effectiveness of his campaigns—and to ensure the truthfulness of his men—Ugarte had issued orders in February of 1789 that all Apaches reported killed were to have their ears cut off "as an unequivocal sign" of the truth of the reports. If the number of the enemy was so great as to keep the soldiers from retrieving their bodies, or if the bodies fell into inaccessible places, then a special certification from the officers present was to be forwarded with the official report.

The policy was quickly implemented. On May 1, 1789, Ugarte wrote to his superior, Viceroy Manuel Antonio Flores, in Mexico City, reporting a successful expedition carried out by Spanish soldiers and Apache auxiliaries from the establecimientos de paz that had obliterated an encampment of Apaches not under Spanish control. Ugarte wrote that on April 25, his forces had killed seventeen people, including twelve gandules. "The proof of this success," Ugarte noted, "is my receiving the heads of the twelve gandules and two women and a living gandul with three women, three boys, and one girl . . . and three officers also certified that they saw another three gandules killed in a place where they could not reach to cut off their heads, which documents I enclose for Your Excellency in proof of the claim."

Ugarte's orders were clearly an attempt to prove the veracity of his officers and to ensure that they were not inflating their battlefield counts. How the commandant general regarded the postmortem mutilation of the slain Apaches personally is unknown, but the policy was by no means a new phenomenon.[1]

Throughout history, many societies practiced the mutilation of slain enemies, especially the taking of heads. Julius Caesar wrote that the Celtic peoples of Gaul and Britain routinely cut off the heads of their foes and displayed them in ceremonial fashion; the Almoravid warriors of North Africa who invaded Spain in the eleventh century reportedly decapitated their Christian enemies and piled their heads in heaps large enough to form a tower for the muezzin to climb up on and issue the Islamic call to prayer; and in the fifteenth century, the Aztecs of Mexico kept the heads of tens of thousands of sacrificial victims displayed on their great *tzompantli*, or skull rack, in the center of the city of Tenochtitlan. In these and numerous other instances, the mutilation was either calculated to terrorize and aid in subjugation, or designed for ritualistic and cultural purposes. Sometimes, as with the Aztecs, it was both. Variations of headhunting included scalping and the slicing off of ears, noses, and lips. In almost all these mutilations, the act was justified as ritualistic, as the head was seen as the repository of the soul or spirit of the slain individual. Taking the head or part of the head of an enemy was seen as transferring the soul matter from the slain to the slayer, increasing the latter's power. Often, mutilation gave proof of an individual's prowess and increased that person's status, and the more heads or scalps one possessed, the greater one's status.

Along the northern frontier, several indigenous groups reportedly practiced the mutilation of their dead enemies for cultural or ritual purposes as a feature of conflict. There is evidence of postmortem mutilation, and perhaps even ritual cannibalism, among some southwestern Indians before the coming of the Europeans. When the Spanish arrived in the region, some native peoples continued to engage in both ritual cannibalism and postmortem mutilation, especially scalping. In 1610, Jesuit missionaries reported that cannibalism and mutilation played a central role in the warfare practices of the Xixime peoples of what is now southern Sinaloa, Mexico. Similarly, in 1764 another Jesuit recounted how it had become a ritual among the Ópatas and Eudebes of Sonora to take scalps, although in earlier times they had taken the severed hands from their dead enemies.[2]

After the Spaniards began to have sustained contact with the Apaches all along the northern frontier, they began to ascribe postmortem mutilations to these people as well. In 1698, the Jesuit Eusebio Francisco Kino reported several instances from Sonora wherein Piman (O'odham) groups and their Apache adversaries scalped enemy dead after raids and battles. Similarly, during the 1720s and 1730s, the Spanish in Texas reported examples of various mutilations by the Apaches of both Spaniards and other Indians. In both of these areas, the Spanish inferred that scalping was done for ritual and cultural purposes. But other postmortem mutilations that the Apaches reportedly practiced, such as smashing the head or genitals, flaying the skin and muscle from arms and legs, and disemboweling the body and stuffing it with beans, were taken as evidence of an innate savagery. The Apaches developed such a reputation that Hugo O'Conor, the first commandant inspector of the Interior Provinces, was able to draw up a voluminous report in the 1770s filled with testimony documenting Apache mutilations. Whether these reports were accurate or not, the Spanish used them as propaganda to justify their own similar actions.[3]

Even for men of the eighteenth-century Enlightenment, such as Ugarte and O'Conor, the taking of heads in combat was a recognized aspect of warfare. As Spaniards, both men knew that the long centuries of violence against the Moors and Turks throughout the Mediterranean had resulted in warfare at times far more brutal than conflicts among European powers. Along the North African coast, Spanish outposts such as Oran and Ceuta were engaged in more or less permanent war with the Muslim rulers of the region. Spanish prisoners taken were immediately enslaved and the dead routinely beheaded, their heads displayed as trophies for which the Muslim rulers would pay bounties in order to motivate their soldiers. For their part, the Spaniards were not loath to reciprocate. In 1732 it was reported that after a battle outside Oran, an English merchant ship's captain was dining with several Spanish officers when "the Soldiers brought in two plates full of Turks ears instead of plates of cherries as is commonly brought after dinner."[4]

Exactly when the Spaniards began to practice the postmortem mutilation of Apaches is unclear. In 1772, Lieutenant Don Camilo Chacón of the Presidio of Janos brought back to his commanding officer a pair of ears taken from an Apache whom his men had killed. In 1775, Hugo O'Conor had stopped at the Presidio of Carrizal at the end of his first general campaign when he received a report from one of his officers:

> On my arrival at the said Presidio I found a letter from Captain Dn. Manuel Muñoz written in the Sierra de Guadalupe on the 8th of November just passed, to whom I had given the Squadrons composed of the detachment under his command and they had made six attacks against the Enemy, the third on a Ranchería of forty-four tents, besides the rancho, and a small bastion of adobes, in the Ojo de San Luis, in which he fortunately succeeded in killing ninety-two Piezas from which he cut the ears as proof of the truth of what he had done.

O'Conor does not seem to have ordered a general policy of slicing ears from the bodies of dead Apaches, as none of his other officers who led detachments in the campaign are recorded as having brought in ears as proof of their killing enemies. But

Captain Muñoz's actions were not seen as out of the ordinary; the Spanish taking of ears, scalps, and whole heads was practiced all along the frontier. Nor was the practice limited to just Apache dead; any Indians deemed as enemies were subject to it. In 1782, during a punitive campaign against the Quechan Indians along the lower Colorado River, the Spaniards took ears from the Indians they had killed. Still, given the constant violence between the Spaniards and the Apaches, postmortem mutilation was most frequent between them.[5]

Many Spaniards were aware of Apache cultural sensibilities and knew that they greatly dreaded being in proximity to the corpses of relatives or kin. Apaches believed that the spirits of the dead remained near their bodies for a period of time. To approach a dead body or body parts of another Apache was to risk contamination and perhaps even possession by a disturbed or malevolent spirit. Capitalizing on this belief, the Spanish used the bodies or body parts of dead Apaches as a deterrent. Captain Pedro de Allande of the Presidio of Tucson boasted of the number of Apache heads that crowned the battlements above the gate to the presidio. Captain Antonio Cordero of the Presidio of Janos hung the heads of slain Apaches from mesquite trees lining the road outside his post. While both officers undoubtedly hoped to terrorize the Apaches, they were also most likely attempting to deter Apaches from approaching areas that might prove vulnerable to attack.[6]

Still, while they clearly hoped to engender terror and psychological dread, the Spaniards, in the main, seem to have taken heads and ears for a much more mundane reason: to verify the number of enemy slain. In 1789, when Commandant General Ugarte issued his order requiring the taking of ears and heads as proof of the number of Apaches killed, he was formalizing an existing practice to substantiate the claims being submitted by his officers.

If these mutilated appendages gave tangible proof of the body counts claimed after punitive expeditions, further evidence of success for the Spaniards lay in the living bodies of the men, women, and children that they took captive and then deported. Even more striking evidence could be found in the number of Apaches who had agreed to settle near the presidios in the establecimientos de paz. For Commandant General Ugarte and his officers, all these tallies not only provided tangible proof of the success of official policies, but a vindication of the prowess of Spanish arms.

However, for Brigadier General Juan de Ugalde, events in the eastern portion of the frontier were not as promising. In the spring of 1788, things had appeared to be going well for Ugalde. The previous fall, he had forged an agreement with eight Mescalero leaders who he claimed represented the whole tribe, and they had settled in rancherías on the Río Sabinas near the Presidio of Santa Rosa in Coahuila. Then, in March of 1788, the Apache leader Picax-ande arrived with his people at Santa Rosa as well. Feeling assured of the relative security of the peace establishments, Ugalde left soon after on an extended inspection tour of the provinces of Texas and Nuevo Santander. But as soon as he departed, the Mescaleros rose up and fled the reservation, leaving a wake of destruction as they headed back into the hinterlands. Convinced after this episode that the Apaches could not be trusted for very long, Viceroy Flores had ordered both frontier commanders not to concede peace unless it was under the most restrictive terms. Taking the viceroy's injunction to heart, Ugalde, returning in December of 1788 from his inspection tour, planned to strike a blow that would reverberate throughout the frontier.

When several Mescalero leaders approached him in early 1789, again requesting peace, Ugalde could not forget that in the previous year the Apaches had quickly broken a peace treaty, "which on our part we committed the error of conceding." Determined not to make the same mistake, Ugalde wrote to the viceroy that he would use "perfidy against perfidy, deceit against deceit, cunning against cunning." To that end, he parleyed with the Mescaleros for several weeks and lured a substantial number of them into the Presidio of Santa Rosa. On March 24, he sprang his trap and seized and imprisoned seventy-eight of the Indians, including three chieftains, twenty-three warriors, twenty-nine women, six boys, seven girls, and six infants. Two of the warriors fought to the death rather than submit, and their heads were cut off and preserved, while the remaining prisoners were locked in the cárcel of Santa Rosa, all the men being placed in leg irons.

When word of what had occurred at Santa Rosa spread throughout the frontier, many Spanish officers were appalled at what they viewed as a dishonorable and unprovoked entrapment, but Viceroy Flores hailed the event as a most successful operation. Flores, maintaining his hard line, in the following month ordered several Mescalero bands that had approached the Presidio del Norte requesting peace to be turned away. Enraged at Ugalde's treatment of their kin at Santa Rosa and unable to find refuge in the west, the Mescaleros increased their raids, enlisting many Lipan groups as well. The conflict escalated to the point that Ugalde even asked permission to attack his erstwhile ally, Picax-ande, who had remained near Santa Rosa but now was reported to have aided the Mescaleros. Vowing to crush the Apaches once and for all, Ugalde launched a protracted expedition in August of 1789 that would see him constantly in the field for almost three hundred days in a largely ineffectual campaign against the Mescaleros and Lipans.[7]

While the situation in the east was deteriorating, in the west, Commandant General Ugarte was engaged in similarly bloody, but eminently more successful, operations against the Apaches, resulting in a higher number of deportations. Throughout 1789, he continued to have his forces launch aggressive attacks into the Apache homelands while simultaneously holding out the prospect of peace for those who agreed to settle at the establishments. By year's end, another 48 Apaches had been killed, with 193 others captured and slated for deportation. Again skirting the harsh directives of the viceroy, Ugarte allowed several of the prisoners to avoid exile, releasing them to kinsmen who lived in the peace establishments.

If Ugarte was concerned that his actions would not meet with the approval of Viceroy Flores, he need not have worried. In October of 1789, Flores handed the office of viceroy over to his successor, the second Conde de Revillagigedo, who soon showed himself of a temperament quite different from that of his predecessor. Within a very short time, the new viceroy came to embrace the policies of the Instructions of 1786, the very same policies that Ugarte had been attempting—despite Viceroy Flores's opposition—to put into effect. But if Revillagigedo was more amenable to conceding peace to the Apaches, he was also not averse to using force. When Ugarte, in the late fall of 1789, requested permission to dispatch another collera of Apache prisoners of war into exile, the new viceroy agreed and made preparations to receive what was perhaps the largest number of captives sent out to date.

When he wrote to Viceroy Revillagigedo on December 11, Commandant General Ugarte explained that originally the group had been extraordinarily large: "This collera was to have had more than two hundred fifty piezas; but many died in prison despite the care with which they were attended." Seeking to explain the loss of almost a third of the Apache prisoners before they had even left the frontier, Ugarte had a ready set of excuses. "This accident," as he termed it, "arose in great part due to the inevitable corruption of a place where many people live confined for some time, and from the melancholy that overpowered their spirits with the loss of their liberty, as well as the variation of their diet." While obliquely acknowledging that cramped and unsanitary conditions, and perhaps a lack of food, had contributed to the high mortality rate, Ugarte still found himself with 180 Apache prisoners to be disposed of. For their journey, he had drawn 3,030 pesos from the royal treasury for the daily rations of the captives at the rate of 1½ reales per person per day. He had also contracted for the use of sixty-seven mules to transport them from the frontier to Mexico City, which was calculated to take seventy days.

Ugarte also informed the new viceroy that, as had occurred with previous colleras, there might be requests from the many towns and cities along the way to distribute some of the Apache prisoners as domestic servants or cheap labor. It might be advisable to grant some of the smaller piezas to "members of the Church of Jesus Christ or to useful vassals," but only if they agreed to "raise them up and educate them Christianly." However, none of the adults or older children "that retain any memory of their Country or [have the] evil intention to return as adults to search for their relatives" were to be let out from the group. Indeed, Ugarte believed that only those Apache children under the age of seven should be considered for release, as they were the most likely to "persist faithfully with their Patrons." Once freed from confinement and supplied with proper clothing and diet, he maintained, "they would little by little . . . become instructed in our customs, acquire Christian instruction, and breathe purer air." That the commandant general should show such concern for Apache children was probably due to the high number present. Among the 180 prisoners, there were only 8 men, with 87 women and 85 boys and girls.[8]

The officer charged with overseeing the deportation of this large Apache group was Don Francisco Xavier de Enderica, *alférez primero*, or first ensign, of the Presidio of Fronteras in northeastern Sonora. Enderica was a twenty-six-year-old bachelor of noble quality, from Logroño, in Spain. He had served as a cadet in the regular army but transferred to the presidial forces to serve along the northern frontier. There he had participated in five campaigns against the Apaches as well as several minor operations and had even killed one warrior with his own hands. His superiors viewed him as having valor and good application, and one even remarked rather caustically that "he has the good inclination to be a useful officer." In commanding the escort for such a large contingent of Apache prisoners, Enderica would need all the skills he could muster.

To contain the Apaches, Alférez Enderica was given an escort of twenty-four men of the Third Flying Company under Sergeant Antonio Griego. These soldiers would escort the 141 Apaches held in Chihuahua as far as the post at Pilar de Conchos. There they would pick up another 39 Apaches along with six troopers from the Presidio of San Carlos, sixteen soldiers from del Norte, and another six from El Príncipe, all under Corporal Fermín Uribes. However, the men under Uribes were only to guard the prisoners as far as the Hacienda de Santa Catarina, at which point they were to join the escort for the general remount herd that supplied the presidios with riding animals, under the command of Sergeant Valentín Moreno. After that, Enderica would have only the men of the Third Flying Company to control the collera all the way to Mexico.

In addition, Commandant General Ugarte ordered Enderica to gather up several Apaches from an earlier deportation. In his written instructions to the young officer, Ugarte noted that "under the power of Militia Captain Don Vicente Olonio and Lieutenant Don Manuel Romano in the Río de las Nazas there are two medium piezas, fugitives from the collera conducted previously under the command of Alférez Don Mariano Varela. These two officers undertook to Christianize and educate them, but feel they are too big to undergo this and too close to the frontier to be prevented from going back, and so they ask for two younger boys instead." After changing out the two older boys for younger ones, Enderica was also to pick up another prisoner,

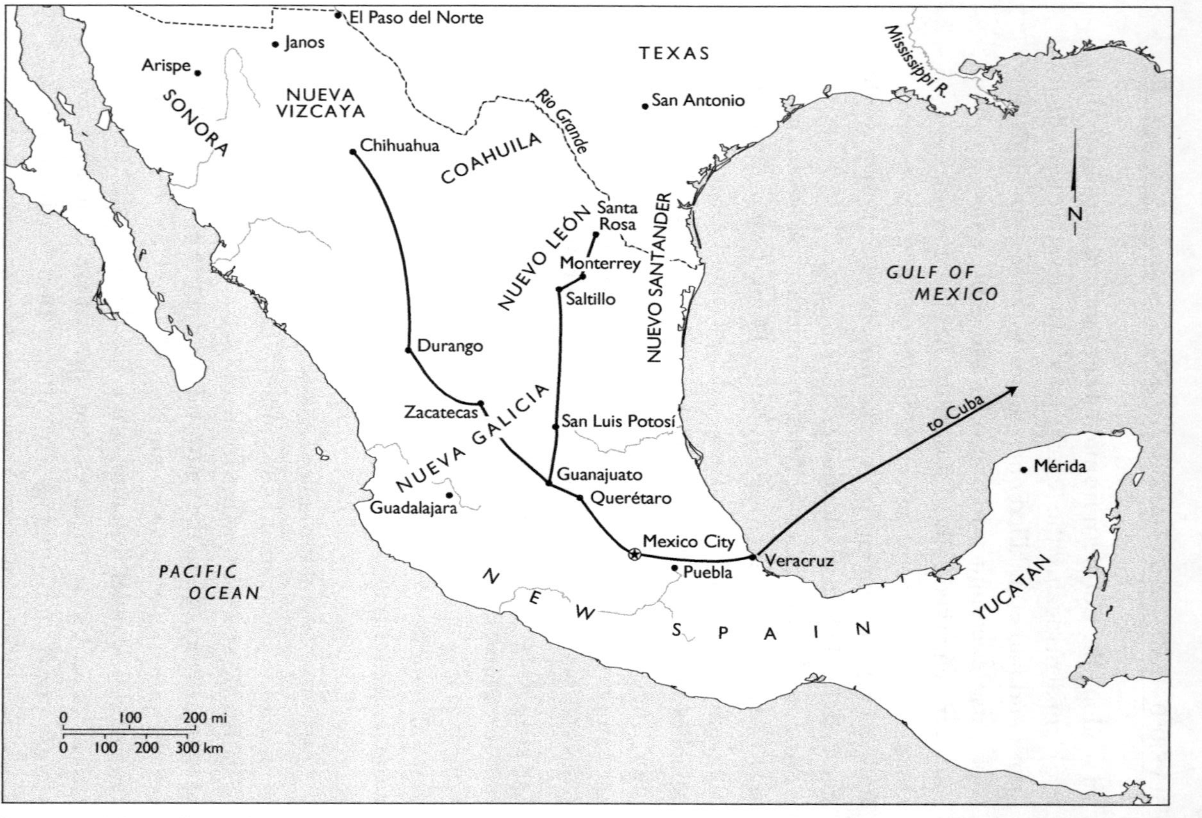

Routes of the *colleras*. Adapted from William B. Carter, *Alliances and the Spanish in the Southwest, 750–1750* (Norman: University of Oklahoma Press, 2009).

an old Apache woman who was left behind sick in the town of Sombrerete, but who had since recovered. She was to be incorporated into the collera as well.[9]

However, the task of gathering additional prisoners receded quickly into the background, for Alférez Enderica soon had enough problems maintaining the ones he already had. On December 9, 1789, two days before the collera was scheduled to leave Chihuahua, a little Apache boy became too sick to move. The next day, another child became gravely ill, and when it was clear he would not survive, he was taken to the chapel of Nuestra Señora de Guadalupe for baptism. The child died that night and was buried in the nearby cemetery. As if these two deaths were not enough, on December 11, as the expedition was getting underway, Enderica noted a particularly disturbing event: "As the mules were being packed for the march, the Sergeant brought me word that an old Indian woman had cut her own throat. I was informed that [the prisoners were asked if] they knew why she would wish to die, and they could not give any reasons. I had her ears cut off and sent them with the news to the Señor Commandant General." When Sergeant Griego reported the suicide, he noted that the woman "had killed herself with a *belduque* [belt knife] that she had." How she came to get the belt knife is unclear, but the circumstances of her death were unnerving. Unfortunately for Enderica, the loss of three of his charges in such quick succession portended a terrible pattern that would plague the rest of the journey.[10]

Moving southeast, the expedition took three days to travel the thirty-four leagues to the military post at Pilar de Conchos, where they were to pick up the rest of the Apache prisoners sentenced to deportation. Along the way, three more captives died, including two children, and two others who were sick were left behind. With the other thirty-nine Apaches now added, the collera continued the journey south from Pilar de Conchos on December 18, making marches of six or seven leagues, or about fifteen to twenty miles, per day. Over the next twenty-two days they traveled through a series of haciendas, ranchos, and small towns, suffering eight more casualties including the death of four little girls and one woman, with a boy, a girl, and another adult woman left behind sick.

On January 10 they reached Durango, the first substantial city along the route, where the expedition spent three days resting and refitting. Still, two more prisoners died during this lull: a boy, given the name of Pedro de la Cruz, and "María, an Apache woman, native of the Gila." Both were baptized before dying and were buried in church cemeteries in the city. Continuing on for the next nine days, the prisoners and their escort moved toward the Real de Sombrerete, where they were to pick up the Apache women left behind from a previous deportation. This they did, but three more boys died in transit and another child and a woman were left behind.

Up to this point, Alférez Enderica had lost a small but steady stream of prisoners. However, when they entered the city of Fresnillo on January 21, the floods burst. Over the next three days, nine of the prisoners died, including four women and girls and five males, among them three boys under twelve and an infant of only two months. In addition, two more women were too sick to go any farther. The onset of what was probably a communicable disease was so sudden that Enderica hired a doctor to attend the prisoners, but whether his ministrations were of any use is unknown.[11]

Pressing onward, the expedition traveled next to the city of Zacatecas, but the change in location did not cause the disease to abate. On January 26 and 27, five more Apaches, all males, were baptized before death and given an ecclesiastical burial. In addition, Don José Francisco de Castañeda, one of the city councilors, took over the care of one infant boy, "orphaned of father and mother, of five or six months old, named José," who was too sick to continue. The councilor agreed to "educate, bring up, and Christianize" the boy after he regained his health. Again, Alférez Enderica vainly sought a solution to the malady, spending a considerable sum of his funds on "medicines" for the sick Apaches.

Two more days' travel continued to see casualties mount. When the party reached the Hacienda de Señor San José de Tlacotes, two more Apaches, "an Adult India of seventy years and a small boy child about six years old," succumbed. The following day, January 29, Mariano Elías Beltrán, a local landowner, drew up a document certifying the deaths and ecclesiastical burials of a prisoner named José Miguel as well as an "India of sixty years, another of fifteen, another of nine, and two *chiquitos,* one of two months and the other of four months, who died at the Puesto de San Francisco and were buried in my Hacienda of San Juan."[12]

On January 30, Alférez Enderica and his party reached the City of Aguascalientes, and here the young officer determined to deal with the sickness plaguing his command. "At this place," he wrote in his diary, "I made a rest as a consequence of the sickness in the collera." He turned to the local churchmen for assistance, contacting Father Pedro Cardozo, Prior of the Convent of San Juan de Dios, the brothers of which operated the Hospital of San Juan. Cardozo agreed to admit ten of the Apache women, all sick with "pains in the side." As Enderica could not linger to monitor the treatment of these women, one of the officials of Aguascalientes, Don Pedro Herrera y Leyva, promised to pay for their upkeep and bill the military authorities after the fact. At the same time, Enderica oversaw the final disposition of those Apaches who had died in the city, including six women, a girl, and a ten-year-old boy, who were all baptized and given ecclesiastical burials. One boy, a "*muchacho* who appeared about fourteen, died without baptism and was placed in el campo." When he continued on his journey, Enderica undoubtedly felt he had done all he could. However, within ten days, Father Cardozo would report that all but one of the women left at the hospital had succumbed to their illness.

The first day of February saw the collera head out yet again, and at this point they were able to stay each night in larger cities and towns. Still, moving into the more densely populated areas did not alleviate the suffering of the Apaches, who continued to fall sick and die. Two boys died in the city of León. In Silao, one man and an infant boy perished, while four other captives, "three small piezas . . . two named José and the other María Josefa," along with a sixteen-year-old girl not yet baptized, were left behind. One man died at Celaya and another at San Juan del Río. In the latter city, "María Francisca, India Apache and her little son" were both baptized before dying. On February 15, two more Apaches, "one the parent and the other a babe in arms," succumbed, as did "José, an infant Apache Indian." Three days later, on the outskirts of Mexico City, "Josef Antonio, an Indian about ten years old of the Apache nation," was baptized before his death. Then, on February 19, when the collera had finally arrived at the capital, the last casualty was recorded, an unnamed woman "who died five hours after she was baptized."[13]

By the time Alférez Enderica turned over the remaining Apaches to the authorities in Mexico City, the losses they had suffered were appalling. Of the 180 that had started the journey, 70 had perished along the way, including all 8 men, 29 of the women, and 33 of the children, including several newborns. In addition, another 11 women and 14 children were left behind sick, and 10 of the former had died soon thereafter. All together, the losses in transit totalled over 50 percent. Records from the expedition show that the prisoners had been adequately clothed, supplied, and fed, and that they had not been forced to march at a quicker pace than was normal. Disease clearly caused the greatest loss of life, but at this distance it seems impossible to discover the nature of the contagion, although it does seem that the soldiers of the escort were immune.

If the Spaniards were unable to heal the physical maladies of the prisoners, they nevertheless evinced constant concern for their spiritual status from the Spanish Catholic perspective. Of the seventy deaths noted, fifty-five were baptized and interred according to Catholic doctrine, with another thirteen probably baptized *in extremis* by the members of the escort. Only two of the prisoners who died were clearly not baptized. Whatever the modern attitudes regarding the imposition of European spiritualism on native peoples, the Spaniards in the escort and in the places along the way regarded their faith as the only true religion, and by their own beliefs were compelled to administer the saving grace of baptism to their charges, even if the ritual was incomprehensible to those who received it. While such attitudes and beliefs may be foreign to the sensibilities of some in the twenty-first century, to Spaniards of the eighteenth century, they were not only understandable but were regarded as righteous. Regardless, the religious ceremonies and ministrations performed for these Apaches were a continuing feature noted in all of the deportations.

While the saving of Apache prisoners' souls was clearly important to the Spaniards, it did little to alleviate their overall plight or to mitigate the enmity between both groups of people. Violence still permeated the Interior Provinces. The brutality of the conflict continued with all the dehumanizing tactics available to the antagonists. For the Apaches, the killing and despoilment of Spaniards became a cultural routine woven into the patterns of society, with success measured by the number of enemies slain, captives seized, and booty taken. For the Spaniards, the visible proof of their success could be measured by the severed heads and rotting ears of dead Apaches enumerated by bureaucrats, as well as the steady stream of captured prisoners of war heading south from the frontier, trudging forlornly into the oblivion of exile.

CHAPTER 6

A Singular Expression of Friendship

Lieutenant Colonel Don Antonio Cordero could not help feeling gratified with the results of the latest campaign. As military commander of the First Division of Nueva Vizcaya and captain of the Presidio of Janos, Cordero was perhaps the most skilled and experienced Spanish commander in the Interior Provinces. For the better part of the year 1790, his soldiers had scoured the mountains and deserts in search of the Apaches and had killed and captured many enemies. Better still, members of several Apache rancherías had joined the Spanish in these attacks, helping to roust their own kinsmen from the mountain fastness of their traditional homeland.

In the thirteen years that he had served along the northern frontier, Cordero had developed an impressive knowledge of the Apaches. He had fought against them in twenty-one major campaigns as well as smaller engagements that he listed as "*salidas, corredurías*, and *mariscadas* without number." In all, Cordero was responsible for the killing of 263 Apache men, women, and children, including 95 warriors, some by his own hand. He had taken another 128 people prisoner. Nevertheless, he had seen them not just as enemies, but also as potential allies. In 1787, when the Spanish began to set up the peace establishments, Cordero had been named *agente de paces*, or peace agent, in which office he was "commissioned . . . to give passports to the Mimbreño and Gileño Indians," which allowed them to travel in areas of Spanish control and identified them as peaceful. "Many times," Cordero wrote, "I visited their . . . rancherías alone" to verify the Apaches' intentions. Over time, Cordero came to understand their language, their religion, and their society. Above all, he came to understand the fluid nature of leadership among the Apaches. He would later write that the Apaches were "jealous of their liberty and independence" and noted that "every family head in his own camp considers himself a sovereign in his district." This fierce independence could reach such an extent, he wrote, that some heads of families "prefer to live completely separated from the others with their wives and children, because thus no one disputes their leadership."[1]

In October of 1790, Cordero was therefore not surprised when he received word that one of the numerous Apache *capitancillos*, "little captains," wished to speak with him. It was Tetsegoslán, the leader of a band of Apaches that had taken up residence outside the Presidio of Bavispe some sixty miles west of Cordero's own presidio at Janos. Over the past two years Tetsegoslán had begun to emerge as one of the most prominent of the leaders helping the Spanish fight the Apaches who were still raiding from the hinterland. The capitancillo was here to crave a special favor from Cordero: the return of several family members taken prisoner by the Spanish.

Like many Apache leaders, Tetsegoslán settled at the establecimientos de paz only after years of open warfare. Indeed, when he first came into Bavispe to accept peace around May of 1787, he had been considered "loyal" by the Spanish for only a relatively short period. Given this fact, it was not surprising that Tetsegoslán had suffered casualties among his own kin. He now asked Cordero for help in retrieving several close relatives, namely his eight-year-old son, Tajuyé; Tetsegoslán's sister, Quineidestín; and her five-year-old son, Matchan. All three had been captured and sent as prisoners to Mexico City in the collera under the command of Alférez Enderica. Whether he was moved by the pathos of the situation or recognized an opportunity to benefit from the situation, Cordero told Tetsegoslán that he would use "the greatest efforts to acquire this grace" and would seek the return of the prisoners.

On October 14, 1790, Cordero wrote to his superior, Commandant General Jacobo Ugarte y Loyola, at his headquarters in Chihuahua on behalf of the Apache capitancillo. Cordero began his plea by remarking on the "singular expressions of friendship" shown by Tetsegoslán in his alliance with the Spanish. He had been of particular assistance in the pursuit and chastisement of three groups of hostile Apaches—the rancherías led by two brothers labeled by the Spanish as Manta Negra the Elder and the Younger and that led by Squielnocten. Cordero noted that Tetsegoslán was a "meritorious person" who had gone out on campaign "in union with our arms" and that the successes enjoyed by the Spanish had to some extent been the result of "this very able, astute, and warlike Indian." With this in mind, Cordero asked that he be allowed to send some representatives of Tetsegoslán along with a detachment scheduled to take another group of Apache prisoners to Mexico City. Once in the capital, the Apaches would be able to search for their captive relatives and seek their recovery, or at least find out if they had died. In light of Tetsegoslán's activities on behalf of the Spanish, Cordero wrote that he hoped Ugarte would agree to this undertaking. Within a few weeks, Commandant General Ugarte approved Cordero's request and passed it on to his superior in Mexico City, Viceroy the Conde de Revillagigedo, on October 27.

Juan Vicente de Güemes Pacheco y Padilla, the second Conde de Revillagigedo, had been serving as the viceroy of New Spain for over a year by the time he received the request from Commandant General Ugarte. During that period, Revillagigedo had embraced the peace policies called for in the Instructions of 1786 as the most cost-effective method of dealing with the Apaches. As a result, he had removed the bellicose brigadier general Juan de Ugalde from command of the Eastern Interior Provinces and temporarily allowed Commandant General Ugarte to assume control of the entire frontier region, albeit under close supervision. Yet, while Revillagigedo favored a peaceful solution, he also endorsed harsh policies against the Apaches who still defied the Spanish. The deportation of Apaches captured in battle, either to Mexico City or to Cuba, was one of those policies. But the request to return Apaches already removed from the frontier also presented some new issues.[2]

Ever since he had assumed office in October of 1789, Revillagigedo had been dealing with issues in the deportation of Apaches, not least of which were requests to return various prisoners already in exile. Revillagigedo fully endorsed the frontier policy of returning captives to their relatives in exchange for the good behavior of the Apaches de paz. The problem lay in the timing. Apache prisoners often died during the harrowing journey south to Mexico City or to the islands of the Caribbean. Others succumbed to illness or died due to overwork once they reached their final destination. Some even vanished from the official records due to carelessness or bureaucratic errors that obliterated their actual physical whereabouts.

The prime example of losing track of a prisoner occurred in the summer of 1790 when the viceroy had been asked to release a prisoner of war who was a close relative of an Apache leader from the peace establishments. Yagonxli, an Apache headman who had recently made peace at the Presidio of Janos, had soon

Juan Vicente de Güemes Pacheco y Padilla, second Conde de Revillagigedo, Viceroy of New Spain, 1789–94. From Manuel Rivera Cambas, *Los gobernantes de México*, 1 (Mexico, 1872–73). Courtesy Special Collections, The University of Arizona Libraries, Tucson.

after his surrender requested that Spanish authorities return his brother, who had been sent to the metropolis from the northern frontier. When Revillagigedo replied on November 15 to Ugarte's letter about Tetsegoslán's request, he cautioned that things might not unfold as all hoped. He explained that he had used "particular diligence in inquiring if the Indian Jasaquechoe, brother of Yagonxli, is in the Plazas of Veracruz or Havana" but could not ascertain his whereabouts. Obviously aware of the importance of keeping Yagonxli at peace, the viceroy appeared willing to return his brother if he could be located, but that did not appear promising. Likewise, Revillagigedo agreed to allow Tetsegoslán's kinsmen to "search the capital and private houses therein," where they might recognize their family members. However, the viceroy cautioned that "they may be redeemed and sent back or it may be as with the cited [brother of] Yagonxli" that they would not be found.[3]

Despite the physical dangers experienced by deported Apache prisoners, Viceroy Revillagigedo seemed more interested in the spiritual ramifications of the request to have Tetsegoslán's family members returned home. Responding to Commandant General Ugarte on November 15, 1790, Revillagigedo wrote that he was concerned that many of the young captives had already been baptized by the time they reached Mexico City. He argued that to return these Christian children to their parents, who were still pagan, would not be just. However, if the parents themselves were to convert, the situation would be different. While he realized that proper instruction in the faith would take time, the viceroy noted that "under these circumstances it might be opportune" to let the indios de paz know that they might secure the release of their kin if they themselves accepted "the responsibility and complications" necessary to become Christians. Nevertheless, he told Ugarte to impress upon Tetsegoslán and the other Apaches at the peace establishments that the prisoners sent to Mexico "were made captive in a declared war and conducted without fault to this capital," where they had been treated well. Revillagigedo was eager to impress the Apaches with the just intentions of the Spanish and wrote that the prisoners had "experienced our humanity [here] the same as they have seen our power on the frontier."

Within several weeks, Revillagigedo's letter granting Tetsegoslán's request reached Commandant General Ugarte. Seeking to assure the viceroy that he had not compromised the conversion to Christianity of any of the Apache captives, Ugarte responded in a letter of December 6 that he had always observed the method that once prisoners were baptized, they would not be returned to their pagan relatives, in spite of the strongest entreaties. He claimed that "it would not be just for Christian persons, following the Straight Road of our Religion, to return amongst those where they would pervert and forget those sentiments which they obtained and were imprinted upon them at Baptism." Ugarte noted that this was the procedure he had followed earlier when Lieutenant Colonel Cordero had passed along the request from Yagonxli for the return of his brother, and that it would be the same now with the three prisoners requested by Tetsegoslán. Whether Ugarte was moved by genuine concern for the spiritual well-being of the Apache captives, or whether he merely echoed the sentiments of his superior, it was obvious that both Spanish officials had set conversion to Christianity as a clear-cut limitation on the choice of captives who might be sent back to their homelands.

Religious considerations aside, within a few days, Commandant General Ugarte forwarded the viceroy's approval to Lieutenant Colonel Cordero, who in turn had word delivered to Tetsegoslán. Now assured of Spanish compliance, the Apache capitancillo determined to press ahead with plans for the return of his family members held in captivity. Sometime over the next several weeks, Tetsegoslán contacted the leaders of two other rancherías at peace with the Spanish. The first was El Compá, a

Chiricahua leader who had made peace in late 1788, after which he and the members of his ranchería settled at the Presidio of Janos, where they served the Spanish loyally, scouting for the white men in the continuous forays against those Apaches still at war. El Compá's actions on behalf of the Spanish were so noteworthy that they eventually bestowed on him formal recognition as Principal Chief of the Apaches de Paz.

The second leader was Yagonxli, whom the Spanish now called Ojos Colorados, or "Hazel Eyes." A leader of the Apaches the Spanish identified as Mimbreños, Ojos Colorados had been among the estimated eight hundred members of that group who settled in an establecimiento de paz outside the Presidio of San Buenaventura in February of 1787. However, in May of that year, the Apaches rose up and fled the reservation, killing five people, including three Chiricahua Apache scouts. Stung by what they regarded as a "treacherous rebellion," Spanish authorities had organized several large-scale expeditions to punish the Mimbreños. Over the next three years, warfare intensified and Ojos Colorados and his people were put under constant pressure. Finally, in the spring of 1790, the Spaniards dispatched El Compá to parley with Ojos Colorados to try to convince him to make peace. In May of the same year, Ojos Colorados decided that this was the better path and settled his ranchería in the Janos peace establishment.[4]

Coming together in conference, Tetsegoslán, El Compá, and Ojos Colorados (Yagonxli) undoubtedly discussed the fact that the Spaniards had in the recent past allowed the Apaches de paz to recover close relatives destined to be exiled. Although attempts by Viceroy Revillagigedo to retrieve the brother of Ojos Colorados had been unsuccessful, El Compá had been a prime beneficiary of this policy. He had originally agreed to make peace with the Spaniards in order to gain the freedom of his wife, who had been captured sometime in the fall of 1788. After almost a full year of loyal service, El Compá was able to rescue more captive kin. In September of 1789, his niece Keoltjan had been taken prisoner during a Spanish raid into the Sierra de los Mimbres. A few weeks later, the same Spanish expedition attacked another Apache camp, and among the prisoners captured was the sister of El Compá's wife. Both women were soon marked for deportation. El Compá had quickly approached Lieutenant Colonel Cordero, who had commanded the Spanish expedition, and asked that the women be delivered to him or other close relatives and not deported. Acknowledging the Spanish chain of command, the Apache had requested that Cordero write to Commandant General Ugarte, who "could grant this mercy" with the stroke of a pen. A little while later, El Compá was proven correct when Ugarte ordered that the two women prisoners be released to the capitancillo "in consideration of his fidelity and correctness on campaigns."[5]

Although El Compá's rescues had occurred before the colleras had departed from the frontier, the Apache headmen Tetsegoslán, El Compá, and Ojos Colorados obviously felt that a precedent had been set, even if those they hoped to recover were now far away. They decided to seek the return of eleven members of their rancherías, one each belonging to El Compá and Ojos Colorados, and the remaining nine to Tetsegoslán. El Compá chose to ask for the return of the woman Vegonz-in-e, while Ojos Colorados asked for a man called Taggaiso-é. Tetsegoslán was particularly eager to recover his young son, sister, and nephew, but he also sought the return of four other women, Chinaggai, Senz-si, Ylche-he, and Lass-é-sen; one girl, Colchinhé; and another man, Tagu-húl. Whether or not all of these individuals were members of the extended families of the three capitancillos is unknown, but clearly they were valued members of the rancherías in which they lived, and the obligations of Apache society required that everything possible be done to try to recover them.

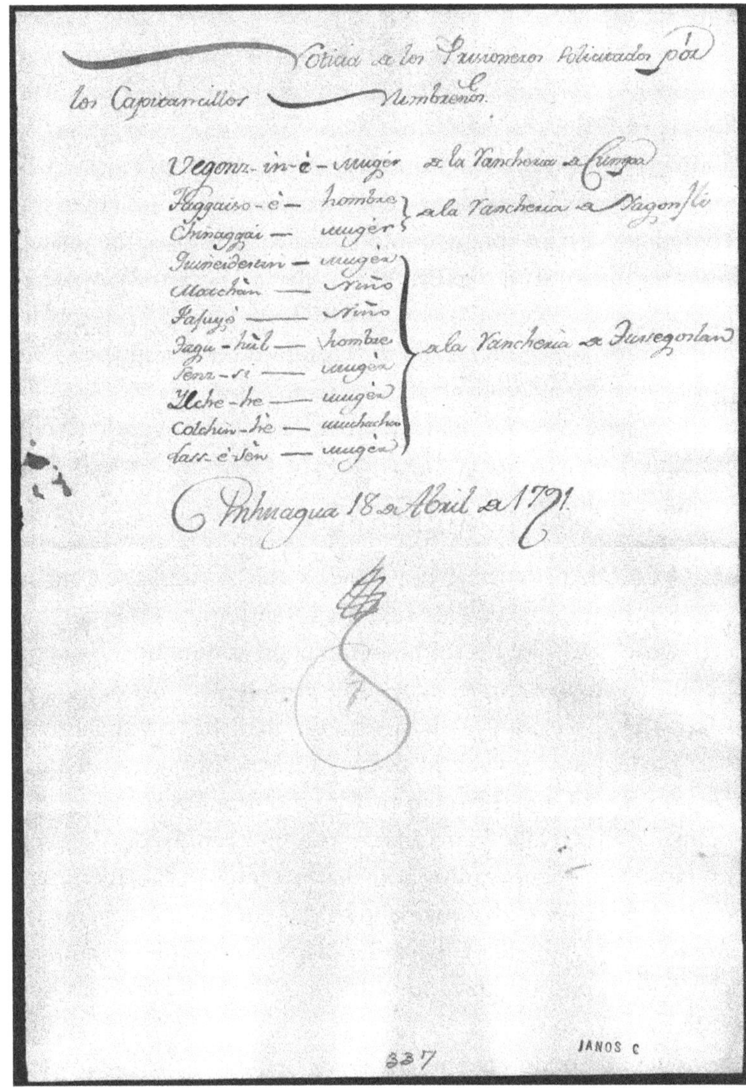

Noticia de los Prisioneros Solicitados por los Capitancillos nombrenos.

Vegonz-in-é - muger de la Rancheria de Compa
Yaggaiso-é - hombre } a la Rancheria de Yagonxli
Chinaggai - muger }
Quineidestin - muger
Macchan - Niño
Yasuyé - Niño
Yagu-hil - hombre } a la Rancheria de Tetsegoslan
Senz-si - muger
Ilche-he - muger
Colchin-he - muchacha
Lass-e'sen - muger

Chihuagua 18 de Abril de 1791.

337

JANOS C

List of prisoners requested by the Apache *capitancillos* Tetsegoslán, El Compá, and Yagonxli (Ojos Colorados), dated April 18, 1791. From the Records of San Felipe y Santiago de Janos, 1706–1858. Courtesy Benson Latin American Collection, General Libraries, University of Texas at Austin.

In addition to drawing up a list of the captives they wished to have returned, each capitancillo also chose which of their own people to send along to search out the captives and lead them back. They selected three men: Eustingé, representing El Compá; Padatssi, representing Tetsegoslán; and Quienastgnan, representing Ojos Colorados. But the dispatch of these men was problematic, as the Spanish would have to guarantee the protection, feeding, and transportation of three "peaceful" Apaches amid a larger group of "enemy" prisoners of war. The Apache capitancillos, however, clearly differentiated between their own people and the bulk of the prisoners, about whom they seemed unconcerned. At some point after their conference, they communicated their request to Lieutenant Colonel Cordero, who issued his approval.[6]

For his part, Cordero had more to occupy his time than just the particulars of sending the Apache delegation to search for their captive relatives in Mexico City. Throughout the fall and early winter of 1790, his soldiers had been conducting constant operations against the Apaches. The results had been, at least as far as the Spanish were concerned, fairly successful. Numerous Apache rancherías had been attacked throughout Nueva Vizcaya and the neighboring province of Sonora; many of the enemy had been killed and a large number captured. After several months of campaigning, Cordero's men had taken enough prisoners to make it worthwhile to ship them out from the northern frontier to Mexico City, to be dispersed as the viceroy saw fit. It was time to organize another shipment of prisoners into a collera.

As warfare between Spaniards and Apaches had escalated throughout the Interior Provinces in the previous four years, the number of colleras of captured prisoners increased to the point that their conveyance south into the heart of Mexico had become a routine military duty, usually detailed to junior officers. Still, this assignment required a degree of administrative and financial ability to handle the food, clothing, and transport expenses of the captives and their escorts, plus a degree of tact and diplomacy to navigate through an array of civil populations. In addition, the possibility of attempted escapes by the prisoners was all too real. In numerous instances, Apache prisoners of war had contrived to break away from their guards and regain their freedom. Some had even been able to return to their homelands and rejoin their families, filled with even more hatred for the Spaniards and seeking retribution. To allow prisoners to escape would be a damning indictment of the abilities of the commander of the escort and could result in a court martial. Still, the potential rewards for the successful delivery of a collera to the viceregal capital outweighed the dangers of failure. For ambitious young officers, the chance of an independent command offered the promise of promotion and advancement, and among the presidios and garrisons of the northern frontier there was an abundance of such officers. It now only remained to choose one.

CHAPTER 7

An Officer Disposed for Commissions

At age twenty-four, Miguel Díaz de Luna sensed that his military career was finally moving ahead. Born in the city of Tehuacán, southeast of Mexico City, Díaz de Luna belonged to a family of such prominence that he could claim "noble" status and be addressed by the honorific "don." On July 16, 1781, when he was fifteen, he was enrolled as an officer cadet in the Regiment of the Dragoons of Spain, one of the premier units in the army of the viceroyalty. Once joined, however, he found himself in a closed society where promotion depended less on talent than on two factors beyond his control: seniority and patronage. The Dragoons of Spain had only a set number of officer positions. The twelve companies of the regiment each had a captain, two lieutenants, and either an alférez or a *portaguión*, the first company being senior and the twelfth company being the most junior. Vacancies due to death, transfer, or promotion within the regiment usually resulted in a reshuffling, with the next most senior man in grade advancing into the vacant slot. But wealth and nepotism might enable an outsider to purchase a commission or have his powerful relatives pull strings to move their favorite ahead of those with more seniority.

After vainly waiting more than five years for a commission in the regiment, Don Miguel Díaz de Luna decided to take matters into his own hands. He managed to secure a transfer to the northern frontier, becoming an officer cadet in the Third Flying Company of Nueva Vizcaya. There was a greater probability of advancement on the frontier, as the individual talents of an officer in a wartime theater would be more quickly recognized and utilized than in a peaceful garrison unit. Vacancies also occurred more frequently—especially among the junior officers—due to their deaths at the hands of the Apaches.

Díaz de Luna labored for two years to prove his mettle and gain the confidence of his superiors. In that time, he participated in six actions against the Apaches and killed two warriors and captured another with his own hands. His superiors pronounced him as having sufficient valor, having bold application, being of regular capacity, and demonstrating overall good conduct. This record proved good enough for Díaz de Luna to finally gain a regular commission, and on October 18, 1788, he received a promotion to first alférez of the Presidial Company of Janos, skipping ahead of the normal appointment, the most junior grade of second alférez. Since then, Don Miguel Díaz de Luna had served so steadily that his commanders simply noted on his service record, *bueno para la guerra*—"good for war."[1]

Among his numerous duties, the young officer was entrusted with the transport of captured Apache prisoners of war from the frontier to the city of Chihuahua, the headquarters of the commandant general of the Interior Provinces. Arriving prisoners were held either in the public jail, in one of a number of public workhouses, or less often, at the homes of private individuals. As far as Díaz de Luna was concerned, the subsequent fate of these prisoners was beyond his control, and he probably gave them little thought once he delivered them to the city.

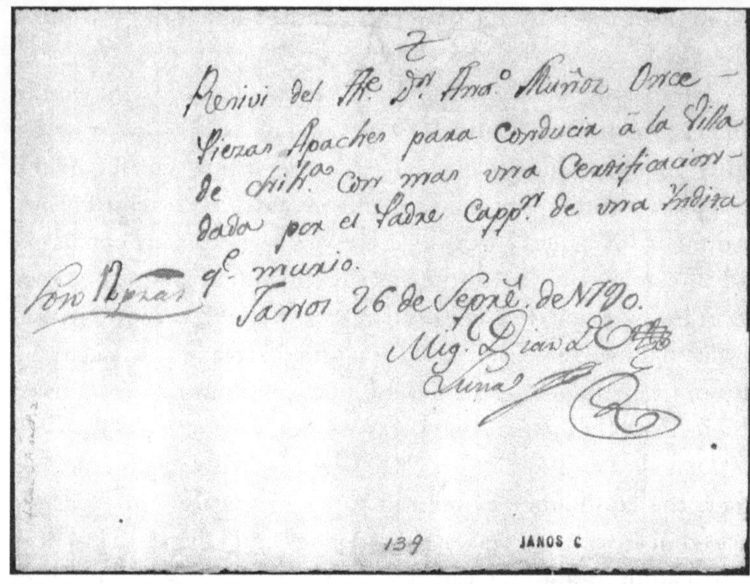

Recivi del Th.e D.n Ant.o Muñoz Once Piezas Apaches para conducir á la Villa de chih.a con mas una Certificacion dada por el Padre Capp.n de una Ynd.a q.e murio.

Son 11 piezas

Janos 26 de Sept.e de 1790.

Mig. Diaz de Luna

139 JANOS C

Receipt for 11 Apache "*piezas*" destined for deportation, signed by Alférez Miguel Díaz de Luna, dated September 26, 1790. Five months later, the young officer would set out in command of a *collera* of 74 more prisoners bound for Mexico City. From the Records of San Felipe y Santiago de Janos, 1706–1858. Courtesy Benson Latin American Collection, General Libraries, University of Texas at Austin.

But that suddenly changed in early November of 1790, when he was informed that he had received a new and more difficult commission—to escort a large number of prisoners all the way from Chihuahua to Mexico City, a journey of almost a thousand miles that would take more than two months. For Díaz de Luna, this duty showed that his superior, Lieutenant Colonel Antonio Cordero, commander of the First Division of Nueva Vizcaya and titular captain of Janos, had enough confidence in him to entrust him with an independent command. Cordero had recently commented that the young officer "had a disposition for commissions," and he was obviously determined to give him a chance to prove it. Cordero had much in common with Díaz de Luna; he, too, had been a young officer in the Regiment of the Dragoons of Spain who had advanced his career by serving on the northern frontier. Whether or not Cordero was influenced by these similarities, he had faith in Díaz de Luna's ability to escort the prisoners to Mexico City. For Díaz de Luna, this opportunity was also a chance to return to his home and perhaps see his family again. But as the young officer undoubtedly knew, for the Apache prisoners he was taking south, the opposite was true — they would most likely never see their homeland and families again.

Sometime during the early winter, numerous Apache prisoners were congregated in Chihuahua City and placed under guard. In December of 1790, Lieutenant Colonel Cordero received word that Viceroy Revillagigedo had been informed of the Spanish military operations of the previous year and that a large group of prisoners was being sent to the capital city for his disposition. By January, Cordero noted that the planning for the expedition was nearly finished. When he received word on February 4 that another group of Apaches had been captured in Sonora, Cordero ordered that their delivery to Chihuahua be hastened so that they, too, could be included with those prisoners already scheduled for deportation.[2]

By February 15, 1791, Cordero was satisfied that all preparations were complete for sending out the collera of Apaches. To serve alongside the young alférez, Cordero selected José Ramírez, the first sergeant of Janos, along with five other veteran soldiers. Another twenty soldiers would be detailed from Janos's sister presidio of San Buenaventura. At some point, the prisoners were given a final inspection, and from this Cordero prepared a formal chart detailing the number contained in the collera: seven adult males, thirty-four women, twenty-five boys, and eight girls, for a total of seventy-four. He then had Alférez Don Miguel Díaz de Luna present himself at headquarters, where Cordero officially handed the young officer his orders. These began by confirming several specifics that the alférez already knew, namely that he would command a force of twenty-six soldiers including Sergeant Ramírez and five troopers from Janos. Twenty of the men were to have the sole responsibility of guarding the prisoners, while Sergeant Ramírez and the troops from Janos were also charged with the safe delivery of reports from the Interior Provinces to the viceroy. The soldiers were also to be accompanied by the three emissaries sent by Tetsegoslán and the other leaders of the Apaches de paz. Cordero enjoined Díaz de Luna to keep careful and formal records of all the expenses he incurred, whether relating to the prisoners or to the escort. He also reminded the alférez that the officers of the Royal Treasury in Chihuahua had issued instructions on the correct method for recording expenses.

Regarding the Apache prisoners, Cordero's orders laid out in specific detail how they were to be treated. As commander of the collera, Díaz de Luna would first and foremost be responsible for the security of the prisoners. If the collera bivouacked in an unpopulated area, the prisoners were to be closely guarded and surrounded by sentinels, who, if need be, were authorized to use "some corporal necessity," meaning that the Apaches could be physically bound, manacled, or shackled. If the prisoners were lodged in populated areas, they were to be housed "in well-lit places with locked doors and sentinels outside, and a guard is to be there as well to quiet any disturbance." If the soldiers of the escort were to find themselves "attacked by a great number of enemies trying to free the prisoners," Díaz de Luna's instructions were crystal clear: "You are ordered to kill all the big ones attempting [this], sparing (if possible) all the medium and small ones." Reiterating this point, the orders stressed that the alférez was "to make a proper defense" and allow none to flee. In other words, he was authorized to kill his prisoners rather than allow them to escape.

Still, Díaz de Luna was also charged with ensuring the well-being of the Apache prisoners; he was instructed to assist them with anything they might require, but to do so economically. He was to "give them blankets if they do not have them to cover their nakedness" and to provide whatever else they might need to endure any inclement weather. If any prisoners should become too ill to continue the journey, they were to be left at the nearest town or hacienda, where they were to be properly cared for, with word sent to the commandant general as well as to any nearby civil authorities, or, if in a rural area, they were to be taken to the nearest owner or overseer of any haciendas. Should any of the prisoners fall ill and die, Díaz de Luna was to record their deaths on the march, noting the day, place, and any burial certificates or other documents he might receive.

Cordero reminded the alférez to make sure his paperwork was in order when the expedition reached the outskirts of Mexico City. He was to present to the viceroy his diary of the journey as well as a detailed register of his expenses to prove that he had not accrued any needless costs and did not make any "inferred extortion on the vassals of His Majesty." A copy of these reports was to be made for the commandant general in Chihuahua as well. Finally, when the collera arrived in Mexico City, Díaz de Luna was to alert the sergeant major of the regiment garrisoning the city to inform him that the prisoners were coming and to arrange for their transfer to the soldiers of the city.

After dismissing Díaz de Luna with his orders, Lieutenant Colonel Cordero penned a series of reports to Viceroy Revillagigedo. In addition to repeating the particulars he had given to the alférez, Cordero sent further details to the viceroy regarding the three Apaches de paz who were accompanying the collera. Cordero called the viceroy's attention to the three Apache men, Eustingé, Padatssi, and Quienastgnan, who were from the rancherías of capitancillos El Compá, Tetsegoslán, and Ojos Colorados, respectively, and who had all provided good service to the

Spanish. "These individuals," Cordero noted, "and all their rancherías have been accredited for a long time in these parts with great fidelity to our alliance. They have accompanied our expeditions with vigor, carrying out the most gallant feats in the combats that have been made against their own compatriots."

In return for this good service, the three Apaches were to seek the return of eleven of their kinsmen, whom Cordero listed in a separate attachment. Cordero noted that these "three emissaries will present [themselves] to Your Excellency and entreat your mercy" for the return of the eleven "made prisoners by our arms and [recently] conducted to the Capital in the cuerdas under the command of the alféreces Don Joseph María del Rivero and Don Francisco Xavier de Enderica." Regardless if the Apache emissaries found the friends and relatives they were seeking, or if they discovered that they had died due to illness, or even if they could not find them at all, Cordero felt that the experiment would be worthwhile, as "they will have the satisfaction to know the Great Captain who commands all the Spaniards on this continent, and carry to their own [people] the news of the good treatment they experienced on their journey."[3]

On February 16, Alférez Miguel Díaz de Luna began completing the final dispositions for his command before heading south to Mexico City. At the Royal Treasury House along the main plaza of Chihuahua, he had an audience with Don Domingo de Bergaña, the ranking treasury official. After inspecting the list of Apaches in the collera, Bergaña filled out a report for Díaz de Luna indicating that each of the prisoners would be assigned a daily stipend of 1½ reales for seventy days, in the amount of 971 pesos 2 reales. In addition, another 2 reales per day would be expended to cover the cost of contracting for fifty-five mules for the same period, as well as the panniers and crates necessary to carry the baggage for the prisoners. All together, Bergaña gave Alférez Díaz de Luna funds in the amount of 1,933 pesos 6 reales that he calculated should be adequate for the total expenses of the collera. Finally, Bergaña gave the alférez 1,000 pesos for his expenses and those of the twenty-six soldiers of the escort for the round-trip journey from Chihuahua to Mexico City, which was estimated to take no longer than five months.

With his accounts confirmed, Díaz de Luna next turned to gathering the soldiers of the escort. From his own company of Janos, the young officer drew Sergeant José Ramírez and five soldiers. Lieutenant Colonel Cordero had also ordered that an interpreter, Nepomuceno Téllez, be included, undoubtedly to assist with the three Apaches de paz. Cordero also described the soldiers to be chosen: "that they not have debts on their accounts, [be] young men of good disposition and conduct, and be completely equipped." The remaining twenty soldiers were to be selected from the Second Flying Company and from the Presidio of San Buenaventura and, presumably, were to be of similar quality.[4]

Each of the twenty-six soldiers would have drawn clothing, arms, and equipment enough to last for five months from their own company stores. Although they could look forward to purchasing rations at various towns along their route, they nevertheless would have stocked up on enough food to cover them in case of emergencies. All of these goods would then have been loaded onto several pack mules held in common by the soldiers of each presidial company, who would be responsible for the animals. Then the soldiers, as ordered, selected "four strong horses" from the seven that each man was required by regulations to own. These horses were regarded as the private property of the soldiers, and if an animal was injured or killed, each man would have to pay for any replacement mounts out of his own pocket.

Having overseen the disposition of the soldiers of his command, Díaz de Luna would then have had to meet with the *arrieros*, the mule drivers who were providing the transport for the collera of Apaches. Arrangements had been made to contract one string of twenty-six mules from José Santos de Analla and another string of twenty-seven from Mariano Analla for the journey to Mexico City. The seventy-four Apaches in the collera were to be mounted two-by-two on forty-two of the mules, with the remaining animals detailed to carry the goods and supplies necessary for the maintenance of the prisoners. Although it is not certain, it would appear likely that José and Mariano Analla were relatives and that their operation was a family business.

After securing the services of the arrieros, the alférez rendezvoused with the three emissaries being sent by Tetsegoslán and the other leaders of the Apaches de paz. However, the three Apaches may have created an unforeseen problem for the young Spanish officer, as it does not appear that any of his superiors had specifically detailed how their daily expenses were to be covered. Perhaps they felt that the amount already given to Díaz de Luna would provide enough surplus funds to meet the needs of the three additional members of the party. In any case, the issue seems to have been ignored for the time being.

All preparations made, Alférez Miguel Díaz de Luna set out on Thursday, February 17, 1791, on his first independent command. With the troopers of his escort and the large herd of mules driven by the arrieros, he headed to the obraje, the public workhouse of Chihuahua, to pick up the collera of Apache prisoners. Almost immediately, things began to go wrong. Father Juan Ysidro Campos met Díaz de Luna and informed him that two young Apache girls, both about seven years old, had died that very day. Father Campos was relieved to report that both had received baptism before they expired and had been given the names María Josepha and María Juaquina. As Christians, they were entitled to burial in consecrated ground, and Father Campos had had both children interred in the cemetery of the Chapel of Our Lady of Guadalupe.

Losing two of his charges before he had even left the environs of Chihuahua does not appear to have delayed Díaz de Luna. He mounted the seventy-two Apaches of the collera on the rented mules and ordered the whole cavalcade of approximately one hundred men, women, and children and over 150 horses and mules south along the Camino Real bound for Mexico City. The young officer undoubtedly viewed the expedition as another step toward advancing his career. For the soldiers of the escort, the journey promised an opportunity to visit several large cities, including the cosmopolitan and opulent capital of the viceroyalty; at the very least it gave them the opportunity to break the tedium of their routine duties. For the three Apaches de paz, there was the hope of finding and being reunited with lost relatives and friends. But for the prisoners of the collera there can only have been a dark descent into the unknown, surrounded by enemies.[5]

CHAPTER 8

Bodily and Spiritual Necessities

Alférez Díaz de Luna was ordered to keep a diary during the journey of the collera under his command, but that document is not found among the other records of the expedition. What does remain is a series of some seventy-one receipts for the purchase of supplies needed by the expedition. All contain the date and location where the expense was incurred, along with a list of the goods provided. These receipts allow us to trace the day-to-day movements of the collera and to gain some insight into the conditions the travelers encountered. It is evident that the Spanish paid attention to the physical needs of the Apache prisoners as well as showing what appears to be a genuine concern for the souls of those who sickened and died. Unfortunately, death occurred all too often along the way.

Setting out from Chihuahua, the collera and its escort headed southwest, skirting the mountains south of the city. As it would for the rest of the journey, the collera moved in relatively easy marches that would average fifteen to twenty miles a day. On February 18, 1791, probably in the late afternoon, the alférez ordered a halt. The party would have left any readily available water behind as they moved away from the Río Chuviscar, but whether this was a dry camp is unknown. The Apache prisoners would have been placed in the center of the encampment, with the soldiers of the escort surrounding them. The horses and mules would have been pastured outside this circle, with the arrieros and a few soldiers detached to guard the herd. Somewhere along the march, Díaz de Luna had purchased an ox and a quantity of candles. The ox was slaughtered and the portions distributed among the prisoners and the soldiers of the escort for their daily rations. As the evening came on, the darkness would have been broken by the cooking fires of the party, along with the candles that were shared out among the sentries guarding the prisoners.

The collera followed the same routine for two more days as they moved south along the Río Santa Isabel, buying their meat on the hoof and a quantity of candles. By February 21, they reached the small town of Babonayagua, a mission community of Tarahumara Indians with about 150 souls. Here the expedition suffered another casualty. An Apache girl, "Michaelia, about fifteen years old, died at Babonayagua." The cause of the young woman's death is not noted, but sickness is most likely. Although she was listed as a Christian who had apparently been baptized on her deathbed, Alférez Díaz de Luna ordered her ears to be sliced from her head before burial as proof of her demise. The soldiers had not removed the ears of the two younger Indian girls who had succumbed as the expedition set out, so it is unclear why the ears of Michaelia were taken. Perhaps there was no suitable person of authority in the area to file a written certification that would suit Díaz de Luna's needs. Regardless, the body of the young Apache girl was quickly buried, probably in the cemetery of the mission church of Santiago.

The next day, the collera again moved south and reached the Río San Pedro, where another prisoner was lost. At this place, the alférez located a literate citizen, upon whom he laid the charge of caring for a small Apache boy who had fallen ill. To ensure just payment for this service, the officer gave Juan Mateo Solís a certificate declaring "that he was left *un Indito chiquito* about four years old who fell gravely ill, and it was impossible for him to continue the march, and whether he lives or dies, Lieutenant Colonel Don Antonio Cordero is to be informed."

The loss of two prisoners to sickness in such quick succession seems to have made an impression on Díaz de Luna, and after another day's travel he attempted to alleviate the situation. By February 24, the collera had reached Pilar de Conchos. Until 1751, this town had contained a presidio and resident garrison, but in that year the presidial company had been suppressed. Nevertheless, a small civilian community remained, and by 1787, the military had returned when the town began to serve as the headquarters for the Third Flying Company, in which Díaz de Luna had served for several years. Assured of support from this detachment, he reported to the company commander and submitted his request for aid.

Captain Manuel Vidal de Lorca's Third Flying Company was one of the larger military units on the northern frontier, with a full complement of 154 men. Combined with the surrounding civilian population, the town was fairly large by frontier standards and had what must have seemed to the Apaches like an abundance of goods. The prisoners were in need of supplies, especially clothing, and Alférez Díaz de Luna approached Captain Vidal de Lorca for help. Over the next five days, Díaz de Luna was able to purchase an amount of raw wool as well as some yards of Querétaro wool cloth, some lighter material for lining, and several yards of cloth "for shirts and skirts." In addition, he acquired a large number of "light sombreros" as well as some silk, ribbon lace, and buttons. The majority of these items were obviously for the Apache prisoners, and it seems that by the time the collera set out again, many, if not all of them, had been given new clothes for the journey.[1]

After five days of refitting and rest, the collera set out again on March 1, heading southwest toward the Río Parral. By the following day, the expedition had reached the river crossing and made camp at the Hacienda de San Gregorio. But death still stalked the prisoners, despite the recent recuperation they had enjoyed at Pilar de Conchos. That night another young Apache girl, "María, a little more than twelve years old, died at the Hacienda de San Gregorio." As had happened earlier, María was baptized a Christian on her deathbed, and as had also happened before, her ears were sliced from her head before she was buried in the chapel of the hacienda.

The next morning, the expedition rode into the Valle de San Bartolomé, one of the oldest Spanish settlements in the Kingdom of Nueva Vizcaya, having been founded in the 1560s. At the time the collera arrived, Valle de San Bartolomé was a prosperous agricultural center with several thousand people living in its vicinity. The town had once contained a presidio, but after the garrison was moved in 1751, the population was still large enough to support a respectable militia establishment of its own. It was with the local military officials that Alférez Díaz de Luna now sought an audience. On March 3, he met with Don Manuel Azque de Armendáriz, a captain in the Provincial Dragoons of San Carlos who also served as the subdelegate of the Royal Junta de Guerra for the Valle de San Bartolomé. Explaining the recent losses suffered by the collera, Díaz de Luna requested verification of the death of the two Apache girls. The captain prepared a terse report that read, "I certify that the Alférez commanding the chain gang of Apaches, Don Miguel Díaz de Luna, presented to me this day four fresh ears—*quatro orejas frescas*—from two Indian girls who died of sickness and who were already Christian."

Díaz de Luna, leaving the severed ears with the captain and with his certification in hand, set out to purchase more supplies for the prisoners of war to help guard them against the elements. Valle de San Bartolomé was of sufficient economic stature to contain a variety of well-stocked merchants, and relatively quickly, Díaz de Luna located and purchased fifty wool blankets that were distributed to the remaining sixty-nine Apache prisoners. More fresh beef was doled out for rations and the expedition had another extended rest period, remaining in the town for a total of three days.[2]

By March 5, the collera and escort were ready to set out again, heading toward the Río Florido. They camped that night in an uninhabited location, but by the following evening, they managed to locate a ranch known as the Hacienda de la Estancia. The Spanish soldiers purchased a head of cattle for their dinner and that of the collera, as they had almost every night of the journey. This time they availed themselves of the hacienda's produce and supplemented their meal by buying half a *fanega*, almost fifty pounds, of corn. The next morning, the party set out again, and two more days of travel saw them make camp at another hacienda, that of San Francisco Xavier del Río Florido. After crossing the river, they came within sight of Cerro Gordo, the "Fat Hill," which lent its name to a substantial town nearby.

Cerro Gordo, like many of the major towns along the party's route, had once housed a presidio, but in 1773, the garrison had been moved north. In 1791, the town had a population of about a thousand, mostly dependent on ranching and agriculture, and several haciendas lay within a short distance of the community. It was at one of these that another Apache prisoner reached the point of death. Sometime on March 9, Alférez Díaz de Luna brought "*una Indita vieja,*" an old Indian woman, to the Hacienda de Xaramillo. The local priest, who ministered to the town as well as the surrounding haciendas, came to baptize the woman, and after receiving the sacrament, she died and was buried that same day in the chapel of the hacienda. Díaz de Luna then contacted José María Hernández y Pareda, either the owner or overseer of the hacienda, and the latter drew up a certificate verifying the woman's death and burial. Apparently this was sufficient, as there is no record that the dead woman's ears were removed before she was buried.

Despite pushing on soon after, it appears that the collera had been infected with some sort of sickness, which may have been what killed the old Apache woman. Four days after her death, the party had reached another hacienda called Sapien. There, Díaz de Luna made an extraordinary purchase, paying more than ten pesos to one Dionisio Escalante "for forty lights for six sick Apaches." Just how the lights were used to help treat the ill patients is not clear, but if they were tapers or other candles, they may have been used in some sort of curing ceremony either by the Apaches themselves or by some local folk healers. Given the Apaches' views on death, it is also possible that the sick persons felt they had become spiritually infected and that their illness was the result of what they believed to be contamination from the dead woman. However, as the same phenomenon did not occur when other members of the collera died, it may be that the sickness was genuinely physical.[3]

Whether the sick Apaches had recovered sufficiently or not, the next day the expedition resumed its southward march, skirting the edge of the thinly populated and barren area known as the Bolsón de Mapimí. Realizing that they were heading into harsh terrain, Díaz de Luna had taken the precaution of buying an extra fanega of maize for rations before leaving Sapien, noting in his receipt books that "we will sleep in an unpopulated area." Another day brought them relief as they reached the Río Nazas; they sheltered at the Hacienda del Señor San Antonio del Río de Nazas on March 15. The next day, they reached an unnamed hacienda, where for unknown reasons it appears the party remained for an extended period of time, as there are no records of any purchases until they reached the mining town of Real de Cuencamé on March 20. Another day brought them to the hacienda of Atotonilco, and soon thereafter, the expedition crossed from Nueva Vizcaya into the Kingdom of Nueva Galicia. From this point, they began to enter into more densely populated areas with many more Hispanicized communities. The party camped at a series of haciendas in rapid succession as they headed toward the large city of Fresnillo, arriving there on March 28.

At this point, there seem to have been some problems with transportation. According to his receipt book, upon entering Fresnillo, Alférez Díaz de Luna bought six mules for the Apaches de paz who accompanied the expedition. Why this purchase occurred here is unknown. It seems unlikely that the three Apache men had been making the journey on foot this whole time. Perhaps they had suffered some accident to their own animals, which might have run off, been killed, become lame and unusable, or even been stolen. Regardless, the three men now turned to the Spanish escort for relief and despite this unforeseen circumstance were soon mounted again.

While the Apaches de paz were being assisted with their mule problem, a far graver situation had developed for one of the woman prisoners, who that same day gave birth to a very sick child. Fortunately, at least for the infant, Fresnillo was a large enough city to have some doctors available to treat the newborn. Alférez Díaz de Luna sought help from the local magistrates and made arrangements for the infant to receive medical care. As always, he needed to verify the arrangements he made, and Don Manuel Joaquín de Bonechea, royal scribe and notary public for the Cabildo of Fresnillo, drew up the paperwork. Bonechea noted that "there entered a collera of Apache Indians from the Interior Provinces being conducted to the capital of Mexico by Alférez Don Miguel Díaz de Luna, and when they arrived and were going through this Villa, there came a newborn Apache gravely ill and in danger of death, for which reason and as a precaution, that if continuing on the journey he might die during it, he was left in this referred-to Villa in order to receive the medical treatment considered necessary." Bonechea closed the certification by noting he had verbal orders to proceed in this matter from the Licenciado Don Miguel Tovar y Cuenca, *teniente de justicia mayor* (lieutenant of the chief justice) of the city.

That Díaz de Luna arranged for medical treatment for the sick newborn indicates that there was some hope that the infant would survive. There is no indication that the Spanish sought to baptize the child, the normal practice with prisoners who died along the march. Nevertheless, if the infant survived, he was never going to see his mother again, as after a few days' rest, she and the rest of the Apache prisoners in the collera continued their journey toward exile.[4]

By April 1, the expedition reached the large and affluent city of Zacatecas. At one time, the city had been the heart of one of the most prolific and wealthy silver strikes in the world, and although output had fluctuated from the end of the seventeenth century, it was still a center for silver mining and production and boasted a population of over ten thousand inhabitants, numerous churches, and even an impressive aqueduct. But the architectural splendors of Zacatecas were soon forgotten amid the realization that yet another young Apache prisoner was too ill to continue. As he had done three days earlier in Fresnillo, Díaz de Luna sought out the municipal authorities with whom to leave the sick boy. That same day, Don Juan José de Escobar, scribe of the royal treasury for the city, prepared a certificate noting "that the Officer Don Miguel Díaz de Luna, in whose charge a cuerda of prisoners is going to the Court of Mexico, has left in this Capital an Indian boy who looks to be about seven or eight years old, sick, and seemingly impossible for him to be moved." The scribe then had three citizens of Zacatecas sign and witness the document before he turned it over to Díaz de Luna. The ultimate fate of the Apache boy is unknown, but if he survived, he most likely was placed as a domestic servant, probably in a private residence somewhere in the city.

The next day, the collera and escort moved out again on their journey. At this point they headed south on the Camino de la Plata, the Silver Road, which conveyed the riches from the mines all the way to Mexico City. The route would now be punctuated not only with numerous haciendas but also with regular lodging places for travelers, called *mesones*, common between the larger cities. After leaving Zacatecas, the collera camped in quick succession at the Mesón de Tlacotes, the Hacienda de San Pedro, and the Hacienda del Pavellón before reining up at the large city of Aguascalientes. This city was substantial, with several thousand people living there, but in recent years it had suffered a devastating plague and subsequent famine that had killed over half the population. Not tarrying, Díaz de Luna had the party press on. On April 7, they reached another large villa, that of Santa María de los Lagos, commonly known as Lagos. The surrounding area was prime agricultural and pastoral land, filled with numerous haciendas and ranchos. Díaz de Luna allowed the collera one day's rest in the villa and then pushed on.[5]

Within a short time of leaving Lagos, the group passed from Nueva Galicia and entered the Kingdom of New Spain proper. The areas they traversed were now densely populated and the roads well maintained and heavily traveled. On April 10, they reached the Villa de León, a large urban center that reportedly contained three thousand houses and ten churches. Here Díaz de Luna took advantage of the local production centers to refit his command. Many of the saddles and horse gear of the soldiers of the escort were becoming worn. León offered a good opportunity to buy these items directly. Dipping into the money he had been given for the maintenance of his soldiers, the alférez purchased 170 pesos' worth of saddlery and other tack from local vendors.

After two days of refitting in León, the party continued onward. The routine of the collera now began to see them stopping almost exclusively in larger cities established by the Spaniards in the sixteenth century. Here in the heartland of New Spain, the Apaches would have been a novelty to the numerous residents. The prisoners and their escort moved down the major road toward the capital, passing in quick succession through the cities of Silao, Irapuato, Salamanca, Celaya, Querétaro, and San Juan del Río, reaching the latter on April 20.

The rapid pace over good roads did not shield the prisoners from the pale horse of death that had plagued the expedition since it began. This time, one of the seven adult Apache men became gravely ill. When it became clear that he would not survive, the Spanish sought to baptize him, but either he expired before a priest could be found to perform the ceremony, or the man refused to undergo the ritual. When Díaz de Luna obtained a certificate from Don Pedro Martínez de Salazar y Pacheco, the justicia of San Juan del Río, concerning the Apache man's death, the justicia noted the failure to baptize the prisoner, writing, "there died in this Pueblo an Apache Indian prisoner . . . who died a pagan on the 20th of the current month." Where the man's body was interred is not noted in the documents of the expedition, but he probably was not buried in the consecrated ground of a church cemetery, although he may have been placed nearby. The death of the Apache man and the disposition of his body seem to have taken some time and may have served to give the party an excuse to slow their pace, as they remained in San Juan del Río for three days. The city also provided a change in fare, as Díaz de Luna did not purchase meat on the hoof to eat, instead buying almost a hundred pounds of dried meat and over thirty pounds of maize, enough to feed all his charges for two days.

Departing from San Juan del Río, the expedition was entering the final phase of its journey. Climbing in elevation, they now passed through an area somewhat thinly settled, and Díaz de Luna had his men and the collera stay at two haciendas along the main road. By April 26, they had reached the town of Tepexis, a mainly Indian community located in a small valley surrounded by mountainous terrain. Soon, however, the mountains opened up into the Valley of Mexico, and they were within reach of the capital. The next day, they went as far as the town of Quatitlán, and two more days brought them to the outskirts of the City of Mexico. All told, the collera and escort had traveled almost one thousand miles in a journey that had lasted seventy-two days. During the sojourn, the original seventy-four Apache prisoners had seen six of their people die: four young girls, one elderly woman, and one adult man. In addition, two little boys and one newborn infant had been left behind, all too sick to finish the journey. Their total losses were slightly over 12 percent. Whether such a casualty rate was considered acceptable to the Spanish authorities is not known. However, for the remaining Apache prisoners, this journey's end represented only the first part, and probably not the worst, of their exile into oblivion.[6]

CHAPTER 9

Reckonings, Rescue, and Return

The sheer size of Mexico City must have made an overpowering impression on the members of the collera and their escort. It was among the largest in the world, with a population of approximately 120,000 people—a huge conglomeration of Indians, mestizos, and other mixed races ruled over by a small but powerful white elite. The city was praised several years later by the renowned German traveler Alexander von Humboldt, who wrote, "Mexico must be counted, without any doubt, among the most beautiful cities the Europeans have built in both hemispheres. . . . There scarcely exists a city of extent which can be compared with the capital of New Spain, for the uniform level of the ground it occupies, for the regularity and wideness of its streets and for the grandeur of its public plazas."[1]

As the capital of the richest colony in the Spanish empire, the city was filled with government buildings, churches, convents, monasteries, and private residences replete with architectural marvels. Among these wonders also sprawled the houses and huts of thousands of poor laborers, many organized into barrios,

City of Mexico from the Convent of San Cosme. N. Currier lithograph, 1847. Courtesy Library of Congress.

or neighborhoods, for the descendents of the Aztecs and other indigenous peoples who had occupied the site before the Spanish came.

The only member of the party who had seen Mexico City before, aside from some of the arrieros, was probably Alférez Miguel Díaz de Luna, who had grown up in the city of Tehuacán to the southeast, and who had served with the Regiment of the Dragoons of Spain that routinely garrisoned the capital. Díaz de Luna's familiarity with Mexico City served him well as he now dealt with several tasks simultaneously: turning over the Apache prisoners in the collera to the proper authorities, delivering to the viceroy the official report of his journey, turning in his receipts and accounts to the royal treasury, and finally, seeing to the disposition of the three Apaches de paz as they searched for their missing compatriots.

Passing along the west side of the capital through the San Cosme gate and parallel to the Santa Fe Aqueduct, Díaz de Luna brought his command to the headquarters of the Acordada, one of the civil authorities that handled criminal cases across a large area of New Spain. The Acordada operated a series of buildings, including offices, a hospital, and a large kitchen, but the main facility was a prison where numerous accused were confined while awaiting trial, and where convicted criminals languished, awaiting the final disposition of their sentence. The prison of the Acordada was infamous for its severe justice, and a grim warning was carved above the entrance: "Passerby, be wary of this place and see that you avoid entering, since once its hard doors close, only for your execution will they open." It was to the Acordada that the members of the collera were to be handed over.

Legal authority over the collera of Apaches, as prisoners of war, rested with the military. Before entering the city, Díaz de Luna had contacted Don Thomas Rodríguez de Biedma, lieutenant colonel of the Royal Armies and sergeant major of the Infantry Regiment of Mexico, the unit garrisoning the capital. The collera of Apaches was officially transferred to the custody of the garrison troops on April 29, 1791, and whether he oversaw the exchange of the prisoners himself or delegated this task to a subordinate, Sergeant Major Rodríguez de Biedma was now responsible for them.

At this point, the records of the expedition grow silent concerning the members of the collera, but from the disposition of other groups of prisoners, we can sketch a rough outline of what happened to them. All of the Apaches would have entered the Acordada, where they would have been counted and registered and then segregated from one another by age and sex. Any that were gravely ill would have been sent to the hospital, but the others would have been sent to prison cells. The six surviving adult men would have been placed together in one area of the prison along with any of the twenty-three boys who were old enough not to need the care of their mothers. The cells of the Acordada were reputedly clean and well maintained, but a prison, however sanitary, was still a prison. Whether or not the members of the collera were placed with other prisoners held in the Acordada is not clear, although it would have been unusual if the place did not contain at least some other *presidarios,* as the inmates were called. The thirty-two remaining women and four girls would have been housed together as well, but they may have been transferred to another facility, the Casa de Recogidas de Santa María Magdalena, the House for Fallen Women. This was a jail for women prisoners, mostly prostitutes, vagabonds, and petty thieves.[2]

The Apaches would endure new and terrible hardships in the days and weeks to come. Younger boys and girls capable of being indoctrinated may have been sent to the homes of private citizens, who, in exchange for the children, would commit to educating and Christianizing them. Older boys and girls, along with some of the women, may also have been employed as domestic servants, while others may have been sent to workhouses, which in Mexico City usually meant being sent to a textile sweatshop to do piecework. However, for the adult men, and probably for many of the women as well, their imprisonment in the Acordada or the Casa de Recogidas was only a temporary situation. At some point, they would have been sentenced, usually for a period of ten years, along with the majority of the other presidarios, to be sent to work on the fortifications that protected the viceroyalty. They then would have been placed in another collera, and escorted by soldiers from the garrison, forced to make another grueling journey to the port city of Veracruz.

Veracruz was the strategic center through which passed virtually all of the exports and imports from New Spain. To safeguard the port, the Spanish had erected a series of massive walls around the city, buttressed by the imposing fortress of San Juan de Ulúa, located on an island just offshore. These fortifications required constant upkeep, and prisoners from all over New Spain, and sometimes even from other Spanish colonies or Spain itself, would be sentenced to hard labor at Veracruz. The city was notorious as a breeding ground for disease, including the dreaded *vómito negro*, or yellow fever, and unacclimated newcomers died in staggering numbers. So many prisoners died soon after reaching Veracruz that the city was constantly bringing in new colleras of presidarios, but often the newcomers died more quickly than they could be replaced. If any of the Apache prisoners of war were sentenced to serve at Veracruz, their chances for survival were poor indeed.

However, it is likely that many, if not most, Apaches who were sent into exile did not remain at Veracruz but were sent off on a third and final journey to Havana, Cuba. After a sea voyage of some weeks, they would have been put to work maintaining the series of forts that guarded Havana's harbor. Although Havana was not as susceptible to disease as Veracruz, the tropical climate, poor nourishment, and backbreaking labor led to a relatively high mortality rate there as well. For the Apache prisoners of war, arrival in Cuba almost certainly meant a long, lingering death. Even if by some miracle they lived to serve out their sentence, they would never be allowed to return to their homelands.[3]

The emissaries sent by Tetsegoslán and the other leaders of the Apaches de paz, the warriors Eustingé, Padatssi, and Quienastgnan, most likely witnessed the transfer of the members of the collera to the prison of the Acordada. They now set about to rescue from this living death their kin who had been deported from the Interior Provinces in earlier colleras. Over the course of the next two weeks, undoubtedly assisted by Alférez Díaz de Luna and Sergeant Major Thomas Rodríguez de Biedma, the three Apaches de paz made numerous inquiries after the whereabouts of the eleven men, women, and children they had been sent to try to find and recover. They were able to locate only one, a teenager, who did not want to come back with them. Determined not to return home empty-handed, Eustingé, Padatssi, and Quienastgnan apparently decided to launch an extraordinary plan.

The three men had undoubtedly come to understand something of the intricacies of Spanish bureaucracy during their journey. Whether they had also developed a working knowledge of the Spanish language or relied solely on the services of interpreter Nepomuceno Téllez of Janos, the three Apaches seemingly decided to formally petition the viceroy for a special request. They secured the services of one José Tapia, a literate individual who agreed to act as their scribe, and on May 16, 1791, Tapia wrote Viceroy Revillagigedo the following:

> The friendly Indians of the Gileño Nation that have come to this City in search of the *piezas* pertaining to the Rancherías of El Compá, Yagonxli, and Tetsegoslán present to Your Excellency that having examined most minutely the residences and houses where they may have been placed, have found none, save one, an Individual of about fifteen or sixteen years old who is already a Christian and thus it is not possible for him to go back.
>
> We beseech Your Excellency that from the *piezas* brought by the Alférez Dn. Miguel Díaz de Luna you command that there be given to serve each of us, one woman, whom we may live with in marriage at the Royal Presidio of Janos, to where we will return.
>
> Therefore, we humbly beseech Your Excellency to grant us this grace, advising Your Excellency that the Indian women for whom we solicit your kindness are found scattered in private houses of this City.[4]

On May 18, two days after the Apaches had submitted their petition, Sergeant Major Rodríguez de Biedma wrote to inform Viceroy Revillagigedo that, as ordered, he had "delivered to the three Apache Indians the three piezas that they pointed out and who were extracted from the households to which they had been ceded by Your Excellency." Whether the three women had formed an attachment to Eustingé, Padatssi, and Quienastgnan during the long journey from the north is not recorded, but their identifying three particular women seems to show that they were not choosing randomly.

At first glance, it appears that Eustingé, Padatssi, and Quienastgnan demonstrated remarkable aplomb in making this bold request to the viceroy. Yet Viceroy Revillagigedo's positive response almost immediately after the request may indicate that the Spanish were planning on making a gesture to secure the goodwill of the Apaches de paz at Janos while simultaneously demonstrating Spanish magnanimity and power. Whether the petition was a piece of Spanish calculation or the result of Apache resolve, the result was the same—three women prisoners from the collera would be spared from permanent exile.[5]

During the weeks that the Apache emissaries had been unsuccessfully searching for their kinsmen and women, Alférez Miguel Díaz de Luna had been a very busy man. After tranferring the prisoners of the collera to the Acordada, he had quickly settled accounts with the arrieros, the mule drivers. Then he ordered the twenty-six soldiers of his command to ride a short distance to the Dragoon Barracks, where they were to be billeted during their stay in Mexico City. However, he was soon informed that the barracks did not have enough room to stable the large number of horses that the soldiers had brought with them and which were their personal property. Somewhat at a loss, the young officer turned for assistance to Sergeant Major Rodríguez de Biedma, who quickly arranged for the soldiers and their animals to occupy three large blocks at the Mesón de San Vicente, a private establishment with the required facilities.

Satisfied that his men were now properly cared for, Díaz de Luna now turned to the exacting task of closing his accounts and preparing reports for the viceroy and the royal treasury officials. The young officer had been entrusted with more than three thousand pesos of the king's money—a very considerable sum—and the agents of the crown were notoriously zealous in keeping track of public expenses. For more than two weeks, Díaz de Luna labored over his reports. By May 19 he had completed the reckoning of the expenses he had incurred for the maintenance of himself and the twenty-six soldiers of his command. To his satisfaction, he reported that from the one thousand pesos he had been given, he had come out in the black, with over thirty pesos remaining that he turned back into the royal coffers.

Within days of completing this first report, however, the young officer was struck by a personal tragedy. A near relative of his, possibly one of his parents, appears to have been in Mexico City and become gravely ill. Leaving Sergeant Ramírez of the Janos presidio temporarily in command, Díaz de Luna hurried to be with his relation, but within days, the person died. Ramírez dutifully passed this news on to Sergeant Major Rodríguez de Biedma, the garrison commander, and in a letter of May 25, Rodríguez de Biedma informed the viceroy of Díaz de Luna's personal loss, noting that the young officer was overseeing "the canonical burial in Guadalupe of a close relative, whom he was with yesterday [and will be with] through tomorrow, and having been overcome with grief it was impossible for him to return and he ordered a servant to advise the sergeant of the escort that he was ill." Despite this, Díaz de Luna said he would return as soon as possible, and the sergeant major regarded his absence without leave as understandable and acceptable.[6]

No sooner had Díaz de Luna returned to duty than he went to work finishing his expense reports that he then forwarded to the viceroy on May 27. As had occurred previously, the alférez was pleased to note that despite spending some 1,896 pesos, he had managed his accounts so economically that he had 77 pesos remaining. However, Viceroy Revillagigedo was not so trusting as to accept the young officer's assertions at face value. He soon passed the reports on to the accountants of the royal treasury, who performed a methodical and time-consuming audit that would last the better part of a year.

The delivery of his written reports to the viceroy signaled that Díaz de Luna and his men were ready to return to their posts in the Interior Provinces. Yet, after thinking that he managed his monetary accounts properly, the alférez was soon confronted with expenses he had not anticipated. First, the owner of the Mesón de San Vicente turned in a bill for twenty-one pesos, the cost of housing the soldiers of the escort in the capital for a period of twenty-eight days. Then he realized that he had allocated no money to transport the three Apache women who had been liberated and would now be sent back to Janos. Fortunately for him, Sergeant Major Rodríguez de Biedma took matters into his own hands. As garrison commander, the sergeant major should have billeted the soldiers in the city's military barracks, but instead he had arranged for private accommodations. He would bear the responsibility for this decision and take over the bill from the mesón's owner. Regarding the costs for the Apaches, Rodríguez de Biedma also saw to that and forwarded forty-eight pesos to Díaz de Luna from his own accounts to cover those expenses.

Undoubtedly glad to be relieved of these extra burdens, on May 26, 1791, Alférez Miguel Díaz de Luna and the twenty-six soldiers of his command set out heading north, back to the Interior Provinces. Alongside them rode the three Apache warriors Eustingé, Padatssi, and Quienastgnan, each now accompanied by an Apache woman they had managed to set free. All were finally heading home after a sojourn of three and a half months. Yet the Apache women, liberated literally at the last moment, must have felt the terrifying reality that for their friends and relatives in the collera, all hope of returning home was now dead.[7]

As they set out on their return journey, the Spanish soldiers and the six Apaches who accompanied them retraced the route they had taken several months before. Marches of approximately twenty miles a day were closed each evening with a stop at a mesón or hacienda and the purchase of local food for sustenance, although it seems likely that they were not buying meat on the hoof as often as they had been when they needed to feed the prisoners in the collera.

For most of the month of June, the journey was uneventful as the expedition moved north through the cities and towns of New Spain and into the Kingdom of Nueva Galicia. By June 28 they reached the city of Fresnillo, but at this point they were experiencing problems. Díaz de Luna had either made a serious miscalculation in the daily expenses his party required, or he had spent too much of his funds along the way. Either way, his men and the Apaches had run out of money, so he decided to approach the municipal authorities in Fresnillo for help, showing them his orders from the viceroy, who obligated all citizens to assist the soldiers as needed. Several members of the Junta Municipal of the Villa of Fresnillo, Miguel Tovar de Cuenca, Joseph Fernández, and Balthasar Mariel, soon investigated the situation for themselves. They later reported that "there came here Don Miguel Díaz de Luna, Alférez, heading for the Presidio of Janos with some troops and Indians, returning through this city, and who were destitute of funds to continue their transit." After some consultation, the members of the junta, "in order not to obstruct the King's Service nor give the Troops and Indians any reason to desert," decided to supply Díaz de Luna with a goodly sum of 250 pesos. Relieved to have received this aid, the alférez pledged that he would see that they were repaid as soon as possible. This was not the first time that citizens of Fresnillo had aided the young officer and his command. Exactly two months previously, he had turned over the sick newborn Apache boy to the municipal authorities of the city in hopes of providing medical treatment for the infant. Whether the alférez recalled that event is unknown, but perhaps the six Apaches who had returned with him remembered.[8]

After receiving aid from the authorities in Fresnillo, the party continued on their journey north. Not being burdened by the collera of prisoners may have meant that they could move at a faster pace on their return journey, but even so, it would have taken approximately forty more days of travel to reach Chihuahua City. By early August, Alférez Miguel Díaz de Luna had completed his first independent command, and after dismissing the soldiers of the escort, he returned to his regular duties at the Presidio of Janos. But if he thought this episode would help advance his career, he was sadly mistaken.

Within two months of his return from Mexico City, Díaz de Luna was confronted by a financial crisis of his own making. In September, the municipal authorities of Fresnillo who had advanced him the sum of 250 pesos to help support his troops on their return had twice written to the commandant general to complain that they had not been paid. Pedro de Nava, the new commandant general, had arrived to replace Ugarte in March of 1790 after Díaz de Luna and the collera had departed. Upon receiving the complaint against Díaz de Luna, Nava forwarded it to Lieutenant Colonel Antonio Cordero, noting that the alférez "has not satisfied this debt even though he offered to execute it after he returned, according to what I have been shown." Nava then ordered that if the charges were true, arrangements were to be made to withhold one-half of Díaz de Luna's salary until the debt was paid. In addition, Nava instructed Cordero to let the young officer know that he was not at all pleased with his actions, writing, "Your Honor should make understood to him the disgrace with which he is seen for failing to keep his word and [for] the silence that has been caused by this business." Cordero echoed this tenor when he wrote from Chihuahua to the temporary commanding officer at Janos, telling him to inform Díaz of the situation, "making known to him the disposition of the Lord Commandant General and having Luna understand the displeasure he has caused . . . by his disorderly management."[9]

Despite everyone agreeing that Alférez Díaz de Luna was at fault, several more months passed and the municipal authorities at Fresnillo still had not been paid. By February of 1792 they had had enough and took a different approach, this time appealing directly to Viceroy Revillagigedo with their complaint. Perturbed by a situation he had thought resolved, the viceroy in no uncertain terms ordered Commandant General Nava to deduct the amount from the royal treasury in Chihuahua and forward the money to Fresnillo as soon as possible. Nava said he would comply and made arrangements to send the amount owed to Fresnillo in March with the next collera of Apache prisoners. Still, it would not be until June of 1792 that the accounts were closed on this issue.[10]

Yet if the journey to Mexico City and back had ended in unforeseen disappointment and frustration for Díaz de Luna, for the three Apaches who had accompanied him, the results were even more dramatic. Eustingé, Padatssi, and Quienastgnan all returned to their rancherías bringing the sad news that they had not recovered any of the captives they had been sent to find. However, they did bring with them three women rescued from exile, whom the men would now include in their own families. The capitancillos El Compá, Ojos Colorados, and especially Tetsegoslán undoubtedly grieved on hearing the news that the relatives and friends they hoped to redeem were probably lost to them forever. Whether the addition of three new women to their extended families brought some comfort is unknown. What was clear to the Apaches de paz, if it had not been beforehand, was the power, wealth, and sheer numbers of people the Spanish controlled. For the Apaches, the resources available to the white men proved that they had been right in accepting the controlled life imposed by the establecimientos de paz. For the Spanish, that had been the whole purpose of the journey in the first place.

CHAPTER 10

Remove Them from Where They Can Be Dangerous

Commandant General Pedro de Nava never really doubted the need to come to terms with the Apaches. It was 1792, and for almost two years he had seen the positive results of offering them the opportunity to settle in the peace establishments. The growing number of warriors who served the Spanish in hounding those who refused bore a direct relation to the steady if unspectacular diminution of violence in the region. Still, many Spaniards refused to countenance peace with the Apaches, preferring instead to wage unceasing war against a people whom they regarded as innately treacherous and incapable of maintaining any agreement. Such diametrically opposed points of view virtually guaranteed that the war between the two sides would continue.

Nava was appointed to command the Western Interior Provinces in March of 1790 and arrived on the northern frontier that fall at a time of great transition, at least in terms of the Spanish military hierarchy. Control of the Interior Provinces had changed rapidly between 1785 and 1790. The commandant general initially enjoyed an authority more or less independent from the viceroy in Mexico City. However, by 1787, the Interior Provinces were divided into two sections, eastern and western, each with a commandant general independent from each other, but both dependent on the viceroy. For a short period in 1790 before Nava's arrival, the eastern and western commands were again united under a single commander, Jacobo Ugarte y Loyola, but by the following year they were once more split in half, with both commanders dependent on viceregal authority, but as before, autonomous from each other.[1]

However, when Nava was appointed commander of the Western Interior Provinces, the eastern commander, Colonel Ramón de Castro, was delayed in assuming his duties. Because Nava was able to reach the northern frontier much sooner than Castro, he received orders to inspect both the eastern and western commands as his first major duty, and for a brief moment he enjoyed control over all the Interior Provinces. In October of 1790 he arrived at the town of Saltillo, where he set out to review the entire frontier from east to west. After several months of firsthand observations, it became increasingly clear to him that the policy of concentrating Apaches at the establecimientos de paz was the most effective method for curtailing their proclivity for raiding.

During his tour, Nava noted that the Mescalero and Lipan Apaches in the eastern portion of the frontier were in a state of constant warfare. He concluded that much of this animosity stemmed from the steadfast refusal of the previous Spanish commander in the east, Brigadier General Juan de Ugalde, to grant the Apaches any quarter. Ugalde had blocked attempts to have them settle in peace establishments, and even after several groups of Lipans had visited him in person and earnestly requested peace, Ugalde had refused, declaring that they could not be trusted to keep their word, as they had broken numerous treaties before.

While there was much truth in Ugalde's opinion, it was in direct contradiction to the policies codified and implemented by Viceroy Bernardo de Gálvez in 1786. Until 1789, Ugalde's actions had been either tacitly or overtly approved by Viceroy Manuel Antonio Flores. Change came quickly, however, when Flores was replaced as viceroy by the Conde de Revillagigedo. The new viceroy was a firm adherent of the Gálvez policies, and he brooked little debate about the matter. In March of 1789, Ugalde had seized a large group of Apaches who were talking peace at the presidio of Santa Rosa in Coahuila, and after killing those who resisted, he had imprisoned the remainder in such squalid conditions that many of them died. This triggered an intensification of warfare in the region. Outraged by what he felt to be a treacherous act that stained Spanish honor, Revillagigedo ordered Ugalde relieved of his command in the spring of 1790.

When Nava arrived in the Interior Provinces that fall, Revillagigedo endowed him with "full freedom to work for that which appears most suitable to the good services of the King." However, the viceroy also enjoined Nava to treat the frontier Indians, whether at war or peace, in accordance with "the prudent dispositions of the late Conde de Gálvez." Foremost among these dispositions was the policy of congregating the Apaches into the peace establishments. Revillagigedo stressed that Nava should accept the "petitions made by various Rancherías of the Apache Nation that they be admitted to peace in different parts of the frontier." No doubt mindful of Ugalde's disgrace, the viceroy exhorted Nava to leave the Apaches in no doubt as to the Spaniards' "good faith, humane conduct, and the exact observance of our word." If the Apaches remained defiant, Nava was to engage them militarily until he had "reduced them by constant war, or [by] breaking them." Revillagigedo concluded that these policies were the best methods to force the Apaches "to lessen their hostility."[2]

In the summer of 1791, Pedro de Nava completed his inspection of the frontier and took up his command in the city of Chihuahua. By this time, he had come to the realization that the admonitions of Revillagigedo were not only correct, but necessary and practical. He had no doubt that many of the Apaches came into the peace establishments only when it suited them and that their acceptance of Spanish control was only for temporary expediency. Nevertheless, he had seen firsthand that in the Western Interior Provinces, where the peace policy had been pursued longer and with greater consistency, the result had been an overall reduction in Apache raiding throughout the area. Large numbers of Mescalero Apaches had settled outside of the Presidio del Norte, while groups of Gileños had congregated around the town of El Paso. Nava was especially impressed by the Chiricahua Apaches who lived near the pueblo of Bacoachi, "where they are helping us in waging war against their compatriots on the frontier of Sonora and Nueva Vizcaya."[3]

From this point onward and throughout his tenure, Nava diligently attempted to implement the policies summarized in the Instructions of 1786: to offer the Apaches the stark choice of either settling in the establecimientos de paz or facing unrelenting war. While Spanish military pressure was undoubtedly used as a threat, the commandant general made sure that those Apaches who settled at the establecimientos knew they would be treated fairly and that they would be able to maintain a large degree of autonomy. If they broke the peace, however, they would be hunted down and deported from their homelands forever. In short, he made it quite clear that Apaches on the reservation had everything to gain and everything to lose from Spanish control.

For Nava, it quickly became evident that the attitudes and actions of the Apaches who were settled in the establecimientos de paz were due in part to the deportation policy. The threat of exile helped guarantee the behavior of the Apaches within the reach of Spanish control, especially leaders such as El Compá and Tetsegoslán, who had been allowed to try to reclaim relatives captured in battle. Soon after he arrived at his headquarters in Chihuahua in June of 1791, Nava was informed of the events surrounding the recent collera led by Díaz de Luna and the attempt by these same Apache capitancillos to redeem their exiled kin. Within just a few weeks, he was asked to personally approve the release of yet another set of prisoners as a reward for the capitancillos' loyalty.

The Spanish had succeeded in capturing more Apaches in the past several months, and as he had done before, El Compá approached Lieutenant Colonel Cordero at the Presidio of Janos and requested the release of some of the prisoners. This time, El Compá not only intervened on behalf of a group of women and children whom he claimed as kin, but he sweetened the offer by indicating that if these captives were returned to him, five Apache warriors from the same families would come into Janos and settle in peace. When he was informed of the offer, Commandant General Nava was favorably inclined but cautious. He ordered that the prisoners be held until "the five Apache men they belong to have come in good faith to settle at Janos." Only then would Nava agree to release the prisoners; however, they were clearly not going to be sent to Mexico City and permanent exile, and this delay was certainly acceptable to El Compá and his relatives.

Within a short time of El Compá's request, his compatriot Tetsegoslán determined to try his luck. Among the captured prisoners were two small boys that he claimed as his nephews, and as before, the Apache leader approached Lieutenant Colonel Cordero seeking the children's release. Cordero wrote to Nava, saying that he was inclined to grant the request, citing Tetsegoslán's past service and his "good behavior in recent days." The commandant general agreed, and the two boys were turned over to their uncle "in good faith." Yet despite granting

Fuerza del Destacamento de Campaña que ha de operar a las ordenes del Capitan Don Manuel de Casanova.

Compañias	Hombres
Janos incluso un Subalterno	20.
San Buenaventura	20.
Namiquipa incluso un Subalterno	50.
Babispe	15.
Apaches de Janos	20.
Total	125.

Nota.

Que cada Compañia dará los Sargentos y Cabos correspondientes a las fuerzas que franquea. San Diego 29 de Octubre de 1791

Nava

Chart showing Spanish forces, including "Apaches de Janos," destined to campaign against hostiles, signed by Commandant General Pedro de Nava, dated October 29, 1791. Apaches hunting other Apaches had become standard practice. From the Historical Archives, 1710–56: Manuscripts and Documents of Janos. Courtesy Special Collections Department, University of Texas at El Paso Library.

this small mercy, Nava was reluctant to make such releases a common occurrence, lest the fear engendered by deportation become diluted. In August of 1791, he issued an order to the presidial commanders that, as a general rule, prisoners bound for exile should not be turned over to the Apaches de paz.[4]

Nava's order was part of a larger effort to ensure that the Apaches were treated uniformly throughout his command, and by October of 1791, he had drawn up a series of instructions for his officers and soldiers, outlining in great detail exactly how the establecimientos de paz were to be operated. In doing so, Nava demonstrated that he had developed a thorough knowledge of much of Apache culture—no doubt supplemented by numerous interviews with the officers, soldiers, and residents of his command—which he turned to his own advantage. Aware of the division of labor based on sex in Apache society, Nava decreed that seed grain, farming tools, and land allotted to sowing crops were to be given to the Apache women, as the men "live in idleness and are only suited for war." Further, "since Apache women are hard workers," Nava felt they could be employed as wage laborers, either working the fields or "grinding pinole or flour for the troops."

As for the Apache men, Nava also knew how to manipulate them. Hunting expeditions and the periodic gathering of mescal would be permitted, but only to those who received a written passport from the officers at the presidio. Further, any man who left to hunt would be required to leave his family in camp as hostages to guarantee his good behavior. Warriors who served as scouts were rewarded with saddles, extra rations, tobacco, and clothing. The headmen of families or bands were to be given extra gifts as signs of Spanish favor and were to be held responsible for their subordinates. Those leaders the Spanish deemed most loyal were given the title of chief and designated as judges for the community. Although the Instructions of 1786 had recommended that guns and alcohol be handed out freely, Nava strictly limited the distribution of both, ensuring that only the most successful and loyal Apache leaders received them.

The commandant general issued orders to govern the behavior of the Spaniards as well. The presidial officers and their soldiers were to learn the Apache language and customs, and Apache children were to be encouraged to play with Spanish children, a practice Nava felt would "lead to mutual confidence that will be difficult to uproot." But the soldiers were cautioned not to let their guard down and never to completely trust the Apaches. "Those who have blindly trusted them," Nava warned, "have repented their decision at great cost because of the Indians' fickleness and other pernicious qualities." Finally, although he hoped that the Apaches would eventually embrace Christianity, Nava gave instructions to avoid actions that might trigger a cultural backlash. He forbade the presidial chaplains to force conversions, or even to engage in vigorous proselytizing, "to avoid exasperating them, lest they return to their errant and wicked ways."

Although he concentrated great efforts on ensuring that the Apaches who accepted life in the peace establishments were treated humanely, Nava always realized that the entire system was inevitably based on the force of arms. As a result, he vigorously pursued unrelenting campaigns against those Apaches beyond the frontier who resisted the Spanish. He was especially vigilant in confronting any groups or individuals that came into the peace establishments but then left afterward to continue raiding. For Nava and other Spanish officers, such actions could only be viewed as perfidious, regardless of the cultural nuances by which the Apaches governed their own behavior.

It often happened that Apaches captured by the Spanish were given into the custody of their compatriots at the establecimientos de paz. As his orders of August of 1791 indicate, Nava realized that these arrangements, far from appeasing the Apaches, only encouraged further outbreaks. As a result, he commanded that "the abusive practice of returning prisoners that Spanish troops or Indian auxiliaries capture to the Indians at peace will be halted"; he further noted that "the Indians at peace will not claim prisoners taken on the field of battle, because they are the true enemy." Nava stressed that Apache prisoners of war, once captured, "must be removed from land where they can be dangerous even to the Indians at peace. Experience has proven this to be all too true with a number of captives who were freed, only to commit new acts of hostility."

The solution for dealing with these Apaches was, of course, to exile them from their homelands to places where they could not escape. Nava did not explicitly state this as his policy; instead, he reiterated that proper care was to be afforded to those captured. "Prisoners will be treated humanely and gently," he wrote. "They will be provided with what they need to eat, but kept secure so that they cannot escape." Only at this point did Nava hint at the final disposition of Apache prisoners: "They will be delivered as quickly as possible to Chihuahua." Nava planned to deport the prisoners from the frontier and exile them to Mexico City or Havana, as had been the Spanish practice for years. The dispatch of regular colleras of captured prisoners southward from the Interior Provinces was the ultimate weapon in Nava's arsenal. Unfortunately for many Apaches, he was more than ready to use it.[5]

During the winter of 1791–92, Commandant General Nava dispatched the usual round of military expeditions into the hinterland to harry those Apaches who were beyond Spanish control. He ordered other detachments to keep a close watch on the Apaches living at the peace establishments and to react quickly to any disturbance among them or any attempt to band together and launch raids of their own. As a result, the Spanish slowly accumulated a number of Apache prisoners captured throughout the area, and as usual, many of these prisoners were to be made an example of by being deported south in a collera.

By early March of 1792, Nava was informed that a sufficient number of captured Apaches had been congregated at Pilar de Conchos, the garrison headquarters of the Third Flying Company, southeast of Chihuahua City. The Conchos location suggests that the prisoners gathered there may have been Mescaleros or Lipans, the two groups most often found in that region. The post was located in eastern Nueva Vizcaya relatively close to the border with the Province of Coahuila and along the edge of the Bolsón de Mapimí, the desolate basin that often served the eastern Apaches as a gateway to attack Spanish settlements. Regardless of their origins, Commandant General Nava determined that this group was ready to form another collera that would be sent to Mexico City. All told, there were eighty-two prisoners of war, including seventeen men, forty-eight women, and seventeen boys and girls under thirteen years of age.

From his headquarters in Chihuahua, Nava proceeded to make arrangements for the collera to be dispatched. He contacted Domingo de Bergaña, the senior minister of the royal treasury in the city of Chihuahua, to once again begin drawing up an account for the expenses of the collera. Nava also began organizing the detachment of troops that would serve to escort the prisoners. Nava chose Sergeant Antonio Valentín Moreno from the Presidio of San Carlos as commander of the escort.

Moreno was a red-haired, cat-eyed veteran who had risen steadily through the ranks over a nineteen-year career. He was somewhat unusual among the noncommissioned officers in the presidial service in that not only could he read and write, but also handle monetary accounts. As the first sergeant of San Carlos, Moreno had also been involved in dealing with the Apaches de paz. He had purchased cattle to feed the Apaches living at Janos and had also dealt with the Mescaleros gathered in the establecimiento outside the Presidio del Norte. As a result, Sergeant Moreno had developed a reputation as a competent soldier, and Nava decided to appoint him as the commander of the collera, "due to his activity and good conduct in commissions for Remounts and others in which he has produced accounts with clarity and regularity."[6]

By March 12, 1792, Sergeant Moreno appeared before Commandant General Nava at the latter's headquarters in Chihuahua to receive his orders. As had occurred with previous colleras, Moreno was given detailed instructions designed to cover any contingency. He was informed that his command would consist of twenty-four soldiers drawn from his own Presidio of San Carlos as well as troopers from the First and Third Flying Companies. Lieutenant Colonel Antonio Cordero had provided Nava with a list of the anticipated costs for the escort, and Nava passed this on to Moreno with instructions to keep the expenses for soldiers and prisoners separate. Next, Moreno was given the sum of 1,852 pesos 4 reales for expenses for the collera. This was calculated as 922 pesos 4 reales for the maintenance of the eighty-two Apache prisoners at 1½ reales per day for seventy days. In addition, another 930 pesos was allocated for the rental of seventy-two mules to convey the prisoners over the same period. Moreno was to keep a formal account of his expenses as well as a diary of his journey, and when he arrived in Mexico City, he was to give them and any other documents that might be needed to Viceroy the Conde de Revillagigedo. Finally, Nava passed on to Moreno the 250 pesos for the municipal authorities of the Villa de Fresnillo to pay off the debt incurred by Alférez Miguel Díaz de Luna on his return journey from the collera of the previous year.

Regarding the Apache prisoners, Moreno was required to report any losses among the piezas, "should they die on the march, noting the day, place, and any burial certificates from the respective justices . . . where this might happen." Should any fall ill, he was to record where he left them and receive the proper certificates from the local authorities. He was to ensure that the prisoners were "well cared for during all the march," and he was to provide them with whatever was needed to guard them from any inclement conditions they might encounter. Whenever the collera should stop to rest, Moreno was ordered "to place the prisoners in the middle with sentinels in view all around the circumference and guard them with the most opportune methods." To prevent escapes, the guards would be allowed to secure the prisoners using "any physical restraints necessary." When the Apaches were passing through populated areas, they were to be held in well-lit quarters "with closed doors where the sentinels can see into and with a guard outside where they can give aid in case of any commotion."

As with all colleras, Moreno's foremost duty was to prevent the prisoners from escaping under any circumstances, even if he found himself attacked "by a great number of the Enemy intent on liberating the prisoners." Nava's orders on this point were explicit: "I order you to kill them beginning with all the big ones, sparing if possible all the medium and little ones; but you are not to employ this measure unless the situation demands the ultimate necessity and there is no other way to prevent the flight of the collera." After receiving this last order from Commandant General Nava, Sergeant Moreno set out to complete his preparations for the journey. Neither man could have possibly known how prescient this last order was to be.[7]

CHAPTER 11

The Greatest Resistance Possible

Per his instructions, Sergeant Moreno kept a diary to document the events he encountered as commander of the collera of Apache prisoners. He began his log on March 21, 1792, with the entry: "I set out from the Villa de Chihuahua as far as el Fresnal, without incident." It was a simple and straightforward narrative formula that Moreno would employ throughout the diary, with a regularity that would seem tedious were it not for the import of what would occur. Some details Moreno omitted can be surmised. For example, he does not mention if any of the soldiers assigned to the escort accompanied him out of Chihuahua or if he rendezvoused with them at Pilar de Conchos, where the Apache prisoners were being held. But it is extremely unlikely that he set out alone on the roads, carrying almost two thousand pesos in cash or drafts on his person, so at least a few soldiers must have escorted him on the first leg of his journey.

After six days of riding, on March 27, Moreno reached Pilar de Conchos, where he was to pick up the collera of Apache prisoners. Moreno reported to Captain Manuel Vidal de Lorca, commander of the Third Flying Company that garrisoned Conchos. The captain informed Moreno that one of the Apache men had become sick and was too ill to travel, so there would be just eighty-one persons in the collera, and he acknowledged this change with an official receipt. The Apaches were to be mounted on a *recua,* or drove, of seventy-two mules provided by the arrieros Don Juan de Dios Martínez and Don Rafael Romero, who had contracted to transport the collera to Mexico City. Both Martínez and Romero would accompany the expedition, along with an unknown number of hired hands.

At the same time, Moreno formally took command of the twenty-three soldiers of the escort, drawn from the Presidio of San Carlos, the First Flying Company, and Captain Vidal de Lorca's own Third Flying Company. As always, the soldiers would each have had several horses and mules of their own for the journey. In addition, Moreno's party had also come to include five soldiers from the Second Company of the Voluntarios de Cataluña, a unit of the regular Spanish Army of the Viceroyalty that had been on detached service in the Interior Provinces for many years. These soldiers were infantrymen and typically had only one horse and one mule as their standard mounts. Although the Voluntarios would ride alongside Moreno's men, they were technically not under his command and seem to have been charged with delivering dispatches to Mexico City. Despite the disparate origins of the groups gathered at Pilar de Conchos, they must have all been prepared for the journey, as Moreno's journal reads that the day after he arrived, "I received from the Señor Captain Don Manuel Vidal de Lorca the cuerda of Apache Prisoners of the quantity of eighty-one piezas and the same day set out for the Hacienda de Sapien without incident."[1]

For the next four days, the eighty-one Apaches, guarded by the mixed escort of twenty-nine soldiers and perhaps half a dozen arrieros, headed south along roads previously traveled by other colleras. At the Hacienda de San Gregorio, they would

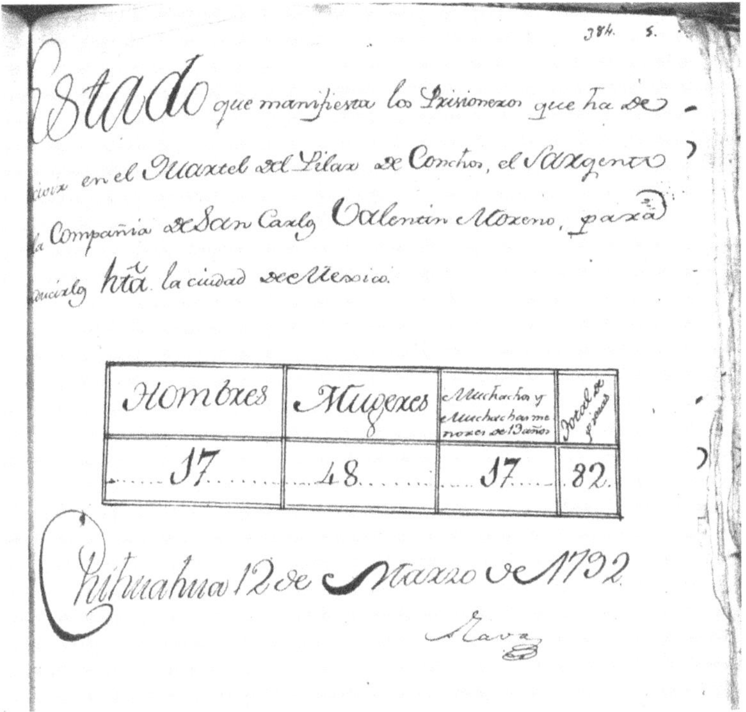

384. 5.

Estado que manifiesta los Prisioneros que ha de … en el Quartel del Pilar de Conchos, el Sargento … Compañía de San Carlos Valentín Moreno, para … hta. la ciudad de Mexico.

Hombres	Mugeres	Muchachos y Muchachas menores de 13 años	Total de piezas
17	48	17	82

Chihuahua 12 de Marzo de 1792

Nava

Chart showing the 82 Apache prisoners to be deported under the command of Sergeant Valentín Moreno, dated March 12, 1792. Most of the men would be killed in the uprising at the Paraje de la Partida. From vol. 142, AGN, PI. Courtesy Special Collections Department, University of Texas at El Paso Library.

have camped near the final resting place of an Apache girl—"María, a little more than twelve years old"—one of the unfortunates carried south with the party of Alférez Miguel Díaz de Luna the year before. Continuing along the same route, they reached the Valle de San Bartolomé the next night, and by the following afternoon of March 30 came to the Estancia del Río Florido, where they sheltered in the hacienda of Don Juan Carrera. At each stop, Sergeant Moreno dutifully noted the expedition's progress, writing in his diary that each day had been "without incident." Unknown to him, that situation was about to change dramatically.

On March 31, the collera and escort came to a place known as the Paraje de la Partida in an unpopulated area one day's march north of the town of Cerro Gordo. Arriving between three and four o'clock in the afternoon, Sergeant Moreno located a campsite relatively near an arroyo that had a good supply of water. As must have been a routine that all members of the party understood, Moreno "had the arrieros form a Plaza with their *jatos* [calfskin trunks] putting the collera in the middle of these." Soon thereafter, Moreno ordered the Apache prisoners to be taken down to the nearby arroyo to be given water, "guarded by the twenty-three men that accompanied me." As they were drinking, many of the Apaches were seen to be gathering up stones. When the guard questioned them about this, "they responded that it was to pound the bones they usually crush for food." When this was reported to Sergeant Moreno, he apparently did not think the actions of the Apaches were out of order and made no attempt to take the stones away.

When the collera returned from the arroyo, Moreno made the final dispositions for that evening's encampment. "It appeared best to me to order that there be placed in the middle the male Indian prisoners with the rest of the Indian women. And around the circle made by the collera, at a regular distance, there dismounted sixteen men, three-by-three, of the twenty-three that came with the party." Moreno then ordered a corporal and four men to be posted as sentinels, while the remaining two soldiers of the escort, along with the five Voluntarios de Cataluña, "were detailed to care for the mules of the arrieros."

With the prisoners and the soldiers positioned, Moreno then ordered Corporal Tiburcio de La O to take three men to "slaughter a bull that we brought from the estancia to feed the Apaches." The bull was most likely brought near one of the groups of three soldiers that were positioned in a ring around the Apaches. Each of the small groups of soldiers would have made a fire to cook their rations and would have placed their saddles, weapons, and horse gear in a pile where they would bed down. Bringing the bull close by would have allowed them access to their lassos and knives, tools they would need to prepare the evening meal. The slaughtering of the bull must have taken some time, even for men who performed such a task regularly. After lassoing the animal's head and horns and hind legs, rendering it relatively immobile, a knife would have been plunged into the bull's throat to sever the major veins and arteries. It would have bled to death within half a minute, with gallons of blood soaking the dirt beneath.[2]

With the bull dead, the soldiers would have now begun the most time-consuming and difficult part of their task, the skinning and butchering of the animal. Once the hide had been removed, the carcass would be ready for carving. As had probably been the case since the beginning of the expedition, the soldiers began to cut the larger sections into smaller portions to be handed out individually. The meat would feed the group of eighty-one Apaches as well as the twenty-nine men of the escort and another half-dozen arrieros, and each person probably received more than two pounds of beef. In addition, the Apaches had obviously been retrieving the cattle bones and crushing them to extract the marrow and most likely would also eat the organs such as the heart and lungs, as well as the eyes and brain from the head if they were particularly hungry.[3]

The prisoners observed the slaughtering and butchering of the bull from a fairly close distance and were prepared for the routine of receiving their rations. Sergeant Moreno then ordered Corporal de La O "to line up all of the Gandules first to give them their meat, which was carried by some soldiers, and the corporal [began] to distribute it among them." At this point, all sixteen of the adult Apache men were gathered close together at the front of the line, with the remaining sixty-five women and children of the collera clustered behind the men. The line of prisoners was close by the saddles and weapons that the soldiers distributing the rations had set up for their own camp. The Spaniards had made a mistake, and the prisoners saw it.

Almost half of the Apache men received their portions of beef without any problem. Suddenly, one man, whom Moreno labeled Pierna Tirante, or "Stiff Leg," let out a shout, and at this signal the Apache men attacked. Sergeant Moreno recalled that "they threw themselves immediately to where there were three saddles with the arms of the same soldiers who were with the squad corporal distributing the meat." Other soldiers nearby attempted to stop the Apaches, but they were unable to contain the rush of sixteen warriors. Some of the Apaches reached the saddles, where there were "three lances which they were able to seize." Quickly turning the Spaniards' own weapons against them, the warriors stabbed and wounded two soldiers: one of the sentinels "that grappled with an Apache" and one of the Voluntarios de Cataluña who had been guarding the mules.

At the same time that the Apache men seized the lances, other Apaches began to hurl the stones they had gathered earlier in the arroyo. Many of the women prisoners joined in the fight. They had concealed a larger number of stones under their clothing and on their persons than was first realized, and they, along with some of the men, began to target the Spaniards. The soldiers were positioned around the Apaches, however, and apparently were able to keep all the prisoners inside the circle they had formed. It seems likely that some of the Apaches attempted to flee into the countryside, but apparently none were able to break through the ring of Spaniards.

For some minutes, the Spanish seemingly stayed at a distance while the Apaches continued to fight with rocks and seek any avenue of escape. One of the arrieros went down, wounded "by a thrown stone that struck him in the head." Unable to restore order, and with his men now standing by with loaded firearms and swords and lances at the ready, Sergeant Moreno had had enough and gave the order to kill the Apaches. As was later reported, the soldiers "commenced fire and entered among them with their lances until they saw that they began to fall and be contained."

The most likely scenario is that the Spaniards first opened fire on the Apaches who wielded the captured lances. At such close range, the soldiers' muskets, carbines, and pistols would have been very effective, and the Apaches would have been shot down. Then the soldiers would have closed in and brought their lances to bear. The men from the Presidio of San Carlos and the First and Third Flying Companies were experts in the use of the lance, and it would have been relatively easy for them to stab and kill any of the Apaches who still resisted, especially if the latter were armed only with stones. With gunshots and lance thrusts, the soldiers brutally crushed the uprising, with Moreno reporting that "in less than a quarter of an hour" his men had "killed twelve of the most daring." The sergeant himself was in the thick of the fighting, noting later, "as is known, I killed three with my own hands." Still, Moreno could not help but praise the desperate courage of the Apaches. "I observed there was no sign of cowardice in them," he reported, "with stones and sticks they made the greatest resistance possible."

Amid the smoke of gunpowder, the screams of battle, and the pools of blood, one can only imagine the terror that gripped the remaining Apache prisoners, especially the women and children, as the battle came to an end. Fear and fury undoubtedly coursed through the Spanish soldiers as well, but the excitement gradually subsided and the soldiers turned to securing their captives. Twelve of the sixteen adult Apache males had been killed, while "an Indian among the younger ones was wounded by a gunshot." The four surviving Apache men, along with the forty-eight women and seventeen boys and girls, were crowded together in the center of the encampment. Nearby, the bodies of the slain warriors were apparently left where they fell. For their part, the Spaniards had suffered four wounded: two soldiers and one arriero stabbed and another arriero hit by a rock. None of their wounds seemed to be life-threatening.

With the afternoon turning into evening, Sergeant Moreno soon realized that he would have to account for the attempted breakout by the Apaches. First he would need to verify the fate of the twelve slain prisoners. Then he would have to compile a report on what had happened and why he had reacted as he did. Obviously, he would need to justify himself and cover up as best he could any mistakes that might be laid to his charge. He drew up a letter to Commandant General Nava, giving a brief but detailed account of the uprising that he would send out as soon as he was able. Then he entered another account of the day's events into his official diary. The two versions were very similar and contained only minor differences, and it was clear that Moreno considered his words carefully.

Yet, when he sat down to compose the official report of the attempted breakout, Moreno visited more pain upon the Apaches. "I ordered the ears cut from the twelve dead Indians to carry to His Excellency, the Viceroy," he noted in his journal. In the gathering twilight, Spanish soldiers pulled the heads of the dead Apaches into position and sliced the ears from each one. The severed ears were then strung in pairs along a leather thong. One of the soldiers then unceremoniously stuffed the grisly record into his saddlebags.

Gathered nearby, the Apache prisoners undoubtedly saw the mutilation of their dead comrades. Adding to their horror, for the rest of the night they were forced to remain in close proximity to the bodies, a phenomenon that according to their own beliefs would have opened them up to both physical and spiritual contamination. Unfortunately for them, the torment of that night would only prove to be a foretaste of what they would endure in the future.[4]

CHAPTER 12

The Jar of Severed Hands

On the morning of April 1, 1792, Sergeant Moreno ordered his troopers to roust the Apache prisoners and get them ready to travel. First light would have revealed the corpses of the twelve Apache men still lying where they had fallen. Rigor mortis would have already come and passed during the night, so the bodies would have been limp. The records, however, do not show whether the Spanish made any effort to collect or bury the bodies or to allow the prisoners to tend them in any fashion. The fear and anger between the Apache prisoners and the Spaniards probably still ran high, and the mood during the preparations for the day's journey must have been tense. Nevertheless, at some point the expedition headed out from the Paraje de la Partida, leaving the dead bodies to the elements and the animals.

By that afternoon, the collera and escort reined up at the town of Cerro Gordo. The one-time presidio was now an agricultural and ranching community, but traces of the military presence remained, not least in the person of Don Juan de Soto, a retired alférez of cavalry who also served as the judicial and political subdelegate for the royal treasury. As a former presidial officer, Soto would have been familiar with the routine of military escorts leading captured Apaches into exile. However, Sergeant Moreno's report of the attempted outbreak must have given Soto pause, as well as stirring up excitement in the community. Sergeant Moreno needed Don Juan de Soto's help, and the old officer complied. First he received Moreno's report on the outbreak and dispatched it in the post bound for Chihuahua and the desk of Commandant General Nava. Then he arranged for lodging and medical treatment for one of the *soldados de cuera* (leather-jacket soldiers) and the member of the Voluntarios de Cataluña who had been wounded in the fight. There is no mention if any special ministrations were offered to the Apache prisoners.

After they rested a full day and night in Cerro Gordo, Sergeant Moreno had the collera and the escort ready to set out again. The two wounded soldiers were left in the care of Soto, who was also put in charge of three horses and a mule for the wounded men, so that they could catch up with the escort after they had recovered sufficiently to ride. On April 3, the cavalcade moved out, heading southeast, reaching the Hacienda de la Zarca by day's end. Pushing on, the group reached the Hacienda El Gallo, where Moreno let his command enjoy a full day's rest. By the afternoon of April 6, the party reached the Río Nazas, where they probably camped in one of several nearby haciendas. The next day, they crossed the river and traveled as far as a location known only as El Paraje, which they reached, as Sergeant Moreno tersely noted, "without incident."

But early the next morning, Moreno suddenly found himself in an exasperating position. Corporal Joseph Antonio Uribes informed Moreno that "the soldier who carried the twenty-four ears of the twelve dead Indians had made known that animals had consumed the ears . . . which he showed me." Most likely the trooper had placed the severed ears among his saddle gear, and sometime in the night, varmints had gotten into them and dragged them out by the leather cord on which they had been strung. Although probably infuriated at the soldier, Moreno soon realized that the loss of the ears posed a far greater problem for him—he no longer had proof that the Apaches had been killed. Without the ears, there was only his word as to what had befallen the men, and if he were accused of allowing them to escape, he would be hard pressed to prove otherwise. He ultimately concluded that he needed more body parts from the dead Apaches.

Consequently, that same day, Sergeant Moreno ordered Corporal Uribes to take one soldier—perhaps the same man who had lost the ears—to ride back to Cerro Gordo and again seek the help of Don Juan de Soto. Moreno sent a message requesting that Soto prepare a certificate verifying the fight at the Paraje de la Partida that would serve "to give proof of the deaths" of the twelve Apaches. At the same time, Moreno asked that "they cut off the right hands and lacking the right, the left," from the bodies, as indisputable proof. Sending Corporal Uribes and the other soldier on their way, the sergeant could now only hope that he could rectify the situation as quickly as possible. With perhaps a sense of resignation, he noted in his diary, "On the same day, I set out as far as Cuencamé, without any other occurrence."

Corporal Uribes and his companion must have ridden hard, for they reached Cerro Gordo about ten o'clock on the morning of April 10, less than forty-eight hours after leaving the collera. They quickly sought an audience with Don Juan de Soto but found the old soldier "gravely ill and in bed." Still, realizing the import of the situation, Soto sent for a trustworthy citizen, Don Ascencio Mendoza, and informed him of what had occurred and about the request from Sergeant Moreno. Soto then commissioned Mendoza "to accompany the said squad corporal and soldier to examine the dead Indians."

Setting out "without loss of time," Mendoza, Uribes, and the other soldier, and perhaps even other citizens from Cerro Gordo, rode out north to the Paraje de la Partida. Although the journey must have taken some hours, they arrived soon enough and quickly found the bodies of the twelve Apaches. The corpses had lain in the open for a week and a half, and decomposition must have been fairly well along. Animal scavengers had been eating at the bodies. Nevertheless, the individual remains were readily identifiable and the joints still fully articulated. Soto's instructions to Mendoza had been to "cut off twelve right hands or if missing, the left." This they did, and with the grisly task completed, they mounted and rode back to Cerro Gordo.

That same day, Mendoza carried the severed hands back to Don Juan de Soto. "Bringing this back to my charge," he noted, "they presented to me twelve left hands with the reason that they found only one of the right." With these body parts secured, Soto began to draw up the formal document detailing what had transpired. In it, he wrote that he had "solicited . . . to know the motive for the flight made by the said imprisoned Indians" by questioning "the same Sergeant conducting them and the squad corporals and soldiers."

Soto had undoubtedly spoken with Sergeant Moreno when the latter had first arrived at Cerro Gordo, and now he took the opportunity to interview Corporal Uribes and the soldier who accompanied him. Further, Soto must have also spoken with the two wounded soldiers previously left in his care. Clearly, all the men seemed to agree on the details of the uprising. The result was that when Soto completed his report, it closely mirrored the earlier accounts written by Sergeant Moreno. Whether Soto merely copied Moreno's accounts or confirmed their accuracy through his interviews, he concluded his own report by affirming the truth of "all, of which I can say and certify with all faith." Then he and Ascencio Mendoza signed the certificate, and soon thereafter he sent Corporal Uribes back on his way along with the severed hands.[1]

While Don Juan de Soto had been collecting the severed hands to send back to Sergeant Moreno, the latter had been dutifully herding the collera of Apache prisoners farther south on their journey. After passing through the mines surrounding the Real de Cuencamé, the expedition reached the region of Atotonilco, the last place they would camp within the jurisdiction of Nueva Vizcaya. The next day, April 11, they entered the Kingdom of Nueva Galicia and passed beyond the "frontier" provinces. For the next four days, the expedition camped each night in a series of lodging houses along the Camino Real, those of Juan Peres, San Marcos, Carvoneras, and Santa Catarina.

Corporal Uribes and his companion managed to catch up with the expedition at the last location, which prompted Sergeant Moreno to note in his diary:

> In Santa Catarina, where the squad corporal and soldier that I had ordered to Cerro Gordo presented themselves to me, and the same brought me the Certification that had been solicited from the Señor subdelegado Don Juan de Soto, and at the same time, a left hand from each of the twelve Indians killed, as they had found only one right [hand] which had not been eaten by animals.[2]

The arrival of the returning soldiers must have broken the routine of the march. When word circulated, as it must have, that the return party carried the severed hands of the men slain during the outbreak, the Apache prisoners would have been exposed to yet more psychological torment. They would again be in close proximity to the physical remains of their dead kinsmen, and once again—according to their beliefs—they were exposed to the spiritual dread visited upon the living by souls not at rest. It was an added burden that they would carry for the remainder of the journey.

Whether Sergeant Moreno or any of the other members of the escort knew or cared about the religious sensibilities of the Apaches cannot be deduced from the records of the collera. All that can be seen at this distance is the continuation of the long journey south. Four days after Corporal Uribes returned with the severed hands, the collera reached the city of Fresnillo. A year earlier, Alférez Miguel Díaz de Luna had contacted the cabildo of the city and sought out medical attention for "a newborn Apache gravely ill and in danger of death." If the child was still alive, he would still be too young to comprehend the passage of this collera through the streets of the city. Of more immediate import to the authorities, Moreno delivered the 250 pesos they had lent Díaz de Luna the year before and that they had experienced so much trouble in recouping.

Two days after leaving Fresnillo, Sergeant Moreno and his command reached Zacatecas, but the silver wealth generated in the city was only glimpsed for a matter of hours, as they continued onward after a single night's respite. They were now mirroring the route taken along the Silver Road that the collera of the previous year had followed, and they stayed in the same series of lodging houses: the Mesón de Tlacotes, the Hacienda de San Pedro de Piedragorda, and the Hacienda de Pavellón. They reached the last hacienda on the afternoon of April 24.

Pavellón was owned by a clergyman, "the señor Bachiller Don José María de Urrucha," as Sergeant Moreno styled him. Urrucha was a presbyter of the Bishopric of Guadalajara who apparently enjoyed a benefice at Pavellón. His priestly services were soon called upon when he was asked to tend to an Apache boy "who had been sick for days." Moreno's journal does not mention any sickness among the Apaches before this, and the only other known casualty was the boy wounded by a gunshot during the uprising on March 31. Whether that child was the same as the one now lying sick is impossible to tell. Either way, Father Urrucha baptized the child that evening, and sometime during the night the little boy died. The next morning, Urrucha had the child given an ecclesiastical burial in the chapel of his hacienda. Demonstrating his business acumen, the priest then drew up a certificate acknowledging the burial along with a bill for one peso for his services. Sergeant Moreno paid the fee, but his superiors would later reject the expenditure, noting that Urrucha should not have required the bill on account of the "notorious indigence of those Indians."[3]

Later that same morning, Moreno, his men, and the Apache prisoners headed out, and by evening, they had reached Aguascalientes. Here the sergeant let the expedition enjoy a full day's rest in the city while he undoubtedly acquired any necessary supplies or rations. On April 26, the journey continued, and for the next two nights, the escort and prisoners sheltered along the road at the Hacienda de San Bartolo and the Mesón de los Sauces. They were now entering densely populated regions near the border of Nueva Galicia and New Spain, and more and more, they found themselves passing through larger cities. After a single night's stay in the Villa de Lagos, the collera pressed on, riding into the prosperous city of León on April 29.

At this place, Sergeant Moreno decided to let the soldiers and prisoners have two full days and nights to recuperate. The soldiers probably took advantage of the hiatus to frequent the town and enjoy any diversions that they could when not guarding the prisoners, while the Apaches were able only to enjoy an all too brief break from riding muleback. At least one of the mules seems to have had ideas of its own. Sergeant Moreno noted in his diary: "There was lost the mule of Soldier José Leyva of the First Company which was turned over to the charge of the Señor subdelegado of said Villa." Whether or not Leyva was reprimanded for losing the mule, he surely felt the loss of this valuable personal possession, and most assuredly, hoped the civil authorities would catch the animal and restore it to him on his return journey. While the soldier lamented his loss, on May 2 the expedition continued south to the city of Silao.

Two days later, they reached the city of Irapuato, and as always, went about the routine of setting up camp in the city for the night. It was noticed that one of the Apache women had an infant girl who was sick, and the child drew the attention of one of the local priests. Moreno noted in his diary that "at the insistence of the señor curate of that place he christened an infant at the breast." Whether the sergeant was irritated by the cleric's zeal or not, soon after the sacrament was received, the new Christian and her unbaptized mother, along with the remainder of the collera, continued on their way.

The expedition was now moving rapidly toward its destination; they passed through a series of large cities in rapid succession along the main road to Mexico City. Evening camps were made over the next week in the cities of Salamanca, Celaya, and Querétaro. The Apaches must have wondered at the number of people and increasing size of the places they passed through. By the evening of May 10, they entered the city of San Juan del Río. However, that night's encampment soon took on a somber tone, due to, as Sergeant Moreno recorded, "an infant at the breast, very ill, who died at eight that night." This infant was not the same as the girl that the unnamed priest had insisted on baptizing several days before in Irapuato; this child was recorded as *un Mequito de días nacido*, "a little Indian boy, only days old." The child's birth was not recorded, but the mother and newborn had obviously not been allowed much time to recover. Still, the child must have been baptized, because Sergeant Moreno wrote, "I remained there to give him burial in said Paraje, as is confirmed by Certification." If he was buried in consecrated ground, the child must have been baptized first. In the morning, Moreno received a certificate from Don Pedro

Martínez de Salazar y Pacheco, justicia mayor of San Juan del Río, recording "the ecclesiastical burial . . . in the Parish of this Pueblo."[4]

The death and burial of the infant Apache boy did not delay the expedition for more than a few hours. The group soon continued along the main route to the capital. After three more days of encampments at mesones along the road, by May 14 they had reached the town of Tepexis and the following day the city of Quatitlán, all the while ascending the mountains that ringed the Valley of Mexico. Finally, on May 16, the expedition entered Mexico City. In his clear, terse style, Sergeant Moreno completed the last entry in his diary, writing that he had arrived "without incident, where I delivered at the same place to the Sergeant Major Don Thomas Rodríguez de Biedma sixty-seven piezas of the eighty-one [received] in the Presidio de Conchos." The journey had lasted some seven weeks. It had begun in the blood and death of the attempted outbreak by the prisoners at the Paraje de la Partida and now ended among the crowded streets of Mexico City. Sergeant Moreno and his soldiers would soon look forward to beginning the journey home. But, for the Apache prisoners of war, the horrors of their sojourn would only continue and most probably increase. The jar of severed hands that still accompanied them gave ample proof of this truth.

As had occurred with other colleras, the Apache prisoners were most likely deposited in the Acordada, where they would have been counted, registered, and locked in prison cells. Within days or weeks they would have been sent to their final destinations—domestic servitude in private houses for some, confinement in the obrajes or textile factories for others, and the most likely destination, hard labor at the fortifications at Veracruz or Havana. For them, there was to be no last-minute reprieve or rescue as had happened the year before. The records of the collera are silent as to their ultimate fate.

Yet for Sergeant Moreno, the duties of his command did not stop with his relinquishing of the prisoners, as he still had to settle his accounts. The troopers of the escort were probably lodged by the garrison commander, Sergeant Major Rodríguez de Biedma, in the Dragoon Barracks, as there is no record of any private accommodations being supplied for the men. With his troopers settled, Moreno could now concentrate on his paperwork. Two days after his arrival in the city, on May 18 he paid off Juan de Dios Martínez and Rafael Romero, the majordomos of the recua of mules that had transported the Apaches. The next day, he submitted to the viceroy his final expense account of the journey. Moreno reported that he had spent 654 pesos 6 reales for the daily maintenance of the prisoners, plus 930 pesos for the rental of the mules to carry them and their baggage, for a total of 1,584 pesos 6 reales. Thus, from the 1,892 pesos 4 reales he had received from the treasury officials in Chihuahua, Moreno still had 268 pesos 3 reales 6 granos left over, which he was going to leave in the charge of the sergeant major of the garrison.[5]

A week after Moreno turned in his expense account and diary for the expedition, Sergeant Major Rodríguez de Biedma forwarded them to Viceroy Revillagigedo along with the 268 pesos that remained. As was his wont, the viceroy passed these along to the officials of the royal treasury for an audit. These bureaucrats soon found several discrepancies in Moreno's accounts. If Sergeant Moreno had hoped to get back quickly on the road home, he was sorely disappointed.

The auditor, Don José del Cabo Franco, indicated on May 30 to the Tribunal de la Contaduría Mayor y Audiencia de Cuentas, the senior accountants of the royal treasury, that while most of Sergeant Moreno's expenses were "legitimate," the sergeant had failed to adjust his expenses for the twelve Apaches killed in the uprising and the other casualties the collera had suffered. According to Cabo Franco, the daily rations for the dead prisoners should have been deducted from the total. Further, as dead men could not ride, the use of several mules should also have been subtracted from the total charged by the owners of the recua transporting the prisoners. Cabo Franco advised that with these adjustments, even after deducting the money Moreno had turned back in, he still owed the treasury just over 265 pesos.[6]

Sergeant Moreno must have been taken aback by the auditor's findings, but he quickly prepared a written response that he delivered to Cabo Franco the next day. In it, Moreno argued that he *had* adjusted his accounts for the daily rations after the twelve Apaches were killed and after the other subsequent losses. However, as to the cost of the mules, Moreno maintained that the contract with the arrieros made by the treasury officials in Chihuahua was for a fixed amount, and he had no authority to alter it. If he had been able to adjust the contract, Moreno reckoned that the actual expense would have been approximately 652 pesos of the 930 he had paid out. Although he did not say so, Moreno obviously felt that if there was any fault in the accounts, it lay not with him, but with the contract drawn up with the arrieros.

Taking his cue from Moreno, the auditor, Don José del Cabo Franco, now turned his attention to the details of the contract entered into by the "*arrieros conductores*," Juan de Dios Martínez and Rafael Romero. In a follow-up to his original audit, Cabo Franco took Moreno's excuses into account and prepared a new document, and this time he decided to go after the two mule drivers. In his second audit, Cabo Franco still maintained that Moreno should have adjusted his accounts, as the collera's journey took only fifty-one days, not the seventy originally anticipated. But the auditor insisted that the greater fault lay with Martínez and Romero, who should have taken it upon themselves to adjust the cost of the mules they had rented to the expedition, especially after the twelve Apaches were slain at the Paraje de la Partida. As a result, he felt they should be ordered to return a total of 277 pesos to the treasury, depositing the amount either in Mexico City or in Chihuahua if they returned to the latter city. Obviously holding Romero as the most culpable of the pair, Cabo Franco recommended that his contract be immediately terminated.[7]

Exactly when Sergeant Moreno learned that he had been absolved of blame by the royal audit is not known, but he apparently left Mexico City in early June and headed back to the Interior Provinces with the men of his escort. It took some time, but by the end of August of 1792, the royal treasury had managed to squeeze the 277 pesos from the two mule drivers, Martínez and Romero. Several months later it also ordered the officials in Chihuahua City to exercise greater caution in drawing up future contracts. Over the same period, the fates of the Apaches of the collera were most likely determined and the prisoners banished to the terrible destinies to which they had been delivered. As for the jar of severed hands, it had served its purpose, and its mummified relics now remained only as curiosities to be gawked at by bureaucrats or as an opportune meal for the animal scavengers that picked through the refuse heaps along the streets of Mexico City.[8]

CHAPTER 13

Hard Lessons

The rotting, decapitated heads of slain Apaches were nothing out of the ordinary for the residents of the Presidio of San Agustín del Tucson. As the northernmost military outpost in the Province of Sonora, Tucson was somewhat isolated, and perhaps to reassure its residents, the soldiers of the presidio routinely placed heads over the main gate as visible proof of their power over the enemy. But the delivery of four more severed heads to post commander Lieutenant José Ignacio Moraga on April 22, 1793, was something new and peculiar. This time they were carried not by Spanish soldiers, but by an Apache. Nautil Nilché, capitancillo of the Apaches de paz at Tucson, had encountered a group of "rebels" along the Río San Carlos, killed four of them, and taken their heads. On his return to Tucson, Nautil Nilché found three more Apaches he regarded as hostile, seized them, and brought them back alive. News of his cargo quickly spread, and two entire rancherías of hitherto warlike Apaches under the capitancillos Quiltolá and Quinanzos, a total of sixty-nine people, came into Tucson to make peace—or so the Spaniards maintained. The truly extraordinary thing about Nautil Nilché's actions was how quickly he had come to copy Spanish habits, as he himself had only made peace three months before. That he would go against some of the most important cultural and religious traditions of his people—exposing himself to the malevolent spirits of other Apaches he had slain by coming into direct and sustained contact with their dead bodies—indicated just how determined he was to prove that he had allied with the white men.

Nautil Nilché was a leader of the so-called Vinictinines, a western Apache sub-group that lived along the Aravaipa Mountains of what is now southeastern Arizona. On January 6, 1793, he had led fifty-one people, including fifteen warriors, into Tucson and agreed to settle outside the post. Two weeks later, another forty-one Aravaipa Apaches had appeared and joined the new establecimiento de paz. Within weeks of presenting himself, the capitancillo Nautil Nilché and his warriors had brought back six heads from "enemy" Apaches and presented them to Lieutenant Moraga as proof of his intentions. Now he delivered four more as further confirmation that he intended to fight for the Spaniards, not against them.[1]

While some may have regarded these actions as evidence of the innate cruelty of the Apaches, for others it was a small sign that things were beginning to change. Ever since the adoption of the Instructions of 1786 of the late viceroy Bernardo de Gálvez, the mailed fist and velvet glove policies had gradually produced acceptable, if not entirely expected, results. Gálvez's hope that these policies would provoke among the Apaches "the ancient hatred, factional interest and inconsistency and perfidy . . . to their mutual destruction" was coming to pass. For proof, one needed only to look at the rotting heads that Nautil Nilché had brought into Tucson.

There were other signs of change as well, and not always as bloody. At the same time that the Aravaipas were settling at Tucson, large numbers of Apaches were already settling in other establecimientos de paz. All told, by January of 1793, the Spaniards counted 1,173 Apaches in eight reservations in three provinces. Sonora had Chiricahuas and Gileños at Bacoachi, Fronteras, and Tucson, each with one ranchería, with a total of 222 men, women, and children. New Mexico had Faraones at two rancherías at Sabinal, containing 226 people. Nueva Vizcaya had the most settlements, mainly Gileños and Mimbreños, with eight rancherías at Janos, four at Carrizal, and one at San Elezario, totaling 725 souls. In addition, eight rancherías of Mescaleros had moved outside the Presidio del Norte, all together containing between 230 and 250 warriors, but they could not be properly counted because they were constantly moving to hunt buffalo on the southern plains. Although there would be fluctuations in the overall numbers, most of these settlements would continue to exist for many years.[2]

Commandant General Pedro de Nava was convinced that the recent and future success in attracting so many Apaches into the peace establishments rested squarely on the consistent application of Spanish policy: military forces would seek out and destroy those Apaches who continued to raid and plunder, while those who passed under government control would be clothed and fed. Indeed, those who came into the Spanish orbit could even continue their raiding traditions as long as they attacked other Apaches not allied with the white men. Still, it was not until the spring of 1793 that Nava was able to apply these policies to the entire frontier. Until then, Colonel Ramón de Castro had held sway in the Eastern Interior Provinces, and he had been convinced that the peace settlements simply would not work.

When he took over as commandant general in the east on April 14, 1791, Castro met with Nava, and both men agreed to cooperate in applying the Instructions of 1786 as required by Viceroy Revillagigedo. During the previous six months during his ad interim tenure as commander over all the Interior Provinces, Nava had attempted to spread into the eastern provinces the peace policies that had proven workable in the west. He had agreed, for example, to a negotiated peace with some of the Lipan groups and had even had them sign a series of carefully prepared "capitulations" regulating their conduct. Castro, however, expressed reservations about trusting the Lipans to keep the peace treaty without having been clearly defeated in battle. But if Castro was initially reluctant to treat with the Apaches, events soon drove him to regard the idea of peace with absolute disdain.[3]

In late April of 1791, Commandant General Castro was at the Valle de Santa Rosa in Coahuila, making preparations for a campaign against the "Lower" Lipans who occupied the territory stretching from the mouth of the Rio Grande north toward the Spanish settlements in Texas. No doubt aware of the military preparations, a capitancillo of the Lower Lipans approached the Presidio of San Juan Bautista asking for peace, saying he was prepared to come in with ten other chiefs and forty more warriors to negotiate. When Castro was informed, he agreed to parley with the Lipans and ordered that they be issued a safe-conduct pass to come and meet him at the Valle de Santa Rosa. The commandant general demanded that the Indians leave their weapons behind and release beforehand all their captives and all the horses they had robbed from the Spanish settlements. The Lipans agreed.

But on the afternoon of May 1, 1791, only one of the Lipan leaders arrived at Santa Rosa, accompanied by thirteen men and three women. They were all quickly brought into the house occupied by Castro, and the commandant general asked where the rest of the Apache leaders were. According to the Spaniards, the capitancillo gave a vague answer that the rest of the Lipans were still gathered at the Rio Grande and made other "suspicious replies." Clearly affronted, Castro "proposed that they send emissaries to the rest of their nation that they come and draw up a peace and that they should give themselves as hostages, the capitancillo and the 13 gandules." The commandant general's proposal was obviously backed by force, and the Lipans "submitted to this, although with some repugnance." Castro then ordered the Indians to be housed in the quarters of Lieutenant Juan de Arrumbide of the presidio and had sentinels placed outside.

Realizing their predicament, the Lipan capitancillo and two warriors slipped out of Lieutenant Arrumbide's room at nine o'clock that night, eluded the guards, and escaped from the presidio. When he was informed of this, an outraged Castro returned to the quarters where the rest of the Indians were housed and began to harangue them over the flight of their companions. Suddenly, one of the Lipans grabbed the commandant general in a bear hug and stabbed him twice in the shoulder with a small knife. After grappling with his opponent for some moments, Castro "finally was able to push him away and kill him at his feet with a pistol shot." The rest of the Lipans began to fight, and the Spaniards recorded that the Indians "entered into a desperate resistance that lasted from nine at night until eight in the morning of the following day, all losing their lives, which with bold faces, they did not relinquish without [killing] a sergeant and a soldier, and wounding another seven and the Lieutenant Don Juan de Arrumbide, whom they left in danger [of death] along with four of the same soldiers."[4]

Although his wounds were not serious, Castro emerged from this encounter furiously angry, convinced more than ever that the Lipans were incapable of making peace and that they should be utterly exterminated. Conversely, the Lipans saw in the encounter a repetition of the deceitful tactics they had seen perpetrated under Brigadier Juan de Ugalde a few years before. Mutual distrust fueled mutual violence, and open warfare escalated throughout the eastern frontier. Castro marshaled his forces and over the next months began to attack the Lipans at every opportunity. In addition, he solicited aid from the Comanches and other Indians in the region, who, taking their cue from the vengeful commandant general, moved against the Lipans. Pressed on all fronts, the Apaches soon became desperate.

Turning to tactics that had served them well in the past, in February of 1792, eight Lipan leaders moved to the west and appeared outside the Presidio del Norte, requesting peace from Commandant General Nava. He was inclined to concede terms but told the Apaches that they were under the authority of Castro, who refused to treat with them. Nevertheless, Nava temporized, and as the Lipans departed, he told them he would seek guidance from his superiors. Five months later, in July, the Lipans again approached Nava to crave peace. Yet again Nava forwarded their request, and yet again Castro refused to allow it. When it became clear they could not obtain what they wanted, in disgust and frustration the Lipans attacked and murdered three Mescaleros settled in peace at the Presidio del Norte and then fled precipitously back into Coahuila and Texas.[5]

The inability of the Lipans to conclude any type of peaceful agreement with the Spaniards was soon surmounted when Nava became sole commander of northern frontier. In November of 1792, King Charles IV of Spain, seeking to economize government expenses on the brink of new European wars, ordered that the Interior Provinces should again become unified under a single commandant general, independent of the viceroy. But unlike the days of the Caballero de Croix, the Interior Provinces were pared down to include only the five core provinces of Sonora, Nueva Vizcaya, Coahuila, New Mexico, and Texas, leaving under viceregal control the Californias in the west and Nuevo León and Nuevo Santander in the east. Despite this diminution of his authority, Viceroy Revillagigedo gave genuine, if reluctant, support to the new administration and concurred with the appointment of Pedro de Nava as the new commandant general.

By March of 1793, Nava had reunited the Interior Provinces under his sole authority, and he soon pressed ahead with his plans for dealing with the eastern Apaches according to the same dictates he had employed in the west. He ordered Adjutant Inspector Don Juan Gutiérrez, stationed in Coahuila, to concede peace to the Lipans should they again importune the Spaniards. Results were soon forthcoming, as a great number of Lipans arrived in April outside the Villa of San Fernando, where the Presidio of Aguaverde was located. They said they desired to conclude peace terms and conduct their seasonal buffalo hunt undisturbed. Nava approved of this arrangement and began to entertain hopes that the pattern of settling Apaches that had proven practicable in the western provinces could be applied to the eastern provinces as well.

Indeed, within a year of the granting of a peace treaty with the Lipans, Nava saw many more signs of hope, some of which pointed to a gradual acceptance of a new order on the part of the Apaches de paz. On May 17, 1794, for example, the commandant general penned a series of letters to Manuel de Casanova, captain of the Presidio of Janos, each of which pointed out the potential for increasing peaceful interaction between the Spaniards and those Apaches settled near his command. Nava first wrote about enrolling Juan José, son of El Compá, the "principal chief of the Apaches," in the school established for the children of the residents of Janos. In an additional missive, Nava asked Casanova about constructing houses for two other leaders of the Apaches de paz, Güero and Vívora. Finally, the commandant general broached the idea of dispatching some of the "faithful Gileños" settled at Janos farther to the east to live outside the Presidio of Carrizal in order to help the Spaniards in that area of the frontier.[6]

If Nava entertained sincere hopes that the Apaches de paz would continue to aid his soldiers in maintaining a modicum of order along the frontier, he knew that naked force would be the ultimate guarantor of their behavior. To that end, military expeditions continued their yearly forays into the homelands of the Apaches, killing and capturing those who maintained their independence beyond the pale of Spanish control. These expeditions increasingly were joined by the warriors from the establecimientos de paz, who often led the Spaniards in scouting out and attacking their kinsmen in the hinterland. Some Spanish officers even grudgingly admitted that their success was due in large part to the services of these Apache auxiliaries.

Yet, while the Spanish were using the Apaches de paz for their own ends, the Apaches themselves just as often manipulated circumstances to their own benefit. Utilizing their newfound status as "allies," many Apaches began to adapt their traditional cultural patterns of seasonal movements to their changed circumstances. For example, residents from one presidio might solicit permission to visit friends or relatives in rancherías located near other presidios or even in the hinterland; others might seek permission to go out hunting, to gather mescal, or, in the eastern frontier, to engage in twice-yearly buffalo hunts. Although the Spanish attempted to regulate these movements by issuing written internal passports, once they found themselves beyond direct control, many Apaches took the opportunity to engage in small-scale raids or illicit trade to supplement the rations they received at the establecimientos de paz. Commandant General Nava and his officers were aware of these activities, but as long as the level of thievery and violence remained low, they chose to tolerate it, considering it a result of the natural inclinations of the Apaches.

Even when Apaches de paz moved about without engaging in surreptitious activities, they still knew how to manipulate the situation. Many capitancillos realized that if they made promises of military aid to the Spaniards, they would often be rewarded. The craving of boons for actual or intended services soon produced a steady stream of Apaches de paz heading to the Villa de

Chihuahua to see the commandant general in hopes of obtaining gifts and favors. At one point, an exasperated Pedro de Nava issued orders for his officers not to issue any more passes allowing Apaches to come to his headquarters, because he was growing tired of their continuous "impertinent entreaties."

If Nava was taxed by the actions of individual Apaches de paz, he was even more disturbed when the entire system became stressed. When war broke out between Spain and Revolutionary France in 1793, the Spanish government quickly exhausted its financial resources and began to make draconian cuts in expenses. The government saw the establecimientos de paz in the Interior Provinces as a drain on revenue and soon ordered Nava to cease supplying monthly food rations to the Apaches and instead to require them to relocate near the presidios, where they could live off the land. When Nava attempted to comply with the order, many of the Apaches simply refused to leave. Others departed from one presidio only to show up several weeks later at another, requesting and sometimes demanding rations. Often, bowing to the implied and sometimes open threat of violence, the Spaniards had no recourse other than to comply. But from this point on, the Spaniards were hesitant to allow more Apaches to settle in the establecimientos de paz, realizing that they had only enough funds to support those already resident. For the remainder of the colonial period, the reservation system seems to have stayed at a fairly standard level of about two thousand Apaches.[7]

Still, while the Spaniards may have been reluctant to support more Apaches in the peace establishments, they showed no compunction in capturing and deporting those who opposed them. During the same period that Commandant General Nava was required to cut back on expenses for the reservations, the government continued to pay for the transportation into exile of large numbers of Apache prisoners of war. In mid-1793, Nava reported that his forces all along the frontier had killed seventy-seven Apaches and captured another seventy of all ages and both sexes. Although there is no record of their final disposition, it seems most likely that Nava had these captives deported from the frontier.

Even though Nava's command was officially independent from the authority of Viceroy Revillagigedo, the constant deportation of Apaches required the two men to cooperate in order to properly dispose of the colleras sent south from the Interior Provinces. In April of 1794, Nava sent out another group of prisoners and wrote to the viceroy with the particulars:

> Esteemed Sir: There left on the 1st of this month from the post at Pilar de Conchos occupied by the 3rd Flying Company a collera of Apache prisoners of war composed of twenty-eight gandules and fifty-six women over eighteen years, guarded by a party of twenty-six men under Alférez Andrés Joseph Mateos. This officer will deliver them to that capital for Your Excellency's disposition, and consequently, it is my hope that you would kindly arrange that the Indios be dispatched to Havana and that the women be placed in a location from which they cannot flee and return to these countries.[8]

Nava had supplied the collera with eighty-three animals for transport and baggage and had drawn a sufficient amount from the treasury of Chihuahua to cover all expenses. However, he asked the viceroy to send a party of cavalry or dragoons to relieve the soldiers of the escort when they reached either the cities of Fresnillo or Zacatecas. Revillagigedo was sympathetic but told Nava he could not comply, because most of his available troops were engaged in the duties of the capital, especially in "escorting the monthly trains of presidarios to Veracruz."

The viceroy did, however, assist the collera when it was beset by illness. On May 6, as they were passing through the Villa of

León, Alférez Mateos was informed that several of the Apache women prisoners had become ill. Mateos quickly contacted the municipal authorities and Father Manuel Bonifacio Navidad, administrator of the Royal Hospital of Saints Cosmas and Damian. Father Navidad and his monks took in the Apache women and found that they were "gravely ill with the plague which they had contracted in the said Villa." The women were soon quarantined, and Alférez Mateos was able to move out within a few days. Over the next three weeks, the women were treated, and, as Father Navidad later reported, eight of them "were well and of a fitness to take the journey to which they had been assigned." However, one woman "was found to have contracted diarrhea, from which she died . . . she was interred in one of the Interior corrals of this Convent, not having asked for the waters of Baptism." When he was informed of the convalescence of the sick women, Viceroy Revillagigedo ordered his accountants to cover the cost of their care while he arranged for a party of militiamen to escort them from León to Mexico City, where they presumably rejoined the other members of the collera.[9]

Within six months of this expedition, more Spanish offensives resulted in the capture of another ninety-five Apache prisoners. Nava ordered these unfortunates to be gathered together for deportation late in the fall of 1794, but before they had even set out for Mexico City, fourteen perished from an undisclosed illness. The other eighty Apaches were exiled.[10]

This same pattern of deportation continued year after year. Spanish attackers killed and captured numbers of "hostile" Apaches, and toward the end of each year, the prisoners were sent south into permanent exile. As had often happened in the past, disease killed off many before they even reached their final destination. In 1796, Nava reported that his men had taken 173 prisoners during the year. One group of at least 61 prisoners, including 57 women and girls and 4 men or boys, is recorded as having reached Mexico City in November of 1796. But when these captives were sent on to Veracruz early in 1797, they were attacked by an illness reported as "putrid fever." Twenty-two more Apaches soon died, with another 11 too sick to move, so that of the original number, only 28 lived long enough to be sent to Cuba. A like fate befell the collera dispatched the following year. Setting out from the frontier on November 7, 1797, this contingent contained 71 prisoners, including 11 men and boys, 57 women and girls, and 3 small children. When they reached Mexico City on December 26, the collera had only suffered a single loss, one woman left behind too sick to travel. But their luck ran out within weeks of their arrival, when smallpox broke out in the capital with devastating results. After two months in Mexico City, and despite the authorities' sending the sick to be treated at hospitals, only 19 of the 57 Apache women survived, while the fate of the men and boys is unknown. Despite these losses, the surviving women were soon marched to Veracruz, again bound ultimately for shipment to Havana.

The situation was repeated in 1798. In April, Spanish soldiers out of Coahuila attacked a large encampment of Mescaleros and Lipans in the Sierra Blanca of southern New Mexico, killing 11 and capturing 54 men, women, and children, while another 20 surrendered voluntarily. By early fall, the 49 Apaches still held captive were dispatched from the Valle de Santa Rosa in another collera bound for Mexico City. But as had occurred the previous year, the prisoners were beset by a contagious illness during their sojourn, and by the time they reached the capital, 20 had perished. The remaining 29 prisoners, joined by 2 more Apaches left behind ill in the capital the previous year, were again sent to Veracruz, destined for Cuba. Whether the 31 Apaches—9 men, 19 women, and 3 children—ever reached the island is unknown.[11]

And so it continued. For the remainder of his term as commandant general, Pedro de Nava continued to oversee yearly deportations of Apache prisoners of war from the Interior Provinces. The specter of their doomed countrymen herded into exile occurred with enough regularity to persuade many Apaches to accept terms from the Spaniards, albeit reluctantly and out of expediency. Nevertheless, it was enough. Nava and the Spanish government believed that at least some of the Apaches had learned and accepted the harsh lessons of military power, despite the need to repeat them over and over. But the Apaches could teach as well, and no single lesson was so often imparted as their ability to escape from a hopeless situation. One of the most striking instances occurred early in 1799.

During October of 1798, Spanish officials in Mexico City were making preparations to dispatch a large number of convicts to Veracruz for dispersal to the public works. According to the viceroy, Miguel José de Azanza, they were "criminals," sentenced by the various legal authorities throughout the city, including "La Capitanía, Sala de Crimen, Tribunal of the Acordada, and Prohibited Beverages." In all, eighty-six men had been sentenced to serve their terms, not just at Veracruz, but other stations, including "Havana and its arsenal, the Vessels of the Royal Armada, and other Presidios." The cuerda of presidarios was to be escorted by an officer and twenty-three men of the Dragoons of Spain along with twenty-three men from the Provincial Militia Regiment of the capital. For greater security, each of the prisoners was to be secured by a pair of iron manacles, wryly called *esposas*, or "wives." Viceroy Azanza, undoubtedly trying to be efficient, had approved that the presidarios be accompanied by yet another collera of ninety-five Apache prisoners of war recently assembled in the capital. This batch of captives comprised twenty-six indios, sixty-six indias, and three *niños*. The viceroy cautioned that the Apaches "should be strongly and carefully guarded" but did not increase the number of soldiers in the escort.[12]

The combined collera of criminals and prisoners of war under command of Lieutenant Mariano Miranda of the Dragoons of Spain departed from Mexico City on January 19, 1799. Miranda marched his prisoners east along well-worn roads until, after thirteen days of travel, the collera reached the city of Perote on January 31. Positioned strategically along the highway leading from the capital to the port of Veracruz, Perote contained a large garrison of soldiers. Soon after his arrival, Lieutenant Miranda turned over command of the prisoners to another officer, Lieutenant Juan de Dios Cos of the Dragoons of Mexico. Lieutenant Cos would now be responsible for the final delivery of the collera into Veracruz. His command included a sergeant, two corporals, and seventeen dragoons from his own regiment, along with a sergeant, two corporals, and eighteen men from the Second Company of the Voluntarios de Cataluña, drawn from the garrison of Perote.

On February 5, 1799, at four o'clock in the afternoon, Lieutenant Cos and his charges arrived at the Venta de la Rinconada, a traveler's inn several leagues outside of Veracruz, where he received a reinforcement of ten mounted *lanceros* (lancers) from the port's garrison. The inn had several large rooms, or *galerías*, each with cane walls and thatched roofs, windowless, and with a single door fronting a common patio. Lieutenant Cos herded all the presidarios and adult male Apaches, or *mecos*, as the Spaniards termed them, into a single room, which must have been substantial to contain all 112 men. The sixty-six females, or *mecas*, along with one small boy, were split up into two other rooms. After feeding them dinner at about seven o'clock, the soldiers performed a routine search of the prisoners and then secured all the men with their manacles. The women were also restrained, tied together at the wrist in pairs with leather cords called *encuerdas*. As night came on, Lieutenant Cos posted sentinels, two inside the men's quarters and two more at the door. Each of the women's quarters contained one sentinel inside and another at the door. Five more men were placed behind all the quarters. In addition to the thirteen sentinels, a corporal's guard of four men made the rounds as *la ronda*, or the watch. The night was overcast with strong, gusty winds that constantly blew out the

City of Vera Cruz from the Road to Mexico. N. Currier lithograph, 1847. Courtesy Library of Congress.

lanterns carried by the sentinels, making it difficult to see clearly inside the prisoners' quarters.

Between midnight and one in the morning, one of the sentinels in the galería of the men noticed that an Apache meco had slipped out of his manacles. In an instant, the Apache jumped up and lunged at the sentinel; the latter raised his weapon to strike the meco and yelled for the watch. Simultaneously, all the Apache men began shouting, while the eighty-six presidarios seemingly stood by in confusion and amazement. The soldiers of the watch and several of the sentinels ran to the room and discovered that six of the Apache mecos had managed to get out of their manacles and were preparing for a fight. Lieutenant Cos quickly arrived on the scene with sword and pistol in hand and immediately ordered that the mecos be tied up with riatas fetched from the soldiers' horses. The Spaniards struck at the

Apaches with their weapons and with wooden sticks to try and regain control.

At the same instant, the Apache women in the two adjoining galerías seized their chance. Screaming in answer to the shouts of their men, all the mecas in both rooms rushed the sentinels. In one room, soldier Manuel Carpintero of the Voluntarios de Cataluña "called out for the Guard, but it availed nothing as all of that troop ran to the gallery of the men." Carpintero shot one woman dead and tried to bayonet another, but the rest of the Apache mecas, "some casting blows with the hand and others clawing," pushed past him. Outside, they literally ran over three dragoons and trampled their firearms into the ground. One of the dragoons was struck several times in the head and seriously wounded. In the other room, the Apache women had rushed the sentinels as well, but the soldiers had grabbed the leather thongs holding some of the women's wrists and managed to hold on to fourteen of them, but the remainder broke free. According to Lieutenant Cos, within a short time after the first outcry, "all of the Mecas [were] in the patio of the Venta with furious outcries and . . . as they could not get the weapons from the sentinels, the Mecas made for the Mountains."

Daybreak revealed that fifty-one Apache women and one boy of about six years old had managed to flee from the Venta de la Rinconada, most while still tied together in pairs. Lieutenant Cos sent out several mounted lancers in pursuit, but these managed to recapture only one meca, and even she did not go back easily. The soldier who captured her had to strike her with his machete, wounding her severely. Cos sent news of the outbreak to the military authorities in Veracruz and the surrounding regions, and although word spread quickly, there is no record that any of the Apache women were recaptured. Viceroy Azanza was furious and ordered Lieutenant Cos to be tried for dereliction of duty, but after a court martial, in July of 1799 he was found not guilty, mainly because it was determined that he had been given too few troops to properly escort such a large number of prisoners.[13]

If the Apache women who fled from the Venta de la Rinconada defied their fate of being sentenced to hard labor, they were extremely fortunate. For the overwhelming number of prisoners, the possibility of escaping from servitude was almost nonexistent. The only hope some had was to accept the Spaniards' teachings and agree to become Christians. In this case, deportation to Veracruz and Havana might be delayed and perhaps even suspended. A list from June of 1801 of Apache women held in the Real Hospicio de Pobres, or Royal Home for Indigents, in Mexico City reveals how this was possible.

The list shows that sixty-seven Apache women were held in the facility, including twenty-year-old María Dolores, a Christian, who had been admitted on December 26, 1797, and had remained there for over three years. Another nine Apaches had arrived on August 20, 1800, including one Christian, twenty-five-year-old María Guadalupe; along with three "gentile" women aged seventy; and five others between ages thirty and fifty. Almost a year later, on June 15, 1801, a large group of fifty-seven Apache women was moved into the facility, including six *Cristianas* between sixteen and thirty-five years. The remainder of the women were gentiles, including three said to be aged at least eighty, six aged fifty, and forty-two others between sixteen and twenty-five. When the time came to ship them to Veracruz, only those "too old or sick to move and to be made Christians" were allowed to remain. Fifty-four gentiles were sent to Veracruz. All eight of the Apaches identified as Christians, along with one sick gentile and several of the oldest women, were allowed to remain. Whether genuine or feigned, the acceptance of Spanish religious beliefs opened one of the few doors left to the prisoners to escape laboring on the fortifications.[14]

But if any of these Apache women ever managed to return to their homeland along the northern frontier, whether through conversion or escape, they would not have found the situation much changed. Spanish officers throughout the Interior Provinces continued the balancing act of alternating between peace with those Apaches who accommodated, and military expeditions against those who refused. Even after Pedro de Nava relinquished his position as commandant general in 1802, his successor, Nemesio Salcedo y Salcedo, continued to oversee campaigns into the Apachería and against any recalcitrants from the establecimientos de paz who openly practiced raiding. Salcedo's men also continued to take prisoners and send them south into exile.

In February of 1802, the new commandant general dispatched a collera of eighty-four captured Apaches, including twenty-one men and sixty-three women, the youngest being two girls of fifteen and the oldest a woman of ninety. The escort of twenty-two soldiers under Sergeant José Antonio Uribes arrived in Mexico on April 1, 1802, and deposited the men in the Acordada and the women in the Hospicio de Pobres. The following year another group of eighty-two Apaches was sent out containing nineteen men, sixty-two women, and one girl of twelve. Both contingents were remarkable in that unlike so many others, they included no young children. The reasons for this are unknown.[15]

Between 1804 and 1809, Salcedo oversaw the deportation of at least three more colleras of Apaches, although the actual number of prisoners seems to have diminished. Nevertheless, the policy had proven so effective that even after the outbreak of the revolt of Father Miguel Hidalgo y Costilla in 1810 that initiated the Mexican War of Independence, Spanish authorities continued to capture and exile Apache prisoners. Amid the tumult of what in many ways was a civil war, authorities in the Interior Provinces still marshaled the military forces necessary to exercise a certain level of control over the Apaches in the region. Punitive campaigns were dispatched into the hinterland to strike at those who harassed the Spaniards, and prisoners continued to be taken and deported, although after 1810 most were sent to areas relatively near the frontier. For example, Apaches captured in the province of Sonora were often sent to the Presidio of San Buenaventura in the neighboring province of Nueva Vizcaya or to the Villa de Chihuahua. The farthest south that the colleras appear to have been dispatched was to the city of Durango. That this expense and effort would be maintained in the midst of such upheavals clearly indicates how valuable the Spanish perceived the policy to be.[16]

With the achievement of Mexican Independence in 1821, the deportation of Apache prisoners of war, like so many other aspects of Spanish policy along the northern frontier, came to an end. The peace establishments continued in place, largely of their own internal momentum, for several years. But the vagaries of Mexican national politics left the administration of the northern frontier on a distinctly secondary tier. The struggles of nationhood saw the newly independent Mexico change from an empire to a confederation of states and back to a centralized republic, all in the span of a few years. Military officers engaged in praetorian coups with alarming regularity, and the weakness of the central government was felt most on the edges, with the frontiers left more and more to their own devices. Bereft of support, the peace establishments began to wither. The Apaches de paz had acquired at least some of the rudiments of Hispanic culture, but without the fear of death and deportation or the inducements of peace and food, their own powerful cultural traditions, especially raiding and warfare, emerged again. The semi-sedentary lifestyle, encompassing limited agriculture and seasonal harvesting of wild plants and game, supplemented by trade, extortion, or theft, became the norm for many Apaches. The general weakness of the Mexican government along the northern frontier accentuated Apache strength, and by 1831 the cycle of violence was renewed with both sides returning to a state of open warfare.

If, in the end, the effort to control the Apaches through the mechanisms of the establecimientos de paz did not last, it did manage to secure an acceptable level of coexistence in the last decades of Spanish rule. Beginning about 1790, the studied application of force and coercion, punishment and reward, and severed heads and full bellies proved to be the most effective strategy the Spanish had ever used against the Apaches. For thirty years, it guaranteed a greater measure of peace along the frontier than either side had ever known. In the context of the application of power—the alternating strategy of the mailed fist and the velvet glove—the deportation of Apache prisoners of war accomplished its purpose by placing a powerful constraint on the behavior of those viewed as enemies or potential enemies. The threat of open war, even as a last resort, was always the base upon which the Spaniards built their structures. Among Spanish tactics of war, deportation was one of the most lasting and effective.

For the Apaches, the generations that lived in this era and fought the Spaniards witnessed in the deportations a policy that was, in effect, a means of applied terror. Death in battle or in the constant series of raids and counterraids was a feature of life that had been part of Apache society for decades, if not centuries. To be slain by an enemy, though to be dreaded, was at least understood; it may even have been embraced and accepted as "normal." Being captured by the enemy was also an intelligible fate that, under certain circumstances, held forth the possibility of being exchanged and redeemed and ultimately reunited with one's family. But the Spanish policy of deportation and exile introduced a new element into the equation, namely that of the unknown. Clearly, the Apaches had some knowledge of circumstances surrounding the deportations. Prisoners did manage to escape (with enough frequency to cause the Spaniards apprehension) and presumably tell their own kin the terrible destiny from which they had been delivered. In at least one instance, Apaches had traveled alongside doomed prisoners and witnessed their dispositions firsthand. But the vast majority of those sent into exile never returned, and their ultimate fate remained unknown and unknowable, leaving their families and friends to lament and to wonder and to dread. For the Spaniards, this represented the ultimate vindication of deterrence. For the Apaches, it was literally a fate worse than death.

Epilogue

The German military theorist Carl von Clausewitz defined war as "an act of violence intended to compel our opponent to fulfill our will." If this is so, the long, cruel war between Spain and the Apaches witnessed an evolution of the "will" on both sides. The centuries of violence forced both peoples to adapt their respective cultures' understanding of the nature of the conflict, not only as to the means employed but also as to the ultimate ends to be achieved.[1]

Regarding the Spaniards, this evolution is most clearly evident in their changing definition of "victory." Their relationship with the Apaches began as an attempt to dominate them. The Spaniards tried to force the Apaches to conform to outside conceptions — to adhere to Christianity and to assume at least the trappings of Hispanic civilization. They had used this template successfully against numerous other Indian peoples, but it gradually became apparent that it would not work against these. The Apache homelands, for the most part, lay beyond the borders of Spanish control, and for a variety of reasons the white men did not seek to conquer them. They engaged instead in a limited struggle designed to stop Apache raiding into regions where the Spanish at least nominally held sway. This tactic resulted in a war of both limited means and limited ends. Victory for the Spaniards thus evolved from domination and assimilation into pacification.

Within the constraints of this limited war, the Spanish policy of the mailed fist and the velvet glove—alternating severe violence with the inducements of food, goods, and protection—was recognized early on as the most effective method to use in the struggle. Yet it would require decades for the policy to be applied with consistency, due to repeated changes in the military command structure of the Interior Provinces and the personal predilections of high-ranking Spanish officers. Nevertheless, in the midst of this "confusion of power," the Spaniards remained consistent in several aspects, chief among them their use of the policy of deportation.

Drawing on their historic dealings with Islamic corsairs, on European perceptions that culminated in the Enlightenment, and on their own practices with other Indian peoples, the Spanish attempted to apply "the rules of war" in their conflict against the Apaches. Treating captured Apaches as prisoners of war freed the captives, theoretically, from the possibility of perpetual enslavement, while deportation mitigated their risk of slaughter by their captors. Although these rules limited the behavior of the Spaniards in the theater of war, they also obliterated the possibility of the prisoners' return to their own people almost as surely as if they had been killed outright.

Beginning with the bellicose commandant inspector Hugo O'Conor in the early 1770s, through the reign of the more bureaucratic-minded commandant general Teodoro de Croix between 1776 and 1783, and lasting through the long duel for power between western commandant general Jacobo Ugarte y Loyola and the eastern commander Juan de Ugalde from 1786 to 1790, the Spanish repeatedly employed deportation as the ultimate weapon against the Apaches. Even after Viceroy Bernardo de Gálvez drew up the "peace policies" enumerated in his 1786 Instructions, Spaniards routinely used deportation despite the seeming changes in policy.

When, over this same period, the Spaniards modified the means by which they waged the war and even changed, or at the very least adapted, the ends of the conflict itself, deportation continued. Tactics designed to crush the Apaches through decisive campaigns gave way to a war of attrition. Raid and counterraid inevitably led to the employment of terror—massacre and mutilation—as a regular feature on both sides. The Spanish eventually modified their aims in the war as well, from seeking to defeat the Apaches militarily into a more pragmatic effort to reduce the violence they perpetrated to an acceptable level. The entire system surrounding the establecimientos de paz revolved around this notion. To use an anachronistic modern concept, what the Spaniards ultimately sought to impose upon the Apaches was the concept of deterrence; and as demonstrated by modern conflicts, the ultimate aim of deterrence is not necessarily peace, but the absence of war.

That the Apaches themselves came to this realization is seen in the adaptations they made in both means and ends during the long history of the conflict. After the implementation of the line of presidios called for in the Regulations of 1772, the Spanish launched large-scale campaigns all along the frontier, and the Apaches responded as they always had. Innumerable members of Apache rancherías conducted innumerable vengeance raids seeking blood for blood. But the Spaniards inexorably adapted their own tactics. The soldiers' continuous small-scale attacks on Apache homelands strained the physical resources of many Apache groups, limited their ability to acquire food and supplies, and steadily diminished their population base. Finally, the deportation policy closed the door on the long-held practice of prisoner exchange and inflicted further losses on groups already reduced by battle casualties.

When offered the opportunity to settle at the establecimientos de paz, many Apaches accepted and gradually came to understand that this provided them with a mixture of security coupled with an ability, albeit reduced and regulated, to maintain many of their traditional cultural practices, including raiding and warfare. Now, however, they would often fight alongside the Spaniards, not against them. During the long tenure of Commandant General Pedro de Nava between 1793 and 1802, Apaches de paz increasingly allied with the Spaniards against their independent kinsmen in the hinterlands, becoming perhaps the single most important component in the entire system surrounding the peace establishments. For these Apaches, at least, the violence that they regarded as an integral part of their traditional lifeway ultimately became a method of accommodation.[2]

For the Spaniards, the system supporting the Apaches de paz was clearly less onerous to the royal treasury than the costs required for military operations, even the successful ones. The diminution of violence—and its concomitant loss of life and property—now enjoyed along much of the frontier was obviously worth the effort. If the Apaches as a whole were not subdued or Christianized, many of them were at least quiescent, and for Spanish officials in the Interior Provinces, in Mexico City, and even in Madrid, that proved to be enough. For the peoples of the northern frontier, both Hispanic and Apache, the great irony was that this realization—the end of countless years of brutal warfare—was only achieved as Spain's control over the area waned and expired in the wake of Mexican Independence in 1821.[3]

Two new nations, Mexico and the United States, would come to control the region, and the hard lessons learned by Spanish and Apache would be renewed, revamped, and replayed over subsequent decades. The United States eventually became the power that most impacted the Apaches and that would come to control their destiny. In 1829, at the same time that the Mexican government still vainly tried to maintain the rump of the peace establishments on the frontier, the United States began a series of "Indian removals" of the native peoples of the southeast, expanding a concept that reflected, however dimly, the Spanish policy of deportation.

Removal and segregation became the model for dealing with all Indians controlled by the United States, a model that the Apaches themselves would come to experience. Over half a century later, in 1886, the Americans would finally vanquish the Apaches, and as the last act in the conflict, declare Geronimo and some three hundred Chiricahua Apaches to be prisoners of war. They were all subsequently deported to Florida, most of them never to return to their homelands. As it had been under the Spaniards, deportation would be the ultimate weapon used against those who resisted the Americans, and like their ancestors in the colleras, their destiny would unfold not in their own country, but as exiles in a faraway land.[4]

Appendix

NUMBER OF APACHES DEPORTED

In the thirty-seven years between 1773 and 1810, thirty-two known colleras were sent out. Of these, twenty-seven have clear, partial, or estimated numbers of prisoners, for a total of 2,266 individuals deported. However, this total is probably low by at least one-third, as many of the records do not give complete figures. Some, for example, give the number of prisoners who arrived at the destination but not how many set out.

Of the 2,266 persons mentioned in the records, 1,330 are clearly delineated as men, women, or children. Of these, 16.9 percent were listed as "men," indicating to the Spaniards that they were capable of bearing arms. This probably included boys who had reached puberty—that is, who were older than twelve or fourteen years of age. The largest percentage of these delineated prisoners, 60.4 percent, were women, indicating females who had reached puberty. Children, including newborns and infants, composed 22.6 percent of the deportees. Some of the colleras listed boys and girls separately, while others did not, often using generic terms like *párvulos,* especially for those under four years of age.

The Apaches who made the journey to Mexico City suffered various fates. Of those whose destiny is recorded, only 5.6 percent managed to escape, the vast majority of them in two mass breakouts in 1783 and 1799. Another 10.3 percent were recorded as having died, mainly due to disease, although 1.1 percent were killed while trying to escape. Many more Apaches, 10.3 percent, were either left behind too sick to continue or were deposited in Spanish households as domestics. The vast majority of the latter were children young enough to be inculcated into Hispanic culture. Among the twenty-seven colleras whose fate is recorded, the number of prisoners who survived the journey from the northern frontier was approximately 74 percent, or just under three-quarters. However, even assuming that the prisoners were not subject to any illnesses in the capital, the mortality rate undoubtedly continued to rise as they undertook at least one more journey to Veracruz. And many of the adults had to endure a third journey overseas to Havana. The survival rate for any individuals unfortunate enough to undergo all three legs of the journey is unknown, but it must have been no better than 50 percent.

Details of Apaches Deported

Year	Origin	Number	Men	Women	Children	Died/ Killed	Left/ Deposited	Escaped
1773	San Saba	14	0	?	?	0	7	8
1775	Carrizal	95	—	—	—	—	—	—
1776	Chihuahua	128	—	—	—	—	—	—
1777	Chihuahua	150	—	—	—	—	—	—
1781	Chihuahua	51	—	—	—	—	—	—
1782	Chihuahua	95	—	—	—	—	—	—
1783	Monclova	28	—	—	—	—	—	—
1783	Chihuahua	142	—	—	—	9	—	38
1783	Monclova	33	6	24	2	—	—	—
1784	Chihuahua	?	—	—	—	—	—	—
1787	Arispe	154	21	47	86	10	45	2
1787	Santa Rosa	?	—	—	—	—	—	—
1788	San Antonio	15	0	13	2	—	—	—
1788	Chihuahua	77	—	—	—	—	—	15?
1789	Chihuahua	108	—	—	63	6	29?	0
1789	Chihuahua	180	8	87	85	67	25	0
1791	Chihuahua	74	7	34	33	6	3	0
1792	Conchos	82	16	48	17	14	1	0
1794	Chihuahua	95	18	72	5	14	—	—
1794	Conchos	84	28	56	0	2	7	0
1796	?	61	4	57	—	22	11	0
1797	Conchos	71	11	57	3	38	17	0
1798	Santa Rosa	49	15	34	0	20	0	0
1798	Conchos	100	—	—	—	—	—	—
1799	?	95	26	66	3	1	0	52
1800	?	?	—	—	—	—	8	—
1801	?	?	—	—	—	—	57	—
1802	Conchos	84	21	63	0	—	—	—
1803	Conchos	82	19	62	1	—	—	—
1804	?	46	10	36	0	—	—	—
1808	Chihuahua	?	—	—	—	—	—	—
1809	?	64	16	47	1	—	—	—
Total	31	2,266	226	803	301	209	210	115

Notes

Archival sources have been identified by the following abbreviations:

AGI, Guad	Archivo General de Indias, Audiencia de Guadalajara
AGN, PI	Archivo General de la Nación, Mexico, Provincias Internas
AGS, GM	Archivo General de Simancas, Spain, Guerra Moderna
AGS, SGU	Archivo General de Simancas, Spain, Secretaría del Despacho de Guerra
JC	Presidio de San Felipe y Santiago de Janos Records, 1706–1858, Benson Latin American Collection, General Libraries, University of Texas at Austin
JMC	Historical Archives, 1710–1856, Manuscripts and Documents of Janos (microfilm), C. L. Sonnichsen Special Collections Department, University Library, University of Texas at El Paso
UNM	University of New Mexico, Albuquerque

Illegible words in documents are indicated by dashes: [—]

INTRODUCTION

1. There are several reasons for speculating that the hands were put into an earthenware jar. First, perishable items shipped between the Interior Provinces and Mexico City were placed in a variety of containers, including boxes, trunks, and earthenware vessels. However, particularly fragile items or those with a high risk of spoilage, such as certain types of foodstuffs and liquids, were most often shipped in jars or jugs. There are records for jars of oil, wine, lard, and even dried shrimp. Second, records from the nineteenth century regarding the preservation of human body parts, specifically whole heads, indicate that they were preserved in jars. An example is the severed head of the American filibuster Henry Crabb, preserved after his ill-fated attack on the town of Caborca, Sonora, in 1857. Finally, the condition of the recovered severed Apache hands would have necessitated a special container, not just one chosen at random. The hands would have been mummified by the time they were retrieved, and they would have needed placement in a hard-sided container. If they were merely wrapped in cloth and put into a bag or sack, they would have been crushed, the skin would have flaked off, and the cartilage and bones would have been jumbled together. In this state, they would have been useless for the purpose of verification. Wooden boxes and trunks might have provided an adequate container, but such items were regarded as furnishings and would have been considered valuable, expensive, and hard to replace—not easily given up, especially on the northern frontier. A much more readily available, inexpensive, and disposable container would have been earthenware, such as an *olla* or *botilla,* filled with sand or liquid that would have cushioned the hands as well as preserved them indefinitely. Thus a jar is the most likely container for the hands. See, for example, "6 pounds of hair powder . . . and bottle; .1 arroba of oil in two botijos, 2 limetas [small bottles] of Castilian aguardiente; 1 pound of saffron in its bottle." College of the Most Holy Cross, August 31, 1779, Account of the assets remitted by the Reverend Father Guardian Fray Sebastian Flores for the new mission, in "Account book for Mission San Lorenzo de la Santa Cruz, Camp Wood, Texas, 1762 to 1769"; and "Purísima Concepción del Río Colorado, near Winterhaven, California, 1779 to 1781," Roll 15, Frames 5009–5041, Celaya Microfilm. For Crabb's preserved head, see Forbes, *Crabb's Filibustering Expedition*, 30.

CHAPTER 1. A CRUEL AND BLOODY WAR

1. Manuel de Echeagaray, "Hoja de Servicio," December 1787, legajo 7278, Archivo General de Simancas, Guerra Moderna (hereinafter AGS, GM), microfilm copy at the Center for Southwest Research, University of New Mexico, Albuquerque (hereinafter UNM); "Diario de la Campaña executada por el Capt. Don Manuel de Echeagaray en el Campo del Enemigo, Santa Cruz, February 13, 1788," certified copy by Juan Gasiot y Miralles, Janos, March 13, 1788, vol. 128, pt. 2, exp. 4, Archivo General de la Nación, Mexico, Provincias Internas (hereinafter AGN, PI), microfilm copy at Center for Southwest Research, UNM.

2. John, *Storms Brewed in Other Men's Worlds*, 20–23, 40–57; Kessell, *Spain in the Southwest*, 32–47, 74–96; Carter, *Indian Alliances*, 118–64.

3. John, *Storms Brewed in Other Men's Worlds*, 70–79; Forbes, *Apache, Navaho, and Spaniard*; Carter, *Indian Alliances*, 184–204.

4. Anderson, *Indian Southwest, 1580–1830*, 57–66, 105–27; Dunn, "Apache Relations in Texas, 1718–1750," 198–269.

5. It is difficult at this distance to determine if the Apaches as delineated by the Spaniards correspond to those groups known at the end of the nineteenth century and in modern times. In 1777, Hugo O'Conor listed the Apaches from west to east under the tribal names the Spaniards had given them (and their own tribal names): Chiricaguis (Sigilandé); Gileños (Setozende); Mimbreños (Chiguende); Mescaleros (Zetosende); Faraones (Selcotisanende); and the rancherías of Pascual (Culchahende), of Ligero (Cachuguinde), of Alonso (Yncagende), of Chief Bigotes (Sigilande); and the Natagés (Zetosende). Whether due to a faulty memory or simple ignorance or confusion, O'Conor repeated several names; did not list the Navajos, Lipans, Lipiyans, Jicarillas, or Llaneros; and counted as independent groups several heads of rancherías that were in fact part of larger entities. O'Conor, *Defenses of Northern New Spain*, 70–71. Almost twenty years later, Lieutenant Colonel Antonio Cordero y Bustamante produced a much clearer, thorough listing of the Apaches, identifying them as Tontos (Vinni ettinen-ne), Chiricaguis (Segatajen-ne), Gileños (Tjuiccujen-ne), Mimbreños (Iccujen-ne), Faraones (Yntajen-ne), Mescaleros (Sejen-ne), Llaneros (Cuelcajen-ne), Lipanes (Lipajen-ne), and Navajos (Yutajen-ne). Cordero had a much longer association with the Apaches and a deeper knowledge of their language and self-identification than O'Conor. Cordero, for some reason, omits the Jicarillas in his listing, although he

does refer to them elsewhere in his report. Matson and Schroeder, eds., "Cordero's Description of the Apache, 1796," 336. A few years after Cordero's report, Lieutenant José Cortés produced another report on the Apaches that provided additional details. Cortés remarked that the Faraones were "believed to be a branch of the Jicarillas" and that the Llaneros were "divided into three categories which are the Natajés, Lipiyanes, and Llaneros." Cortés y de Olarte, *Views from the Apache Frontier*, 49–53. A brief discussion of the eighteenth century Spanish terms can be found in Opler, "Apachean Culture Pattern and Its Origins," in Ortiz, *Southwest*, 388–89. Our ability to link eighteenth century Spanish names with modern Apache identities is imprecise. The Tontos or Coyoteros are the ancestors of the Western Apaches that today inhabit the White Mountain and San Carlos reservations of Arizona. Goodwin, *Western Apache Raiding and Warfare*, 487–88. Of the four primary band identifications of the Chiricahuas, the Chiricaguis are best associated with the Chokonen, the Mimbreños with the Bedonkohe, and the Gileños with the Chihenne. The Spaniards do not seem to have distinguished the Nednhi, or Southern Chiricahuas, as a separate group. Opler, "Chiricahua Apache," in *Southwest*, 416–18. The Faraones and Natages appear to be historic names for a northern and southern division of the present-day Mescaleros or distinct groups that amalgamated with the Mescaleros. Opler, "Mescalero Apache," in *Southwest*, 420, 437–38. The Jicarillas were identified as such by the Spaniards as early as 1700; by the late 1780s they were joined by the Lipiyans and Llaneros, previously independent groups that had been driven to seek refuge with the Jicarillas as a result of pressure from the Comanches. Tiller, "Jicarilla Apache," in *Southwest*, 447–50.

6. Opler, "Apachean Culture Pattern and Its Origins," 368–76; Goodwin, *Western Apache Raiding and Warfare*, 14–18, 253–63; John, *Storms Brewed in Other Men's Worlds*, 57–64; Griffen, *Apaches at War and Peace*, 1–18.

7. Moorhead, *Presidio*, 3–47.

8. Albi, *Defensa de las Indias*, 45–49, 53–67; Kuethe, *Cuba, 1753–1815*, 4–29; Segovia, *Lake of Stone*, 132–61.

9. Navarro García, *Don José de Gálvez*, 134–48; Moorhead, *Presidio*, 55–61.

10. Moorhead, *Presidio*, 64–68.

11. Brinckerhoff and Faulk, *Lancers for the King*, 31, 33, 35. The Spanish used the term "gentile" to refer to those Indians who had not been Christianized or Hispanicized.

CHAPTER 2. PRISONERS

1. Daniel, "Diary of Pedro José de la Fuente," *Southwestern Historical Quarterly* 60:260–61, 266, 271–72, 274–280.

2. Karsten, *Laws, Soldiers, and Combat,* 2–21; Fooks, *Prisoners of War,* 7–12; Contamine, *War in the Middle Ages,* 255–302; Barker, *Agincourt,* 288–94; Keegan, *Face of Battle,* 46–51, 107–12; Montesquieu, *Spirit of Laws,* bk. 15, ch. 2, 109.

3. Fooks, *Prisoners of War,* 7–12; Burrows, *Forgotten Patriots*; Braudel, *Mediterranean and the Mediterranean World,* 2:865–91; Barrio Gozalo, *Esclavos y Cautivos.*

4. Hanke, *Spanish Struggle for Justice in the Conquest of America*; Powell, *Soldiers, Indians, and Silver,* 109–11, 252–57; Carter, *Indian Alliances,* 129–31, 137, 171, 176–77; Weber, *Bárbaros,* 144–45, 234–35.

5. Brooks, *Captives and Cousins,* 31–36, 50–55, 123–25; Naylor and Polzer, eds., *Pedro de Rivera and the Military Regulations for Northern New Spain 1724–1729,* 279; Barr, *Peace Came in the Form of a Woman,* 168–70.

6. Jackson, ed., *Imaginary Kingdom,* 205.

7. Brinckerhoff and Faulk, *Lancers for the King,* 33.

8. I have used the term "deportation" to include individuals sent into exile or banished for criminal or political reasons, as well as the forced relocation of large groups or populations mainly to ensure governmental control of conquered areas. In this usage, the removal is compulsory and is distinct from colonization. Kamen, *Spanish Inquisition,* 18–28, 214–29; Butler, "British Convicts Shipped to American Colonies," 12–33; Hughes, *Fatal Shore,* 36–42.

9. Pike, "Penal Servitude in the Spanish Empire," 21–40.

10. Powell, *Soldiers, Indians, and Silver,* 109.

11. Nentvig, *Rudo Ensayo,* 134.

CHAPTER 3. REGULATIONS AND INSTRUCTIONS

1. Juan Joseph Lemus to Don Pedro Antonio Quiepo de Llano, Real de Santa Eulalia de Chihuahua, February 12, 1770, in "Testimonio de Diligencias sobre insultos de los Indios Bárbaros Enemigos," vol. 42, AGN, PI.

2. Santiago, *Red Captain,* 35.

3. Navarro García, *Don José de Gálvez*, 209–38; Moorhead, *Presidio*, 68–71; Santiago, *Red Captain*, 5–65; Bobb, *Viceregency of Antonio María de Bucareli*, 128–38.

4. Moore and Bean, "The Interior Provinces of New Spain," 276–77; Navarro García, *Don José de Gálvez*, 238n108; "Cuenta de Real Hacienda del Año de 1775," Chihuahua, May 18, 1775, legajo 458, AGI, Guad.

5. Navarro García, *Don José de Gálvez*, 238–42; Santiago, *Red Captain*, 65–73.

6. Manuel de Escorza, "Estado que manifiesta los caudales que se han acopiado y gastado en el Real Thesoreria de Chihuahua con los Piquetes de Dragoñas y Cuerpo Volante y Caballería que sirven en estas fronteras desde de primero de Henero hasta último de Marzo de Mil setecientos setenta y seis," Chihuahua, April 1, 1776; Manuel de Escorza, "Estado que manifiesta los caudales que existen oy día de la fecha en la Thesoreria de Chihuahua que es de mi cargo, pertenecientes a la Expedición de estas Fronteras de Nueva Vizcaya," Chihuahua, May 2, 1777, both in vol. 71, AGN, PI.

7. Navarro García, *Don José de Gálvez*, 275–93; Moorhead, *Presidio*, 75–80; Bobb, *Viceregency of Antonio María de Bucareli*, 143–55.

8. Thomas, *Teodoro de Croix*, 19.

9. Navarro García, *Don José de Gálvez*, 293–318, 351–62; Moorhead, *Presidio*, 80–84; Moorhead, *Apache Frontier*, 119–23; Weber, *Bárbaros*, 156–58; Manuel de Escorza, "Estado, Corte, y Tanteo de los caudales que se han acopiado y gastado en el Real Thesorería de mi cargo, pertenecientes a la Expedición Militar en estas Fronteras todo el Próximo anterior mes de Diciembre de Mil Setecientos setenta y ocho, y de que existen en la Moneda de Nueva Estampa: formado con intervención Sr. Correxidor de esta Villa Don Francisco Menocal," Chihuahua, January 1, 1779, countersigned by Menocal, vol. 71, AGN, PI; Caballero de Croix to Juan Baptista Perú, Arispe, January 20, April 2, and April 17, 1781, in folder 4, sec. 2, Presidio de San Felipe y Santiago de Janos Records, 1706–1858, Benson Latin American Collection, General Libraries, University of Texas at Austin (hereinafter JC).

10. Moorhead, "Spanish Deportation of Hostile Apaches," 211–12; Starnes, "Juan de Ugalde," 50–51; Moorhead, *Apache Frontier*, 202, 204–206.

11. Pedro Tueros to Viceroy Mathias de Gálvez, Villa de Santiago de la Monclova, September 11, 1783, vol. 24, AGN, PI. "*Indios Gandules*" was a derogatory term the Spanish used for Apache males capable of bearing arms.

12. Navarro García, *Don José de Gálvez*, 429–40; Moorhead, *Presidio*, 95–98.

13. Phelipe de Neve to Captain Juan Bautista Perú, Arispe, January 28, 1784, reel 4, Historical Archives, 1710–1856, Manuscripts and Documents of Janos (microfilm), C. L. Sonnichsen Special Collections Department, University Library, University of Texas at El Paso (hereinafter JMC); Griffen, *Apaches at War and Peace*, 39–52.

14. Manuel Delgado, Monthly review of the Presidio of San Buenaventura, February 1, 1785, reel 9, JMC.

15. Moorhead, *Apache Frontier*, 123–32; Weber, *Spanish Frontier in North America*, 227–30; Weber, *Bárbaros*, 183–85.

CHAPTER 4. THE CONFUSION OF POWER

1. Méritos y Servicios de Don Domingo de Vergara, October 17, 1785, legajo 521, AGI, Guad; Navarro García, *Don José de Gálvez*, 438.

2. Moorhead, *Apache Frontier*, 19–24, 42–49, 59–72, 123–33; Starnes, "Juan de Ugalde," 1–61; Navarro García, *Don José de Gálvez*, 376–80, 387–90, 450–57.

3. Nelson, "Campaigning in the Big Bend," 200–27; Moorhead, *Apache Frontier*, 182–92, 206–17.

4. Nelson, "Juan de Ugalde and Picax-Ande Ins-Tinsle," 438–64; Moorhead, *Apache Frontier*, 217–36.

5. Moorhead, *Apache Frontier*, 72–80; Navarro García, *Don José de Gálvez*, 460–64.

6. Moorhead, *Apache Frontier*, 240–45; Ugarte, "Relación del Numero de los Enemigos Apaches que han muerto y aprisiona las Armas del Rey; y de los Cautivos que han libertado en las Provincias internas desde 9 de Mayo de 1786 en que tomé el mando General de ellos," Arispe, September 30, 1787, enclosed with Ugarte to Flores, Arispe, October 1, 1787, vol. 112, AGN, PI.

7. Ugarte to Flores, Arispe, November 9, 1787; enclosed with "Noticia de los Apaches de ambos sexos Prisioneros de Guerra remitidos en Collera de Guadalaxara a cargo del Teniente del Regimiento de Dragonas de España Don Ygnacio Ullate, Alférez del mismo Don Joseph Loredo, y Sargento de la Compa. de Voluntarios Manuel Terminel," Flores to Ugarte, Mexico, December 18, 1787, vol. 106, AGN, PI.

8. Moorhead, *Apache Frontier*, 82–86, 192–98, 237–46.

9. Ugalde, Presidio de San Antonio de Bexar, April 28, 1788,

vol. 111, AGN, PI; Rivero, "Cuenta de gastos de conducción de Apaches a México, hecha por el cadete del presidio del Pitic, don José María del Rivero," Pitic, August 17, 1788, vol. 230, AGN, PI.

10. Moorhead, *Apache Frontier*, 194–96; Griffen, *Apaches at War and Peace*, 62.

11. Cordero to Ugarte, Janos, December 4, 1788, reel 9, JMC; Ugarte to Cordero, Chihuahua, December 13, 1788, folder 5, sec. 2, JC.

12. Domingo de Bergaña, "Estado que manifiesta el número de Piezas Apaches Prisioneros a quienes les pasé revista en dos del corriente mes de la fecha, y conduce el Teniente de Voluntarios Don Juan Sartorio a la 3a. Compa. Volante situada en el Pilar de Conchos," Real Caxa de Chihuahua, January 9, 1789, enclosed with Bergaña to Flores, Chihuahua, January 9, 1789; Ugarte to Bergaña, Valle de San Bartolomé, December 14, 1788, certified copy by Bergaña, Chihuahua, March 9, 1789; Flores to Bergaña, Mexico, February 3, 1789; Sartorio, "Formado cargo y data que yo Don Juan Sartorio, Teniente de la Compañia de Voluntarios de Cataluña, rindo del caudal que he recivido en la Villa de Chihuahua para mantener las Piezas Apaches que se pusieron a mí desde 24 inclusive de Diciembre de 1788 hasta inclusive 26 de Enero de 1789 que las entregué al Sargto. Nicolás Tarín del Orden del Sr. Comte General caudal sobrante," Hacienda del Río Florido, January 27, 1789, certified copy by Juan Gassiot y Miralles, Chihuahua, February 14, 1789, with twenty-three receipts attached; "Relación que expresa el número de Piezas Apaches que se ha puesto y el entrado al cargo del Teniente de Voluntarios Don Juan Sartorio desde 22 de Diciembre de 1788 hasta el hoy día de la fecha salidas que ha habido por muerte y demás causas," with seven accompanying documents; Sartorio, receipts as follows: No. 1, Chihuahua, December 24, 1788; No. 2, Chihuahua, December 24, 1788, through January 2, 1789; No. 3, Chihuahua, same period; No. 4, Chihuahua, January 3 and 4, 1789; No. 5, Chihuahua, December 24, 1788, through January 3, 1789; Sartorio, documents as follows: Doc. 1, Don Juan Francisco García, Theniente de Cura, Chihuahua, December 30, 1789; Doc. 3, Don Juan Francisco García, Theniente de Cura, Chihuahua, January 1, 1789; Doc. 4, Antonio Mendes, Chihuahua, January 1, 1789, vol. 156, AGN, PI.

13. Sartorio, receipts as follows: No. 6, Rancho de Fresno, January 5, 1789; No. 7, Rancho de la Noria, January 6, 1789; No. 8, Rancho de Borbolla, January 7, 1789; No. 9, Rancho de San Antonio, January 8, 1789; No. 10, Rancho de San Pedro, January 9, 1789; No. 11, Rancho de

Tres Hermanas, January 10, 1789; No. 12, Rancho de la Voca, January 11, 1789; No. 13, Presidio de Conchos, January 12 and 13, 1789. Sartorio, documents as follows: Doc. 5, Antonio Mendes, Chihuahua, January 5, 1789; Doc. 6, Sebastián Florez, Conchos, January 13, 1789, vol. 156, AGN, PI.

14. Sartorio, Doc. 7, Mariano Oviedo, Valle de San Bartolomé, January 19, 1789; Sartorio, receipts as follows: No. 14, Rancho de Sapien, January 14; No. 15, Hacienda de San Gregorio, January 15; No. 16, Valle de San Bartolomé, January 16; No. 17, Valle de San Bartolomé, January 16 and 18; No. 18, Valle de San Bartolomé, January 18; No. 19, Hacienda de la Concepción, January 19; No. 20, Río Florido, January 21; No. 21, Hacienda de San Francisco de el Río Florido, January 20–25; No. 22, Estancia del Río Florido, January 26; No. 23, Hacienda de el Río Florido, January 26, vol. 156, AGN, PI.

15. "Cuenta y cargo y data que yo Sargento Nicolás Tarín del [——]-guido del caudal que recivi del Teniente de Voluntarios Don Juan Sartorio para mantener desde el día 27 de Enero de 1789 noventa y ocha Piezas Apaches que de orden del Sr. Comte. Gerl. [——]uyo a el cadete Don Mariano Varela por haverme enfermo en Serrogordo," Cerro Gordo, January 31, 1789; Tarín, receipts as follows: No. 1, Hacienda de San Francisco Xavier de el Río Florido, January 27; No. 2, same place, January 28; No. 3, no location, January 29; No. 4, Cerro Gordo, January 30 and 31, 1789, vol. 156, AGN, PI.

16. Ugarte to Flores, Chihuahua, February 14, 1789; Mariano Varela, "Cuenta y cargo y data que yo Dn Mariano Varela Cadete de la 1ra Compañía Volante he seguido del caudal que recivi en Serrogordo del Sargento Nicolás Tarín para mantener las Piezas Apaches que vinieron en mi cargo, Mexico, March 28, 1789; Varela, receipts as follows: No. 1, Rancho de la Zarca, February 1; No. 2, Hacienda de la Zarca, February 2 and 3; No. 3, San Pedro del Gallo, February 4; No. 4, San Antonio de Río de Nazas, February 5 and 6; No. 5, Hacienda del Pasaje, February 7 and 8; No. 6, Hacienda Atotonilco, February 9; No. 7, Hacienda de Juan Peres, February 10; No. 8, Hacienda de San Marcos, February 11; No. 9, Hacienda de las Carsenaral, February 12; No. 10, Hacienda de Santa Catarín, February 13; No. 11, Hacienda de la Lavorcita, February 14; No. 12, Hacienda del Río de Medina, February 15; No. 13, Hacienda de Nra. Sra. de los Bolces[?] de la Sanja, February 16; No. 14, Fresnillo, February 19; No. 15, Fresnillo, February 21; No. 16, Fresnillo, February 23; No. 17, Rancho Gemalesos[?], February 24; No. 18,

Rancho de Seguro, February 25; No. 19, Hacienda de San [——] de Tlaco, February 26; No. 20, Hacienda de Pavellón, February 27; No. 21, Villa de la Encarnación, March 2; No. 22, Pueblo de Buena Vista, March 3; No. 23, Hacienda de Xaramillo, March 4; [No. 24 missing from archive]; No. 25, Hacienda de Mendoza, March 7; No. 26, Celaya, March 9; No. 27, Querétaro, Hacienda de la Calera, March 10; No. 28, Querétaro, March 12; No. 29, Hacienda de Juchitla, March 13; No. 30, San Juan del Río, March 14; No. 31, Rancho de San Antonio, March 15; No. 32, Pueblo de San Francisco Sayaniquilpam[?], March 17; No. 33, Pueblo de Tepexi del Río, March 18; No. 34, Pueblo de Quatitlán, March 19; No. 35, Mexico City, March 24; Varela to Flores, Tepexi, March 18, 1789; Flores to the Sergeant Major of the Garrison, Mexico, March 19, 1789, vol. 156, AGN, PI.

17. Ugarte to Viceroy, Chihuahua, November 27, 1789, in "Copias que contiene los partes Justificados del Capitán Don Antonio Cordero sobre efectos de su campaña y varias órdenes comunicadas a este oficial," vol. 193, AGN, PI.

CHAPTER 5. SEVERED HEADS AND CHAINED NECKS

1. Jacobo Ugarte y Loyola to Manuel Antonio Flores, Chihuahua, May 1, 1789. Ugarte had given the original order in a letter of February 19, 1789, sent from Chihuahua to Don Roque de Medina and Don Diego de Borica, the Commandant Inspectors under Ugarte; certified copy by Juan Gasiot y Miralles, Chihuahua, May 1, 1789, vol. 193, no. 528, AGN, PI. Ugarte reported the arrival in the city of twenty-three Chiricahua Apaches from Bacoachi under Alférez Graduado Don Joseph María González, to be used for several expeditions in Nueva Vizcaya around the mountains near the Presidio of San Buenaventura. Then they were to be used in a formal campaign under the command of Lieutenant Don Joseph Manuel Carrasco, scheduled to begin in May. Ugarte to Flores, Chihuahua, April 24, 1789, vol. 193, no. 519, AGN, PI. Ugarte to Flores, Chihuahua, May 1, 1789, notes the success of the campaign under Carrasco and contains the certificates for the Apache heads and prisoners. Receipt from Antonio de Barrios, San Buenaventura, April 25, 1789; receipt signed by Don José Ignacio Escageda, Don Miguel Díaz de Luna, and Don José María González, Presidio of San Buenaventura, April 29, 1789, vol. 193, no. 529, AGN, PI.

2. LeBlanc, *Prehistoric Warfare*, 44–54, 84–91, 122–24, 140–45, 234–35. Naylor and Polzer, eds., *Presidio and Militia on the Northern Frontier of New Spain*, 150, 200, 215, 222–23. Deeds, *Defiance and Deference*, 22–23, 45–46. Nentvig, *Rudo Ensayo*, 64–65.

3. Kino, *Kino's Historical Memoir of Pimería Alta*, 1:178–83, 2:28–31. Dunn, "Apache Relations in Texas," 198–269; Barr, *Peace Came in the Form of a Woman*, 163–66, 170–73; Hugo O'Conor, "Testimonios de diligencias sobre insultos de los indios bárbaros enemigos, 1770," vol. 42, AGN, PI, cited in Blyth, "Presidio of Janos," 140.

4. Jenkins, *New Hampshireman Transports Spanish Troops to Oran*, 7.

5. Hugo O'Conor, "Diario," Carrizal, September 1, 1775, vol. 88, AGN, PI; Santiago, *Massacre at the Yuma Crossing*, 163; Smith, "Spanish 'Piece' Policy in West Texas," 7–24.

6. McCarty, ed., *Desert Documentary*, 43–46; Blyth, "Presidio of Janos," 141–42.

7. Moorhead, *Apache Frontier*, 251–55; Navarro García, *Don José de Gálvez*, 469–71; Ugalde to Flores, Valle de Santa Rosa, March 4 and April 1, 1789, vol. 159, AGN, PI.

8. Ugarte to Revillagigedo, Chihuahua, December 11, 1789; Ugarte, "Estado de las Piezas Apaches que hay en esta Villa y en Conchos por las aconducirse en collera a México acargo del Alférez Francisco Xavier de Enderica," Chihuahua, December 9, 1789, certified copy by Juan Gassiot y Miralles, Chihuahua, December 11, 1789; Domingo de Bergaña, "Estado que manifiesta el número de Piezas Prisioneros Apaches a quienes les pasé revista en 9 del corriente mes y de la fecha y conducido por el Alférez Don Francisco Xavier de Enderica," Real Caxa de Chihuahua, December 9, 1789, both in vol. 155, AGN, PI.

9. Cadet Francisco Xavier de Enderica, Hoja de Servicio, Santa Cruz, December 31, 1787; First Alférez Francisco Xavier de Enderica, Hoja de Servicio, Fronteras, December 31, 1790, both in legajo 7278, AGS, GM; Ugarte to Enderica, Chihuahua, December 11, 1789; Ugarte, "Detal de la Tropa que el Alférez Don Francisco Xavier de Enderica lleva a sus órdenes para custodiar la collera de Prisioneros de que está encargado y convoyar los Atajos y Platas que salen de esta Villa," Chihuahua, December 9, 1789, certified copy by Juan Gassiot y Miralles, Chihuahua, December 11, 1789, vol. 155, AGN, PI.

10. "Diario que forma el Alférez de Presidio de Fronteras, Don Francisco Xavier de Enderica, comisionado a la conducción de Apaches prisioneros a la Capital de México," Mexico, February 20, 1790; receipts as follows: No. 1, Juan de Pagazaurtundua, Chihuahua, December 9,

1789; No. 2, Fr. Juan Ysidro Campos, Chihuahua, December 10, 1789; No. 3, Antonio Griego, Yrigoyen, December 11, 1789, vol. 155, AGN, PI.

11. "Diario que forma el Alférez de Presidio de Fronteras, Don Francisco Xavier de Enderica, February 20, 1790"; Enderica, "Estado de las Piezas Apaches de que me entregué en la Villa de Chihuahua y Pilar de Conchos," Mexico, February 24, 1790; "Cuenta de cargo y data que forma el Alférez Don Francisco Enderica de la collera que conduce para la capital de México," Mexico, February 24, 1790. Enderica, receipts as follows: No. 4, Antonio Griego, San Antonio, December 13, 1789; No. 5 [two], Antonio Fernández, Rancho de Tres Hermanos, December 15, 1789, and Antonio Griego, Rancho de Tres Hermanos, December 15, 1789; [No. 6 missing from archive]; No. 7, Fray [——], Tres Hermanos, December 16, 1789; No. 8, Joaquín Perú, Pilar de Conchos, December 18, 1789; No. 9, Antonio Griego, La Sapien, December 20, 1789; No. 10, Pedro Manuel Asuce de Armendáriz, no location, no date; No. 11, Pedro Manuel Asuce de Armendáriz, no location, December 22, 1789; No. 12, Fr. Joseph Verando Villaseñor, Hacienda de la Zarca, December 28, 1789; No. 13, Juan Bautista Fausdoas, Hacienda de la Zarca, December 20, 1789; No. 14, Antonio Griego, Paraje el Patio, December 27, 1789; No. 14[15], Fr. Juan Francisco de Pazos, Durango, January 11, 1790; No. 14[16], Fr. Juan Francisco de Pazos, Durango, January 13, 1790; No. 17, Fr. Santiago Gándara, San Isidro de la Punta, January 15, 1790; No. 15[18], Fr. José Mariano Campo Cos, Hacienda de San [——], January 16, 1790; No. 16[19], Phelipe López Moreno, Hacienda de San Juan Bautista, January 16, 1790; No. 20, Joseph Martín de Salas, Real de Sombrerete, January 17, 1790; No. 21, José María Fernández y Parada, Hacienda de Xaramillo, January 4, 1790 [date out of sequence]; No. 18[22], Nicolás Mijares Solórzano, Real de Sombrerete, January 18, 1790; No. 23, José Cayetano Caseras, Real de Sombrerete, January 18, 1790; No. 24, Antonio Griego, no location, January 19, 1790; Nos. 25–26, José María Díaz, Fresnillo, January 21, 1790; No. 27, José María Diaz, Fresnillo, January 22, 1790; Nos. 28–29, José María Díaz, Fresnillo, January 23, 1790; Nos. 30–31, José María Díaz, Fresnillo, January 24, 1790; Nos. 32–33, José María Díaz, Fresnillo, January 25, 1790; No. 34, Juan de Ledesma y Sotomayor, Fresnillo, January 25, 1790, vol. 155, AGN, PI.

12. "Diario que forma el Alférez de Presidio de Fronteras, Don Francisco Xavier de Enderica, February 20, 1790"; Enderica, receipts as follows: No. 35, José Francisco de Castañeda, Zacatecas, January 26; No. 36, Fr. José Antonio Bugarin, Zacatecas, January 27; No. 37, Mar-

iano Elías Beltrán, Hacienda de San Diego, January 27; No. 38, José Miguel Villagranal, Hacienda del Señor San José de Tlacotes, no date; No. 39, Mariano Elías Beltrán, Hacienda de San Juan, January 29, vol. 155, AGN, PI.

13. "Diario que forma el Alférez de Presidio de Fronteras, Don Francisco Xavier de Enderica, February 20, 1790"; Don Francisco Xavier de Enderica, "Estado de las Piezas Apaches," February 24, 1790; Enderica, receipts as follows: [Two unnumbered], Fr. Pedro Cardozo, Aguascalientes, February 13; No. 40, Pedro Acareza y Leyva, Aguascalientes, February 1; No. 41, José Antonio Griego, Mesón de San Juan, February 2; No. 42, Br. [Bachiller] Thomas Ybarra, León, February 5; No. 43, José Calletano Aguirre, February 6; Nos. 44–45, Br. Francisco Vergara, Silao, February 6; No. 46, Juan José de Michelena, Celaya, February 8; No. 47, José Mariano Ramírez de la [——], San Juan del Río, February 12; No. 48, Br. José Miguel Picaso, San Juan del Río, February 14; No. 49, Luis José Carrillo, San Gerónimo Aculco, February 15; No. 50, José de Piña, San Gerónimo Aculco, February 15; No. 51, José de Piña, San Gerónimo Aculco, February 18; No. 52, Juan Manuel Cassal y Avarado, San Buenaventura Quatitlán, February 19, 1790; No. 53, Joseph Antonio de León, Rancho de Carboneras, January 30; No. 54, Br. Miguel Martínez de los Ríos, Aguascalientes, January 31 [latter two receipts out of chronological sequence], vol. 155, AGN, PI.

CHAPTER 6. A SINGULAR EXPRESSION OF FRIENDSHIP

1. "Don Antonio Cordero y Bustamante, Teniente Coronel de los Reales Ejércitos y Capitán del Presidio de Janos. Certifico que los servicios contenidos en este libro están arreglados a los despachos certificaciones que me han presentado las interesadas a las hojas de servicios anteriores y pública notoriedad," Chihuahua, February 28, 1791, legajo 7047-124, AGS, GM; Matson and Schroeder, eds., "Cordero's Description of the Apaches," 339, 341.

2. Antonio Cordero to Commandant General Ugarte y Loyola, Chihuahua, October 14, 1790, and Ugarte to Viceroy Revillagigedo, Rancho de Palau, October 27, 1790, both in vol. 142, AGN, PI; Moorhead, "Spanish Deportation of Hostile Apaches," 205–20.

3. Revillagigedo to Ugarte, Mexico, November 15, 1790, vol. 142,

AGN, PI; Griffen, *Apaches at War and Peace*, 57, 60; Archer, "Deportation of Barbarian Indians," 378–79.

4. Ugarte to Revillagigedo, San Fernando, December 6, 1790, vol. 142, AGN, PI; Griffen, *Apaches at War and Peace*, 55–63, 70–78, 102–103.

5. Cordero to Ugarte, Janos, October 12, 1789, and El Paso, October 31, 1789; Ugarte to Cordero, Chihuahua, November 8, 1789, vol. 193, AGN, PI.

6. "Minuta de los Prisioneros cuya devolución solicitan los Capitanes Mimbreños," attached with Cordero to Revillagigedo, Chihuahua, February 15, 1791, vol. 142, AGN, PI; Antonio Cordero, "Noticia de los prisioneros solicitados por los capitancillos mimbreños," Chihuahua, March 31, 1791, folder 7, sec. 1, JC.

CHAPTER 7. AN OFFICER DISPOSED FOR COMMISSIONS

1. Hoja de Servicio of the Cadet Miguel Díaz de Luna, December 31, 1788, signed by Manuel de Casanova, reel 9, JMC; Hoja de Servicio of the First Alférez Don Miguel Díaz de Luna, signed by Manuel de Casanova and enclosed in packet entitled "Don Antonio Cordero y Bustamante, Teniente Coronel de los Reales Ejércitos y Capitán del Presidio de Janos. Certifico que los servicios contenidos en este libro están arreglados a los despachos certificaciones que me han presentado las interesadas a las hojas de servicios anteriores y pública notoriedad," Chihuahua, February 28, 1791, legajo 7047-124, AGS, GM.

2. Antonio Cordero to José María Tovar, Chihuahua, September 17, 1790; Cordero to Janos Commander, Chihuahua, October 13, 1790; Cordero to Janos Commander, Chihuahua, October 19, 1790; Cordero to Manuel de Casanova, Chihuahua, November 9, 1790; Cordero to Janos Commander, Chihuahua, December 8, 1790; Cordero to Manuel de Casanova, Chihuahua, December 21, 1790, all in folder 6A, sec. 1; Cordero to Manuel de Casanova, Chihuahua, January 25, 1791; Cordero to Manuel de Casanova, Chihuahua, February 4, 1791, both in folder 7, sec. 1, all in JC.

3. Antonio Cordero, "Estado que manifiesta el número de Prisioneros que conduce a México el Alférez Don Miguel Díaz de Luna con distinción de hombres, mugeres y niños de ambos sexos," February 15, 1791; Cordero to Don Miguel Díaz de Luna, Chihuahua, February 15,

1791; Cordero to Revillagigedo, Chihuahua, February 15, 1791 [two letters], vol. 142, AGN, PI.

4. Antonio Cordero to Janos Commander, Chihuahua, October 19, 1791; Cordero to Manuel de Casanova, December 21, 1790, both in folder 6A, sec. 1, JC.

5. Domingo de Bergaña, "Estado que Manifiesta el número de Piezas de Prisioneros Apaches que les pasé Revista de diez y seis del corriente Mes de la fecha, y conduce el Alférez Don Miguel Díaz de Luna a la Capital de México," Real Caja de Chihuahua, February 16, 1791; Domingo de Bergaña to Revillagigedo, Chihuahua, February 16, 1791; Miguel Díaz de Luna to Revillagigedo, Mexico, May 19, 1791; Miguel Díaz de Luna, receipts nos. 70 and 71, no location, April 30, 1791; Juan Ysidro Campos, two certificates for ecclesiastical burial, Chihuahua, February 17, 1791, vol. 142, AGN, PI.

Chapter 8. BODILY AND SPIRITUAL NECESSITIES

1. Jackson, *Following the Royal Road*, 116–26, 130–34, 197–98; Gerhard, *North Frontier of New Spain*, 184–85, 195–201; Griffen, *Indian Assimilation*, 60–63, 72–73; Hendricks, "Massacre in the Organ Mountains," 169–77; Miguel Díaz de Luna, receipts as follows: No. 2, no location, February 18; No. 3, no location, February 19; No. 4, San Antonio, February 20; No. 5, Río de San Pedro, February 21; No. 6, Rancho Nuevo, February 23; No. 7, no location, February 23; No. 8, [Pilar de Conchos], March 1 [date out of sequence]; No. 9, [Pilar de Conchos], February 27; No. 10, [Pilar de Conchos], no date; No. 11, no location, February 28; No. 12, Pilar de Conchos; February 28; No. 13, no location, March 1; certificate, Miguel Díaz de Luna from Juan Mateo Solís, Río de San Pedro, February 22, vol. 142, AGN, PI.

2. Miguel Díaz de Luna, receipts as follows: No. 13, no location, March 1; No. 14, Hacienda de San Gregorio, March 2; No. 15, no location, March 3; No. 16, no location, March 3; No. 67, Valle de San Bartolomé, March 3; certificate, Manuel Azque de Armendáriz, Valle de San Bartolomé, March 3, 1791, vol. 142, AGN, PI; Gerhard, *North Frontier of New Spain*, 241–43; Jackson, *Following the Royal Road*, 136–38.

3. Miguel Díaz de Luna, receipts as follows: No. 17, no location, March 5; No. 18, Hacienda de San Francisco Xavier del Río Florido, March 8; No. 19, Hacienda de la Estancia, March 6 [date out of se-

quence]; No. 20, Cerro Gordo, March 8; No. 21, Cerro Gordo, March 9; No. 22, Cerro Gordo, March 10; No. 23, Hacienda de la Zarca, March 11; No. 24, no location, March 11; No. 68, Sapien, March 13; certificate, José María Hernández y Pareda, Hacienda de Xaramillo, March 9, 1791, vol. 142, AGN, PI; Gerhard, *North Frontier of New Spain*, 179–81; Jackson, *Following the Royal Road*, 139–40.

4. Miguel Díaz de Luna, receipts as follows: No. 25, no location, March 14; No. 26, Hacienda del Sr. San Antonio del Río de Nazas, March 15; No. 27, [illegible] Hacienda, March 16; No. 28, Real de Cuencamé, March 20; No. 29, Atotonilco, March 21; No. 30, no location, March 21; No. 31, Hacienda de San Marcos, March 23; No. 32, no location, March 23; No. 33, Santa Catarina, March 24; No. 34, Santa Lucía de las Casas, March 25; No. 35, Santa Mónica, March 26; No. 36, unnamed hacienda and rancho, March 28; No. 37–38, Fresnillo, March 28; certificate, Don Manuel Joaquín de Bonechea, Fresnillo, March 29, 1791, vol. 142, AGN, PI; Gerhard, *North Frontier of New Spain*, 84–86, 192–95; Jackson, *Following the Royal Road*, 189–90.

5. Miguel Díaz de Luna, receipts as follows: No. 39, Zacatecas, April 1; No. 40, Mesón de Tlacotes, April 2; No. 41, Hacienda de San Pedro, April 3; No. 42, Pavellón, April 4; No. 43, Aguas Calientes, April 4; No. 44, Hacienda de Sr. San Bartolomé, April 7; No. 45, Hacienda de San Antonio de los Sauces, April 6; No. 46, Villa de Lagos, April 7; certificate, Don Juan José Escovar, witnessed by Don Juan Francisco Vásquez, Don Juan Calderón, and Don Pedro Sánchez, Zacatecas, April 1, 1791, vol. 142, AGN, PI; Gerhard, *North Frontier of New Spain*, 62–66, 104–108, 157–60; Jackson, *Following the Royal Road*, 147–53, 159–60, 189.

6. Miguel Díaz de Luna, receipts as follows: No. 47, Hacienda de Jaramillo, no date; Nos. 48–49, Villa de León, April 10; No. 50, Silao, April 11; No. 51, Irapuato, April 12; No. 52, Salamanca, April 13; No. 53, no location, April 14; No. 54, Mesón de Celaya, no date; No. 55, Celaya, no date; No. 56, Querétaro, April 17; No. 57, Querétaro, April 18; Nos. 58–60, San Juan del Río, April 20; No. 61, Hacienda del Casadero, April 24; No. 62, Arroyo Sarco, April 26; No. 63, Tepexis, April 26; No. 64, Quatitlán, April 27; No. 65, no location, April 28; No. 66, San Francisco de la Venta, April 28; certificate, Don Pedro Martínez de Salazar y Pacheco, San Juan del Río, April 21, 1791; Miguel Díaz de Luna to Revillagigedo, Mexico, May 19, 1791, vol. 142, AGN, PI; Jackson, *Following the Royal Road*, 166–69, 185–87; Fora, *Nicolás de Lafora*, 37–45.

Chapter 9. RECKONINGS, RESCUE, AND RETURN

1. Humboldt, *Political Essay on the Kingdom of New Spain*, 2:38.

2. MacLachlan, *Criminal Justice in Eighteenth Century Mexico*, 34, 77–78. Whether the women were moved into the Casa de Recogidas is unclear. Between December 1788 and September 1789, a total of eighty-nine Apache females were housed there, but when Don Joseph Antonio de Hogal, the director, complained of the crowded conditions and extra expense, Viceroy Flores ordered the women moved to the Acordada or the Real Hospicio de Pobres, the Royal Home for Indigents. Hogal to Viceroy, Mexico, no date; Flores to Sergeant Major Thomas Rodríguez de Biedma, Mexico, September 19, 1789; Rodríguez de Biedma to Flores, Mexico, September 23, 1789, vol. 155, AGN, PI.

3. Archer, *Army in Bourbon Mexico*, 2–4, 38–44; Pike, "Penal Servitude in the Spanish Empire," 21–40; Archer, "Deportation of Barbarian Indians," 377–81.

4. José Tapia to Revillagigedo, Mexico, May 16, 1791.

5. José Tapia to Revillagigedo, Mexico, May 16, 1791, with appended notation of Revillagigedo to Thomas Rodríguez de Biedma, no date, and appended notation of Biedma to Revillagigedo, Mexico, May 18, 1791, vol. 142, AGN, PI.

6. Miguel Díaz de Luna, receipts as follows: No. 70 to José Santos de Analla, Mexico, April 30; No. 71 to Mariano Analla, Mexico, April 30; Díaz de Luna to Revillagigedo, Mexico, May 19, 1791; Thomas Rodríguez de Biedma to Revillagigedo, Mexico, May 25, 1791; certificate, Rodríguez de Biedma, México, May 26, 1791, vol. 142, AGN, PI.

7. Díaz de Luna, "Relación de los caudales que he recivido de cuenta de Rl. Hazda. para la Suministración y Bagages de la Collera de Apaches de ambos sexos que conduge desde la Villa de Chiha. hasta la Ciudad de Mexico por ord. del Sor. Comandte. Gral. de Provs. Ynterns. Brig. Dn. Pedro de Nava. Rindo al Exmo Sr. Virrey Conde de Revillagigedo con justificativos de los gastos que erogaron," Mexico, May 27, 1791; Díaz de Luna, "Noticia del gasto que se necesita para transportar a Chihuahua los tres Yndios Gentiles de Paz con las tres Mugeres de quenta de la Rl. Hazienda," Mexico, May 27, 1791; Rodríguez de Biedma to Revillagigedo, Mexico, May 27, 1791; Rodríguez de Biedma, Ramón Gutiérrez del Mazo, and José María Martínez del Campo to Revillagigedo, Mexico, May 30, 1791, vol. 142, AGN, PI.

8. Members of the Municipal Junta of Fresnillo to Revillagigedo, Fresnillo, February 9, 1792; Revillagigedo to the Junta Municipal of Fresnillo, Mexico, February 19, 1792; Revillagigedo to Pedro de Nava, Mexico, February 19, 1792; Pedro de Nava to Revillagigedo, Chihuahua, March 22, 1792; Revillagigedo to Nava, Mexico, April 17, 1792, vol. 142, AGN, PI.

9. Cordero to Janos Commander, Chihuahua, October 14, 1791, folder 7, sec. 1; Adjutant Inspector Diego de Borica to Janos Commander, Chihuahua, November 28, 1791, folder 8, sec. 1, both in JC.

10. Municipal Junta of Fresnillo to Revillagigedo, Villa de el Fresnillo, February 9, 1792; Revillagigedo to the Junta Municipal of Fresnillo, Mexico, February 19, 1792; Revillagigedo to Nava, Mexico, February 19, 1792; Nava to Revillagigedo, Chihuahua, March 22, 1792; Revillagigedo to Nava, Mexico, April 17, 1792; Revillagigedo to the Sr. Intendente of Durango, Mexico, June 11, 1792, vol. 142, AGN, PI.

CHAPTER 10. REMOVE THEM FROM WHERE THEY CAN BE DANGEROUS

1. Moorhead, *Presidio*, 95–112.

2. Moorhead, *Apache Frontier*, 253–57. Revillagigedo to Conde de Alange, Mexico, September 26, 1790, "El Virrey de Nueva España avisa la llegada de Comte. Gral. de Provincias del Poniente Don Pedro de Nava, y remite copia de oficio instructivo que le ha pasado," legajo 7045-31; Nava to Revillagigedo, Mexico, September 17, 1790; certified copy, Mexico, September 26, 1790, legajo 7045-30, AGS, GM.

3. Nava to Revillagigedo, Mexico, September 17, 1790; certified copy, Mexico, September 26, 1790.

4. Nava to Janos Commander, Chihuahua, June 7, 1791; Nava to Janos Commander, Chihuahua, July 1, 1791; Cordero to Janos Commander, Pueblo del Paso, August 12, 1791, folder 7, sec. 1, JC.

5. Pedro de Nava, "Instructions to be observed by the commandants of outpost charged with dealing with the Apache Indians who are currently at peace in various places in Nueva Vizcaya, and with those who may seek it in the future," Chihuahua, October 14, 1791, translated in Hendricks and Timmons, *San Elizario*, 102–109.

6. Pedro de Nava, "Estado que manifiesta los Prisioneros que ha de recivir en el Quartel del Pilar de Conchos, el Sargento de la Compañía de San Carlos Valentín Moreno para conducirlos hasta la Ciudad de

Mexico," Chihuahua, March 12, 1792; Nava to Revillagigedo, Chihuahua, March 22, 1792, vol. 142, AGN, PI; Antonio Cordero to Manuel de Casanova, Chihuahua, March 9, 1791, folder 7, sec. 1, JC; Cordero, "Extracto de Revista de Inspección . . . de San Carlos de Cerrogordo," February 25, 1792, legajo 7047-124, AGS, GM. Sergeant Antonio Valentín Moreno's physical description can be found in his *filiación*, or service sheet, enclosed in a packet from Pedro de Nava to Viceroy the Marques of Branciforte, Chihuahua, July 1, 1796, legajo 7025-2, AGS, GM. Moreno would continue to rise in the service and would ultimately retire with the rank of captain after a 45-year career. Manuel Ruano, "Extracto de la Revista pasada por mi Dn Manuel Ruano Teniente en la 4a compa. Volante y Comandante Ynterino de este de Principe a los Oficiales, Capellan, Tropa y Ynbalidos de que se compone," Coyame, August 1, 1818, vol. 233, AGN, PI.

7. Pedro de Nava to Sergeant Valentín Moreno, Chihuahua, March 22, 1792; Nava to Revillagigedo, Chihuahua, March 22, 1792 [two letters]; Domingo de Bergaña to Revillagigedo, March 22, 1792, vol. 142, AGN, PI. The order to kill the prisoners in case of escape was not unique to the Spaniards. A contemporaneous order from military officers from the state of Maryland in the United States regarding the actions of guards holding prisoners reads: "You are to take especial care that the prisoners do not make their escape in case they attempt it—and (if) you find it impracticable to prevent it by any other means than firing on them you are immediately to give the Guard Orders for that purpose. You are likewise to be watchful that the prisoners be not rescued. And, if any persons attempt it . . . [and] if you find there is a real danger of their letting the prisoners loose, you are to give immediate Orders to the Guard to fire on the person offending." Quoted in Fooks, *Prisoners of War*, 262–63.

CHAPTER 11. THE GREATEST RESISTANCE POSSIBLE

1. Valentín Moreno, "Diario que manifiesta las novedades en la Partida de mi cargo destinada ala conducción de la cuerda de Apache Pricioneros para la Ciudad de Mexico desde hoy 21 Marzo de 1792"; Receipt from Captain Manuel Vidal de Lorca, Pilar de Conchos, March 27, 1792, vol. 142, AGN, PI. Although not explicitly mentioned, several references to "Voluntarios" in the documents of this collera categorize

them as "soldiers." In 1792, the Second Company of the Voluntarios de Cataluña was the only unit on the frontier with the appellation of volunteers. The Second Company was at this time garrisoning the city of Chihuahua but by that summer would be recalled from the frontier. Nava to Revillagigedo, Chihuahua, [May–June ?] 1792; Pedro de Gorostiza to Revillagigedo, Mexico City, July 4, 1792, vol. 266, AGN, PI.

2. Moreno, "Diario"; Valentín Moreno to Pedro de Nava, Paraje de la Partida, March 31, 1792, certified copy by Manuel Merino, Chihuahua, April 5, 1792, vol. 142, AGN, PI.

3. Records from the establecimientos de paz show that for weekly distributions, beeves were usually divided into 32 portions. With a beef yielding 280 pounds of meat, this would calculate to a weekly ration for an adult couple of 8.75 pounds, or a little over 4 pounds each. "Each Apache male who has a wife will be given . . . 1 ration of meat (when available). The meat ration is to be 1/32, which is how beefs are divided. . . . Each additional adult in a family will be given one-half of a family portion; a boy or girl under the age of thirteen will receive one-quarter, and nursing children nothing." Pedro de Nava, "Instructions for dealing with the Apaches at peace in Nueva Vizcaya, Chihuahua, October 14, 1791," quoted in Hendricks and Timmons, *San Elizario*, 106.

4. Moreno, "Diario"; Moreno to Nava, Paraje de la Partida, March 31, 1792; receipt signed by Juan de Soto and Acensio Mendoza, Cerrogordo, no date, vol. 142, AGN, PI.

CHAPTER 12. THE SEVERED HANDS

1. Moreno, "Diario"; Moreno to Nava, Paraje de la Partida, March 31, 1792; Receipt signed by Juan de Soto and Ascencio Mendoza, Cerrogordo, no date, vol. 142, AGN, PI.

2. Moreno, "Diario."

3. Ibid.; certificate from Br. Don Joseph María Urracha, Hacienda del Pavellón, April 24, 1792, with a marginal note from Cabo Franco of the Contaduría Mayor de Tribunal de Cuentas de México, May 30, 1792, vol. 142, AGN, PI.

4. Moreno, "Diario"; certificate from Don Pedro Martínez de Salazar y Pacheco, San Juan del Río, May 11, 1792, vol. 142, AGN, PI.

5. Receipt from Juan Díaz Martínez and Rafael Romero, Mexico, May 18, 1792; Antonio Valentín Moreno, "Cuenta que forma el Sargento Antonio Balentin Moreno conductor de la cuerda de sesenta y

siete mecos que condujo con la Partida de veinte y quatro soldados hasta esta capital, sin incluir en el total de Yndividuos quince mecos, catorce que quedaron muertos en el camino y uno vivo en Concha," Mexico, May 19, 1792, vol. 142, AGN, PI.

6. Rodríguez de Biedma to Revillagigedo, Mexico, May 26, 1792; Antonio Tórrez de Córdova to Don José del Cabo Franco, Mexico, May 29, 1792; José del Cabo Franco to Señores Contadores Mayores, May 30, 1792, Mexico, vol. 142, AGN, PI.

7. Antonio Moreno to Cabo Franco, Mexico, May, 31, 1792; Cabo Franco to Tribunal de la Contaduría Mayor y Audiencia de Cuentas, June 1, 1792, Mexico, vol. 142, AGN, PI.

8. Revillagigedo to Don Thomas Rodríguez, Mexico, August 21, 1792; Revillagigedo to the Ministers of the Royal Tribunal, Mexico, August 21, 1792; Revillagigedo to Don Diego Bergaña, Mexico, August 21, 1792. In a letter from Rodríguez de Biedma to Revillagigedo of August 23, 1792, the sergeant major informed the viceroy that as the arrieros Martínez and Romero had already left the city, the amount of 277 pesos 4 reales was covered by one Don Rafael Villagrán, "Padre y amo de los mencionados," who was the actual owner of the recua of mules and was also "Alcalde del Quartel no. 15," vol. 142, AGN, PI.

CHAPTER 13. HARD LESSONS

1. Nava to the Conde del Campo de Alange, Chihuahua, May 30, 1793, Indios, Provincias Internas, legajo 7022-2, Archivo General de Simancas, Secretaría del Despacho de Guerra (hereinafter AGS, SGU), housed at Spanish Ministry of Cultures, Madrid, Spain, available online at Portal de Archivos Españoles, http://www.mcu.es/archivos/CE/PARES.html; McCarty, *Desert Documentary*, 62–63.

2. Pedro de Nava, "Estado que manifiesta el número de Rancherías Apaches existentes en paz en varios Parajes de las Provincias de Sonora, Nueva Vizcaya y Nuevo México y el número de personas de ambos sexos de que se compone cada uno," Chihuahua, May 2, 1793, Indios, Provincias Internas, legajo 7022-2, AGS, SGU; Griffen, *Apaches at War and Peace*, 63–64, 69–74, 267–68.

3. Nava to Revillagigedo, Villa de San Fernando, February 9, 1791, attached with "Convenio ajustado por el Brigadier Don Pedro de Nava Comandante General de Provincias Internas con los Yndios de la Nación Lipana conocida por los de Arriba . . . ," Villa de San Fernando,

February 8, 1791; Nava and Castro to Revillagigedo, Saltillo, March 28, 1791, certified copy by Bonilla, Mexico, May 27, 1791; Nava to Revillagigedo, Saltillo, March 28, 1791 [two letters], certified copy by Bonilla, Mexico, May 27, 1791; Castro to Revillagigedo, Saltillo, March 28, 1791, certified copy by Bonilla, Mexico, May 27, 1791, Provincias Internas de Oriente, Indios Lipanes, legajo 7021-2, AGS, SGU.

4. Castro to Revillagigedo, Valle de Santa Rosa, April 16, 1791; Revillagigedo, no recipient, Mexico, May 27, 1791; Juan Gutiérrez de la Cueva to Revillagigedo, Valle de Santa Rosa, May 2, 1791, Provincias Internas de Oriente, Indios Lipanes, legajo 7021-2, AGS, SGU.

5. Navarro García, *Don José de Gálvez*, 481–84; Nava to Conde del Campo de Alange, May 30, 1793, Chihuahua, Provincias Internas de Oriente, Indios Lipanes, legajo 7021-2, AGS, SGU.

6. Navarro García, *Don José de Gálvez*, 486–88; Nava to Conde del Campo de Alange, Chihuahua, May 30, 1793, Provincias Internas de Oriente, Indios Lipanes, legajo 7021-2, AGS, SGU; Nava to Don Manuel de Casanova, Chihuahua, May 17, 1794 [three letters], folder 10, sec. 1, JC.

7. Griffen, *Apaches at War and Peace*, 73–82, 267–71; Nava to Janos Commander, November 10, 1795, folder 11, sec. 1, JC.

8. Nava to Conde del Campo de Alange, Chihuahua, April 24, 1793, with two reports attached, and May 30, 1793, with one report attached, Indios Provincias Internas, legajo 7022-2, AGS, SGU; Nava to Revillagigedo, Chihuahua, April 16, 1794, vol. 141, AGN, PI.

9. Nava to Revillagigedo, Chihuahua, April 16, 1794; Revillagigedo to Nava, Mexico, May 7, 1794; José Fernandes de Molina to Revillagigedo, Villa de León, May 12, 1794; Revillagigedo to Molina, Mexico, May 21, 1794; Molina to Revillagigedo, León, June 1, 1794; certificate, Father Manuel Bonifacio Navidad, Leon, June 1, 1794; Revillagigedo to Molina, Mexico, June 18, 1794; Revillagigedo to Juan Antonio de Riano, Intendent of Guanajuato, Mexico, June 18, 1794; Riano to Revillagigedo, Guanajuato, June 23, 1794, vol. 141, AGN, PI.

10. Pedro de Nava to the Marquis de Branciforte, Chihuahua, November 27, 1794, vol. 238, AGN, PI.

11. Nava to Don Miguel Joseph de Azanza, Chihuahua, November 7, 1796; Nava to Azanza, Chihuahua, January 30, 1797, Provincias Internas de Oriente, Indios Lipanes, legajo 7021-2, AGS, SGU; Moorhead, "Spanish Deportation," 213, 216–17; Pedro de Nava to Juan Manuel Álvarez, Chihuahua, June 5, 1798, Competencias, Audiencia

de Guadalajara, legajo 7027-10, AGS, SGU; Archer, "Deportation of Barbarian Indians," 380. The collera dispatched from the Valle de Santa Rosa was not the only group deported in 1798. In October of that year, Valentín Moreno, now promoted to alférez, delivered another collera of one hundred Apache prisoners to Mexico City. "Pagos a Indios Apaches: Año de 1798," Chihuahua, October 25, 1798, legajo 459, AGI, Guad.

12. Governor of Perote [José Joaquín de Posada] to Viceroy Miguel José [de] Azanza, Perote, October 15, 1798; Azanza, Mexico, January 17, 1799; José María Laso and José Vildosola, Ministers of the Royal Hacienda, to Azanza, Mexico, January 19, 1799; Azanza to the Governor of Perote, January 19, 1799, all in "Testimonio del Proceso criminal formado al teniente de Dragonas de Mexico Don Juan de Dios Cos por la fuga que le hicieron de la Venta de la Rinconada cincuenta y una Indias Apaches Prisioneros de Guerra y muchacho de la misma nación menor de edad que conduce en Cuerda a la Plaza de Veracruz," attached with Azanza to Don Juan Manuel Albarez, Mexico, July 27, 1799 [two letters]; legajo 6980-13, AGS, GM.

13. José Joaquín de Posada to Azanza, Perote, January 31, 1799; Summary Inquiry of Don Francisco Norma, Lieutenant Colonel of the Royal Armies and Sergeant Major of the Plaza of Veracruz, with Francisco Saliza, Grenadier of the Regiment of the Crown as scribe, Veracruz, February 11, 1799; "Parte" of Lieutenant Juan de Dios Cos, Antigua, February 6, 1799; "Testimonios" of Sergeant José Palacios, First Corporal Agustín Severiche of the Dragoons of Mexico, and Corporal José Milani of the Voluntarios de Cataluña, February 11, 1799; "Testimonio" of soldier Manuel Carpintero of the Voluntarios de Cataluña, February 22, 1799; Findings of the Council of War, Mexico, June 25, 1799, all in "Testimonio del Proceso," legajo 6980-13, AGS, GM.

14. Manuel Antonio de Araujo, "Estado de las Indias Apaches que existen en este Real Hospicio de Pobres de Mexico depositadas de Orden del Excelentissimo Señor Virrey hoy de Junio de 1801," Mexico, vol. 238, AGN, PI.

15. Joaquín Perú, Pilar de Conchos, February 4, 1802, "Estado que manifiesta el Número de Piezas Prisioneras de Guerra que ha recivido en este Quartel el Sargento José Antonio Uribes para conducir a México"; Francisco Noriega to Viceroy, Mexico, April 1, 1802; Pedro de Allende, "Estado que manifiesta el Numero de Piezas Prisioneras de

Guerra que el Alférez Don Pedro Armendariz conduce a Mexico y ha recivido en este Quartel con expression de Sexos y Edades," Pilar de Conchos, September 27, 1803, attached with Salcedo to Viceroy, Chihuahua, October 3, 1803; receipt, Ygnacio Rodríguez Calvo, Acordada, November 18, 1803, vol. 238, AGN, PI.

16. [Viceroy?] to the Governor of Veracruz, Mexico, November 16, 1804, legajo 238, AGN, PI, records the dispatch of a collera of ten men and thirty-six women to Veracruz under Lieutenant Don Felipe de Andrade of the Dragoons of Mexico with an escort of one sergeant, two cabos, and sixteen dragoons of his regiment, and from the Regiment of the Crown one sergeant, two cabos, and fourteen men. Salcedo to Janos Commander, December 2, 1808, reel 15, JMC, notes that two Indians named Janos and Voluntad do not deserve to be freed, due to their treachery, and are to be dispatched with a collera and strongly secured. Unfortunately, the total number of prisoners is not given. José Montes and Diego Madolevo[?] to Viceroy, January 5, 1810, vol. 238, AGN, PI, records the events surrounding a collera of sixty-three Apaches sent from Mexico City to Veracruz bound for Havana between April 4, 1809, and January 2, 1810. Lieutenant José Solis of the Dragoons of Querétaro conducted sixteen males (all secured with manacles) from the Acordada along with forty-seven women and one small child from the Hospital de Pobres to Veracruz via Perote between October 1809 and January 1810.

Commandant General Nemesio Salcedo to the commandant of Janos, Chihuahua, July 2, 1803; Salcedo to the commandant of Janos, Chihuahua, July 9, 1803, folder 17, sec. 1; Salcedo to the Commandant of Janos, Chihuahua, February 7, 1804, folder 17, sec. 2; José María Tovar, Janos, July 18, 1803, folder 17, sec. 3; Salcedo to Juan Francisco Granados, Chihuahua, February 4, 1809; Salcedo to the commandant of Janos, Chihuahua, March 8, 1809; Salcedo to Granados, Chihuahua, April 7, 1809, folder 19, sec. 2; [Unknown] to the governor intendent, Janos, July 18, 1812; [Unknown] to the commandant of Fronteras, Janos, July 18, 1812; [Unknown] to the commander of the Third Flying Company, Janos, March 20, 1813; [Unknown] to the commandant of San Buenaventura, Janos, June 5, 1813, folder 19, sec. 4; Guillermo Limón to the commandant of Janos, Fronteras, July 13, 1812; Salcedo to the commandant of Janos, Chihuahua, January 8, 1812; both in folder 20, sec. 3; all in JC.

EPILOGUE

1. Von Clausewitz, *On War*, 101.

2. Babcock, "Rethinking the Establecimientos," 377–81.

3. The financial cost for each collera averaged approximately 2,000 pesos for the support and transport of the prisoners, with another 1,000 pesos for the maintenance of the escort. This cost was relatively low in comparison with the overall military expenditures of the Interior Provinces. On examining the expenses from the Royal Treasuries located in Arispe, Sonora, and Chihuahua, Nueva Vizcaya, the overall costs for supporting the reservation system, listed as "*gastos de Apaches,*" have been calculated to be approximately 4 percent of the total overall military budget. For example, adding up the expenses from Arispe and Chihuahua for the period 1796–1800, the total was 5,207,019 pesos, of which 100,194, or 1.9 percent, was for gastos de Apaches. Calculating a conservative expense of 3,000 pesos per deportation for each of the five years yields 15,000 pesos expended for deportations, or 0.29 percent of total costs.

For the overall cost of maintaining the Apaches on the establecimientos de paz as a percentage of the overall military budget (as reflected in the royal treasuries of Arispe and Chihuahua), the totals are as follows:

ARISPE

1791–1795 = 48,651 reales de ocho for gastos de Apaches, or 5 percent of total expenses of 1,217,151

1796–1800 = 41,490 reales de ocho for gastos de Apache, or 4 percent of total expenses of 1,232,142

1801–1805 = 35,935 reales de ocho for gastos de Apache, or 3 percent of total expenses of 1,575,472

1806–1810 = 27,295 reales de ocho for gastos de Apache, or 4 percent of total expenses of 1,271,917 (includes 1807–1809)

1811–1815 = 6,614 reales de ocho for gastos de Apache, or 24 percent of total expenses of 580,841 (includes 1813 only)

CHIHUAHUA

1791–1795 = no data

1796–1800 = 58,704 reales de ocho for gastos de Apache, or 4 percent of total expenses of 3,974,877 (includes 1797–1800)

1801–1805 = 103,373 reales de ocho for gastos de Apache, or 5 percent of total expenses of 4,981,868

1806–1810 = 113,577 reales de ocho for gastos de Apache, or 5 percent of total expenses of 5,589,800

1811–1815 = 23,653 reales de ocho for gastos de Apache, or 2 percent of total expenses of 3,996,184 (includes 1811, 1813, and 1814)

Adapted from Jones, "Comparative Raiding Economies," 102–105.

4. Remini, *Andrew Jackson and His Indian Wars*; Kraft, *Gatewood and Geronimo*, 186–220.

Bibliography

ARCHIVAL SOURCES

Archivo General de Indias. Audiencia de Guadalajara. Microfilm copy at Bancroft Library, University of California, Berkeley.

Archivo General de la Nación, Mexico. Provincias Internas. Microfilm copy at Center for Southwest Research, University of New Mexico, Albuquerque, and at C. L. Sonnichsen Special Collections Department, University Library, University of Texas at El Paso.

Archivo General de Simancas, Spain. Guerra Moderna. Microfilm collection at the University of New Mexico, Albuquerque.

Archivo General de Simancas, Spain. Secretaría del Despacho de Guerra. Ministerio de Cultura. Madrid, Spain. Online access at "Portal de Archivos Españoles," http://www.mcu.es/archivos/CE/PARES.html.

Celaya Microfilm. Old Spanish Missions Historical Research Library. Our Lady of the Lake University, San Antonio, Texas.

Historical Archives, 1710–1856. Manuscripts and Documents of Janos. Microfilm. C. L. Sonnichsen Special Collections Department, University Library, University of Texas at El Paso.

Records of the Presidio de San Felipe y Santiago de Janos, 1706–1858. Benson Latin American Collection, General Libraries, University of Texas at Austin.

PUBLISHED PRIMARY SOURCES

Brinckerhoff, Sidney B., and Odie B. Faulk. *Lancers for the King: A Study of the Frontier Military System of Northern New Spain, with a Translation of the Royal Regulations of 1772.* Phoenix: Arizona Historical Foundation, 1965.

Bringas de Manzaneda y Encinas, Diego Miguel. *Friar Bringas Reports to the King: Methods of Indoctrination on the Frontier of New Spain 1796–97.* Translated and edited by Daniel S. Matson and Bernard L. Fontana. Tucson: University of Arizona Press, 1977.

Cortés y de Olarte, José María. *Views from the Apache Frontier: Report on the Northern Provinces of New Spain.* Edited by Elizabeth A. H. John. Translated by John Wheat. Norman: University of Oklahoma Press, 1989.

Fora, Nicolás de la. *Nicolás de Lafora: Relación del viaje que hizo a los presidios internos, situados en la frontera de la América septentrional, perteneciente al rey de España.* Edited by Vito Alessio Robles. Mexico City: Pedro Robredo, 1939.

Gálvez, Bernardo de. *Instructions for Governing the Interior Provinces of New Spain, 1786.* Edited and translated by Donald E. Worcester. Berkeley: Quivira Society, 1951.

Goodwin, Grenville. *Western Apache Raiding and Warfare, from the Notes of Grenville Goodwin.* Edited by Keith H. Basso. Tucson: University of Arizona Press, 1971.

Jackson, Jack, ed. *Imaginary Kingdom: Texas As Seen by the Rivera and Rubí Military Expeditions, 1727 and 1767.* Austin: Texas State Historical Association, 1995.

Kino, Eusebio Francisco. *Kino's Historical Memoir of Pimería Alta: A Contemporary Account of the Beginnings of California, Sonora, and Arizona.* Edited by Herbert Eugene Bolton. 2 vols. in 1. Berkeley: University of California Press, 1948.

Matson, Daniel S., and Albert H. Schroeder, eds. "Cordero's Description of the Apache, 1796." *New Mexico Historical Review* 32, no. 4 (October 1957): 335–56.

Moore, Mary Lu, and Delmar L. Beene, trans. and eds. "The Interior Provinces of New Spain: The Report of Hugo O'Conor, January 30, 1776." *Arizona and the West* 13, no. 3 (Autumn 1971): 265–82.

Naylor, Thomas H., and Charles W. Polzer, eds. *Pedro de Rivera and the Military Regulations for Northern New Spain 1724–1729: A Documentary*

History of His Frontier Inspection and the Reglamento de 1729. Tucson: University of Arizona Press, 1988.

———, eds. *The Presidio and Militia on the Northern Frontier of New Spain: A Documentary History. Vol. 1, 1570–1700*. Tucson: University of Arizona Press, 1986.

Nentvig, Juan. *Rudo Ensayo: A Description of Sonora and Arizona in 1764*. Translated by Alberto Francisco Pradeau and Robert R. Rasmussen. Tucson: University of Arizona Press, 1980.

O'Conor, Hugo. *The Defenses of Northern New Spain: Hugo O'Conor's Report to Teodoro de Croix, July 22, 1777*. Edited and translated by Donald C. Cutter. Dallas: DeGolyer Library, Southern Methodist University Press, 1994.

Thomas, Alfred Barnaby, trans. and ed. *Teodoro de Croix and the Northern Frontier of New Spain, 1776–1783. From the Original Document in the Archives of the Indies, Seville*. Norman: University of Oklahoma Press, 1941.

BOOKS AND ARTICLES

Albi, Julio. *La defensa de las Indias (1764–1799)*. Madrid: Instituto de Cooperación Iberoamericana, Ediciones Cultura Hispánica, 1987.

Anderson, Gary Clayton. *The Indian Southwest, 1580–1830: Ethnogenesis and Reinvention*. Norman: University of Oklahoma Press, 1999.

Archer, Christon I. *The Army in Bourbon Mexico, 1760–1810*. Albuquerque: University of New Mexico Press, 1977.

———. "The Deportation of Barbarian Indians from the Internal Provinces of New Spain, 1789–1810." *The Americas* 29 (1973): 376–85.

Babcock, Matthew. "Rethinking the Establecimientos: Why Apaches Settled on Spanish-Run Reservations, 1786–1793." *New Mexico Historical Review* 84, no. 3 (Summer 2009): 363–97.

Barker, Juliet. *Agincourt: Henry V and the Battle That Made England*. New York: Little, Brown, 2005.

Barr, Julianne. *Peace Came in the Form of a Woman: Indians and Spaniards in the Texas Borderlands*. Chapel Hill: University of North Carolina Press, 2007.

Barrio Gozalo, Maximiliano. *Esclavos y cautivos: Conflicto entre la Cristiandad y el Islam en el siglo XVIII*. [Valladolid]: Junta de Castilla y León, Consejería de Cultura y Turismo, 2006.

Blyth, Lance R. "The Presidio of Janos: Ethnicity, Society, Masculinity, and Ecology in Far Northern Mexico, 1685–1858." Ph.D. diss., Northern Arizona University, 2005.

Bobb, Bernard E. *The Viceregency of Antonio María de Bucareli in New Spain, 1771–1779*. Austin: University of Texas Press, 1962.

Braudel, Ferdinand. *The Mediterranean and the Mediterranean World in the Age of Philip II*. 2 vols. New York: Harper & Row, 1973.

Brooks, James F. *Captives and Cousins: Slavery, Kinship, and Community in the Southwest Borderlands*. Chapel Hill: University of North Carolina Press, 2002.

Burrows, Edwin G. *Forgotten Patriots: The Untold Story of American Prisoners during the Revolutionary War*. New York: Basic Books, 2008.

Butler, James Davie. "British Convicts Shipped to American Colonies." *American Historical Review* 2 (October 1896): 12–33.

Carter, William B. *Indian Alliances and the Spanish in the Southwest, 750–1750*. Norman: University of Oklahoma Press, 2009.

Contamine, Philippe. *War in the Middle Ages*. Translated by Michael Jones. 1980. Reprint, New York: Barnes & Noble, 1998.

Daniel, James M. "Diary of Pedro José de la Fuente, Captain of the Presidio of El Paso del Norte, January–July, 1765." *Southwestern Historical Quarterly* 60 (October 1956): 260–81.

———. "Diary of Pedro José de la Fuente, Captain of the Presidio of El Paso del Norte, August–December, 1765." *Southwestern Historical Quarterly* 83 (January 1980): 261–78.

Deeds, Susan M. *Defiance and Deference in Mexico's Colonial North: Indians under Spanish Rule in Nueva Vizcaya*. Austin: University of Texas Press, 2003.

Dobyns, Henry F. *Spanish Colonial Tucson: A Demographic History*. Tucson: University of Arizona Press, 1976.

Dunn, William Edward. "Apache Relations in Texas, 1718–1750." *Southwestern Historical Quarterly* 14, no. 3 (January 1911): 198–269.

Fooks, Herbert C. *Prisoners of War*. Federalsburg, Md.: J. W. Stowell, 1924.

Forbes, Jack D. *Apache, Navaho, and Spaniard*. 2nd ed. Norman: University of Oklahoma Press, 1994.

Forbes, Robert H. *Crabb's Filibustering Expedition into Sonora, 1857*. [Tucson]: Arizona Silhouettes, 1952.

Gerhard, Peter. *The North Frontier of New Spain*. Rev. ed. Norman: University of Oklahoma Press, 1993.

Griffen, William B. *Apaches at War and Peace: The Janos Presidio, 1750–1858*. 1988. Reprint, Norman: University of Oklahoma Press, 1998.

———. *Indian Assimilation in the Franciscan Area of Nueva Vizcaya*. Anthropological Papers of the University of Arizona 33. Tucson: University of Arizona Press, 1979.

Hanke, Lewis. *The Spanish Struggle for Justice in the Conquest of America*. Philadelphia: University of Pennsylvania Press, 1949.

Hendricks, Rick. "Massacre in the Organ Mountains: The Death of Manuel Vidal de Lorca." *Password* 39, no. 4 (Winter 1994): 169–77.

Hendricks, Rick, and W. H. Timmons. *San Elizario: Spanish Presidio to Texas County Seat*. El Paso: Texas Western Press, 1998.

Hughes, Robert. *The Fatal Shore: The Epic of Australia's Founding*. New York: Alfred A. Knopf, 1987.

Humboldt, Alexander von. *Political Essay on the Kingdom of New Spain*. 4 vols. London: Printed for Longman, Hurst, Rees, Orme, and Brown, 1822.

Jackson, Hal. *Following the Royal Road: A Guide to the Historic Camino Real de Tierra Adentro*. Albuquerque: University of New Mexico Press, 2006.

Jenkins, Lawrence Waters. *A New Hampshireman Transports Spanish Troops to Oran, 1732*. Salem, Mass.: Peabody Museum, n.d. Reprinted from *The American Neptune* 6, no. 3 (1946).

John, Elizabeth A. H. *Storms Brewed in Other Men's Worlds: The Confrontation of Indians, Spanish, and French in the Southwest, 1540–1795*. 2nd ed. Norman: University of Oklahoma Press, 1996.

Jones, Kristine L. "Comparative Raiding Economies: North and South." In *Contested Ground: Comparative Frontiers on the Northern and Southern Edges of the Spanish Empire*, 97–114. Edited by Donna J. Guy and Thomas E. Sheridan. Tucson: University of Arizona Press, 1998.

Kamen, Henry. *The Spanish Inquisition: A Historical Revision*. New Haven: Yale University Press, 1998.

Karsten, Peter. *Laws, Soldiers, and Combat*. Westport, Conn.: Greenwood Press, 1978.

Keegan, John. *The Face of Battle*. 1976. Reprint, New York: Barnes & Noble, 1993.

Kessell, John L. *Spain in the Southwest: A Narrative History of Colonial New Mexico, Arizona, Texas, and California*. Norman: University of Oklahoma Press, 2002.

Kraft, Louis. *Gatewood and Geronimo*. Albuquerque: University of New Mexico Press, 2000.

Kuethe, Allan J. *Cuba, 1753–1815: Crown, Military, and Society*. Knoxville: University of Tennessee Press, 1986.

LeBlanc, Steven A. *Prehistoric Warfare in the American Southwest.* Salt Lake City: University of Utah Press, 1999.

Lozano Armendares, Teresa. "Recinto de maldades y lamentos: La cárcel de la Acordada." *Estudios de Historia Novohispana* 13 (1993): 149–57.

MacLachlan, Colin M. *Criminal Justice in Eighteenth Century Mexico: A Study of the Tribunal of the Acordada.* Berkeley: University of California Press, 1974.

McCarty, Kieran. "Bernardo de Gálvez on the Apache Frontier: The Education of a Future Viceroy." *Journal of the Southwest* 36 (1994): 103–30.

——, ed. *Desert Documentary: The Spanish Years, 1767–1821.* Historical Monograph 4. Tucson: Arizona Historical Society, 1976.

Mirafuentes Galván, José Luis. "Los dos mundos de José Reyes Pozo y el alzamiento de los apaches chiricahuis (Bacoachi, Sonora, 1790)." *Estudios de Historia Novohispana* 21 (2000): 67–105.

Montesquieu, Baron de (Charles de Secondat). "The Spirit of Laws." In *Great Books of the Western World,* edited by Mortimer J. Adler. Vol. 35. 2nd ed. Chicago: Encyclopedia Britannica, 1990.

Moorhead, Max L. *The Apache Frontier: Jacobo Ugarte and Spanish-Indian Relations in Northern New Spain, 1769–1791.* Norman: University of Oklahoma Press, 1968.

——. *The Presidio: Bastion of the Spanish Borderlands.* Norman: University of Oklahoma Press, 1975.

——. "Spanish Deportation of Hostile Apaches: The Policy and the Practice." *Arizona and the West* 17, no. 3 (Autumn 1975): 205–20.

Navarro García, Luis. *Don José de Gálvez y la comandancia general de las Provincias Internas del norte de Nueva España.* Seville, Spain: Escuela de Estudios Hispano-Americanos de Sevilla, 1964.

Nelson, Al B. "Campaigning in the Big Bend of the Rio Grande in 1787." *Southwestern Historical Quarterly* 39, no. 3 (January 1936): 200–27.

——. "Juan de Ugalde and Picax-Ande Ins-Tinsle, 1787–1788." *Southwestern Historical Quarterly* 43, no. 4 (April 1940): 438–64.

Opler, Morris E. "The Apachean Culture Pattern and Its Origins." In Ortiz, *Southwest.*

——. "Chiricahua Apache." In Ortiz, *Southwest.*

——. "Mescalero Apache." In Ortiz, *Southwest.*

Ortiz, Alfonso, ed. *Southwest.* Vol. 10 of *Handbook of North American Indians*, edited by William C. Sturdevant. Washington, D.C.: Smithsonian Institution, 1983.

Pike, Ruth. "Penal Servitude in the Spanish Empire: Presidio Labor in the Eighteenth Century." *Hispanic American Historical Review* 58, no. 1 (February 1978): 21–40.

Powell, Philip Wayne. *Soldiers, Indians, and Silver: North America's First Frontier War.* Tempe: Arizona State University, Center for Latin American Studies, 1975.

Remini, Robert V. *Andrew Jackson and His Indian Wars.* New York: Viking, 2001.

Santiago, Mark. *Massacre at the Yuma Crossing: Spanish Relations with the Quechans, 1779–1782.* Tucson: University of Arizona Press, 1998.

———. *The Red Captain: The Life of Hugo O'Conor, Commandant Inspector of the Interior Provinces of New Spain.* Museum Monograph 9. Tucson: Arizona Historical Society, 1994.

Segovia, Rodolfo. *The Lake of Stone: The Geopolitics of Spanish Fortifications in the Caribbean (1586–1786).* Bogotá: El Áncora, 2006.

Slatta, Richard W. "Spanish Colonial Military Strategy and Ideology." In *Contested Ground: Comparative Frontiers on the Northern and Southern Edges of the Spanish Empire*, 83–96. Edited by Donna J. Guy and Thomas E. Sheridan. Tucson: University of Arizona Press, 1998.

Smith, Ralph A. "The Spanish 'Piece' Policy in West Texas." *West Texas Historical Association Yearbook* 68 (1992): 7–24.

Starnes, Gary B. "Juan de Ugalde (1729–1816) and the Provincias Internas of Coahuila and Texas." Ph.D. diss., Texas Christian University, 1971.

Tiller, Veronica E. "Jicarilla Apache." In Ortiz, *Southwest.*

Von Clausewitz, Carl. *On War.* Edited by Anatol Rapoport. London: Penguin, 1968.

Weber, David J. *Bárbaros: Spaniards and Their Savages in the Age of Enlightenment.* New Haven: Yale University Press, 2005.

———. *The Spanish Frontier in North America.* New Haven: Yale University Press, 1992.

Index

References to illustrations appear in italic type.

www.ingramcontent.com/pod-product-compliance
Lightning Source LLC
Chambersburg PA
CBHW032346280326
41935CB00008B/467
* 9 7 8 0 8 0 6 1 6 4 5 6 4 *